Departures

Departures

A Reader for Developing Writers

Randall Popken
Alice Newsome
Lanell Gonzales
Tarleton State University

Allyn and Bacon
Boston London Toronto Sydney Tokyo Singapore

Editor-in-Chief, Humanities: Joseph Opiela
Editorial Assistant: Brenda Conaway
Marketing Manager: Lisa Kimball
Production Administrator: Rowena Dores
Editorial-Production Service: Colophon
Cover Administrator: Linda Knowles
Composition Buyer: Linda Cox
Manufacturing Buyer: Louise Richardson

Library of Congress Cataloging-in-Publication Data

Departures : a reader for developing writers / Randall Popken, Alice
Newsome, Lanell Gonzales.
     p.   cm.
     ISBN 0-205-16249-5
     1. College readers.   2. English language—Rhetoric.   3. English
language—Grammar.   I. Popken, Randall.   II. Newsome, Alice.
III. Gonzales, Lanell.
PE1417.D47   1994
808'.0427—dc20   94-29358
                                                                   CIP

This textbook is printed on
recycled, acid-free paper.

Acknowledgments

"Measuring Up" by Donna Kato. *Fort Worth Star-Telegram*, March 7, 1993. Copyright 1993 by the *Fort Worth Star-Telegram*. Reprinted courtesy of the *Fort Worth Star-Telegram*.

"Look At Me Now!" by Andrea Heimann. *Los Angeles Times*, September 10, 1992. Copyright 1992, *Los Angeles Times*. Reprinted by permission.

"Oh Mom!" by Barbara Meltz, as it appeared in the *Fort Worth Star-Telegram*, October 13, 1992. Copyright 1992. Reprinted courtesy of *The Boston Globe*.

"The Fine Art of Changing One's Image" by Loraine O'Connell. *Orlando Sentinel*, July 22, 1989. Copyright © 1989 by the *Orlando Sentinel*. Reprinted by permission.

Acknowledgments continue on page 357, which constitutes a continuation of the copyright page.

Printed in the United States of America

10 9 8 7 6 5 4 3 2 1   99 98 97 96 95 94

Contents

Part I: Profiles of Modern America

1   Image   1

2   Heroism   29

3   Stereotypes   51

4   Generation X   69

5   Crime and Violence   91

6   Relationships   107

Part II: Education in Modern America

7   Women in Education   131

8   Innovations in Education   151

Part III: Home Life in Modern America

14   Television and Children   313

Preface to Teachers

Two special considerations have guided us in developing, field testing, and finally assembling *Departures*. First, our book is based on the idea that college students—from developmental to advanced—must read texts, discuss them, and ultimately respond with texts of their own. Being able to respond in writing to the texts of others is, after all, fundamental for survival in academic life: as part of the "credentialization process" for "membership in the academic community" but, more importantly as a way of learning.

We think what makes *Departures* unique among readers for developing writers is that nearly all of the readings in it come from the popular media: newspapers, news magazines, and other popular magazines. We believe that these discourses serve as an excellent bridge for many of our students from precollege and extra-college experiences to their academic lives because the readings contain topics that are of concern to both sides: the academic culture and the home culture. From the academic side, many of the readings in *Departures* report on academic research, adjusted to the interests of the popular reader. From the home culture side, the readings report on the world the students know best. As Rose Marie Kinder points out ("A Piece for the Streets," *Journal of Basic Writing,* 10 (1991): 67–72), popular media writing constitutes "the students' material, their world" and thus, they feel free to interact with it, to "love it or rip it apart" (p. 71). In contrast to bleak reports about reading that students *don't* do, research by Carol Severino ("Where the Cultures of Basic Writers and Academia Intersect: Cultivating the Common Ground," *Journal of Basic Writing,* 11 (1992): 4–15) suggests that most students do read popular media. A good many of the readings in *Departures* are about young people in one way or another, though we haven't slighted the older, nontraditional students either (for instance, see Part III, "Home Life In America").

Our second special consideration in developing *Departures* was that we were determined to give plenty of flexibility for you as teachers to use it. Therefore, we have included nearly 100 readings, enough to allow you to use the book several semesters without boring yourself with repetition and enough to help you adjust for students who may repeat your class. We have also tried to allow you plenty of flexibility in how we have arranged the readings: All readings appear in thematic chapters, which can be used in their entirety or from which individual articles can be selected. Though there is an overall order to the chapters (the readings in the final chapter are longer and somewhat more complex than those in the first), we suggest that you skip around (like we do), using chapters or individual readings that suit your own interests and those of your students.

This same flexibility was in our minds as we put together discussion questions ("Questions for Thinking and Discussion"), which appear after each reading, and writing assignments ("Writing Projects"), which appear at the ends of each chapter. Quite frankly, we have included both of these somewhat reluctantly: We really don't want to imply that teachers *have* to use them. In particular, we hope that you will invent your own writing tasks designed with your own students' needs in mind. Please write to us and let us know about the kinds of writing assignments you have had success with to accompany *Departures* articles.

If you do choose to use our writing assignments, though, we think you will find plenty of flexibility to adjust to the needs of your course and to the levels of your students. For instance, we have included one assignment per chapter that asks students to discuss how the readings are related to their own experiences. Most assignments, however, are not about the self. Some ask for summaries of chapter readings; some require students to conduct interviews or informal surveys to challenge or affirm concepts in readings; some ask students to do library research for further reading on topics; some ask students to search for other evidence to support a thesis.

While we are proud of our work with *Departures,* we also realize that we are indebted to many people for the way it finally came together in theory and practice. For instance, a guiding spirit throughout our work on this book has been Mina Shaughnessy's special concern for her students' predicament: "they were . . . strangers in academia, unacquainted with the rules and rituals of college life, unprepared for the sorts of tasks their teachers were about to assign them" (*Errors and Expectations,* p. 3).

We also owe debts to theoretical influences as varied as Charles Bazerman, Richard Coe, Stephen Goldman, Stephen Krashen, and

Mike Rose. Moreover, articles by Rose Marie Kinder and by Carol Severino (both mentioned previously) have helped shape our notions of what we were doing in *Departures*.

Finally, we want to acknowledge the help of several other people. Special thanks to teachers who helped us field test earlier manuscripts of *Departures:* Stan Coppinger of Howard Payne University; and Sandra Beaty, Terrie Lewis, and Ruben Rodriguez, all of Tarleton State University. We also thank in particular two of our reviewers for helpful suggestions: Tom Dasher of Valdosta State College and Tahita Fulkerson of Tarrant County Community College Northwest. And, we are indebted to Alice Cushman for helping us get financial support for the early version of the book. Finally, we have also been helped immensely by those who worked with manuscript preparation and proofreading: Mary Etzel, Amy Neeb, Shirley Popken, Kristal Sappington, and Grace Ussery.

Randall Popken
Alice Newsome
Lanell Gonzales

Preface to Students

The first thing you might have asked yourself when you saw that this book was being used for your writing class this semester was, "Why is it called *Departures*"? We used this title for our book because three different meanings of the word *departures* refer to the role we hope this book will play in your development as a writer this term.

First, a *departure* is an act of "starting out" or "starting from." In this sense, our book is about ways that other pieces of writing can be the starting points for your own writing. Writing in response to what you have read is commonly what you will do in other courses in your college career. Throughout your college career, in fact, your instructors will ask you to produce summaries, critiques, research papers, think pieces, analytical papers, reports, and essay exams of all sorts. In many of these cases, the writing will be a response to someone else's writing.

We have assembled a book made up of readings for you to respond to by writing. The readings in *Departures* all deal with issues that are important to Americans: Part I gives some profiles of modern America, Part II is about education, and Part III is about home life. Each of these three larger parts of the book is made up of individual chapters on more specific topics such as stereotyping, the value of college, and the influence of television on children. All readings in a chapter are on the same topic, which we think allows you to build your knowledge about a topic in order to be able to write more confidently about it.

The term *departure* also means "setting out in a new direction." For each of you, the decision to come to college has certainly set you out in a new direction. Stop for a minute to think about what this departure means: You are entering a very new place where the primary activities are learning and talking about learning. In this new place, writing is a crucial part of that process of learning. In many ways, then, we think of this book as a point of departure for the rest of your academic and professional career.

A *departure* can also be a "deviation or divergence, as from an established rule or procedure." In this sense, we hope that this book will be a departure from what you might have thought a writing textbook must contain, especially if you have not gotten much out of writing textbooks in the past. *Departures* has no grammar exercises, no rules for writing, no workbook with blanks to fill in. Instead, the departure we offer you centers on reading; your writing instructor will make writing assignments and work with you on them. We think you will enjoy the readings in our book and that the readings will make your writing tasks very meaningful.

We hope you will be as serious and devoted to this book as we have been in assembling it and using it with our own students. We sincerely believe that *Departures* in your hands—and the very important guidance you receive from your writing teacher—will help you improve your writing in preparation for the rest of your college career.

Randall Popken
Alice Newsome
Lanell Gonzales

Departures

1

Image

IN HIS BOOK *Future Shock,* Alvin Toffler speaks about how the
modern era is a time of personal freedom for many people. Because of
technology, people today are able to take on many different images,
many different "selves." For instance, a person might project the image
of a business person at work but also take on the image of an artist,
poet, or member of a musical group during his or her spare time.
Toffler's point is that we are free to take on many different images
throughout our lives.

The image we project is made up of such things as how we act,
how we look, and whom we associate with. This image, which we
create either consciously or unconsciously, provides a way for people
to interpret who we are and what we are.

The readings in this first chapter deal with personal images in a
variety of ways. For instance, the first article reports on a study of
female college students' responses to the images created for them in
women's magazines. The next article shows how not only women are
concerned about ways to create their own images. The third article
examines how children develop a sense of image through the clothes
they wear. The final three readings in the chapter are about reactions

to images: how to change one's image, how some people go through rather extreme measures to change their image, and how some overweight people have rejected society's preferred image of the slim, fit person.

Measuring Up

DONNA KATO

THE COVER BLURBS PROMISE WOMEN "Surprising Tips for Sharpening   1
Your Lovemaking Skills" and "Great Places to Meet a Mate." They
herald "The Latest, Truest Update on What to Eat and Avoid," luring
women who worry about their weight.

Readers snap up more than 7 million copies a month of maga-   2
zines with headlines like those.

Yet what those circulation figures don't reveal is how women feel   3
after reading publications such as *Cosmopolitan* and *Glamour,* according
to a Palo Alto, Calif., social psychologist. Surprisingly, these specialty
magazines—traditionally touted as confidence builders—actually can
lower women's self-esteem, says Debbie Then, who researched the role
these publications play in women's lives.

The detailed answers for her recent study came from 75 female   4
Stanford students, between the ages of 18 and 30, who answered a
confidential survey. It didn't seem to matter that they were students at
such an intellectually elite institution—their answers are consistent
with how most American women feel, experts believe.

"When you're talking about gut-level feelings, you're going to   5
find that women react as women first, without regards to age or
education," explains Ann Kearney-Cooke, a Cincinnati psychologist
who specializes in women's issues. Her self-esteem workshops for
women include such exercises as going to a mall to prove that most
women don't look like actresses or air-brushed models.

Overwhelmingly, the women in the study said they felt worse   6
about their bodies and looks after reading the magazines, says Then,
who started the research while still a graduate student at Stanford.

Respondents indicated a "love-hate" relationship with the maga-   7
zines: They hated the pictures of the thin, gorgeous models, but loved
reading the articles—especially those addressing issues of sex, health
and relationships.

"I had no idea that women's self-esteem would be so diminished   8
by the photographs," says Then, who works with Stanford's psychological faculty and also is affiliated with UCLA's Institute for the Study

of Women. "On one level, they know that the photos are unrealistic, but they're still affected by them."

However, the women told Then that the magazines also gave them a nonthreatening way to get answers to what can sometimes be embarrassing questions, and to be assured that other women were having the same concerns. 9

Cosmopolitan editor Helen Gurley Brown, who introduced the "Cosmo Girl" with her first issue in 1965, believes the use of flashy models, ample cleavage and suggestive cover blurbs is perfectly justifiable. She's also proud of the magazine's story selections. 10

"Our criteria for stories is that we always ask ourselves: 'Will it do something for the reader?' " says Brown, adding that people like looking at beautiful women. 11

Then, who's in her 30s, started reading such magazines as *Teen* and *Seventeen* as an adolescent, mesmerized by the promise of clearer skin, more dates or thinner thighs. She moved on to *Glamour* and *Cosmopolitan* in high school and college. A few years ago, she was startled to see the contents in the *Seventeen* magazine of a friend's 15-year-old daughter. 12

"I thought that the articles were so advanced," and perhaps even harmful to impressionable young girls, says Then. She recalls that the stories told how to be more attractive to boys and whether to have sex on a first date. 13

It raised a question that eventually grew into her research project. Initially, the study's objective was to find out what articles women read so that she could encourage her fellow psychologists to be more aware of how such stories influence young women. Then presented her findings at the annual convention of the American Psychological Association last fall. 14

"Academicians and clinicians who conduct research on women and who treat women need to understand the unique relationship between women and their magazines, as well as the influence such magazines can have on a woman's self-esteem and body image," she says. 15

The Stanford women rated *Glamour, Cosmopolitan, Elle, Mademoiselle, Vogue, Ms., New York Woman, Mirabella*, and *Self* as their favorites. *Glamour, Cosmopolitan, Vogue, Mademoiselle* and *Elle* are the top five sellers with a combined circulation of more than 7 million readers. 16

The women provided Then with a wealth of information she wasn't expecting. For instance, one woman wrote: "*Cosmopolitan* is my favorite magazine. I can't say I actually like it. Reading the magazine is more of a self-torture in that I often use it to see how I am doing in comparison to current beauty standards. It angers me that I put myself up to comparison with such unrealistic ideals." 17

Says Kearney-Cooke, the psychologist: "[The findings from the   18
Stanford women are] very consistent with what women everywhere
think because they've been trained to look outside themselves for body
image instead of looking inside. Somehow, the message has been that
if you change your body, you can change your life."

Although 68 percent of the women said they felt worse about   19
their looks after reading a magazine, they exhibited mixed emotions
about whether the publications hurt or help women, Then's study
found.

What the women were clear on was their preference for articles   20
on men, sex and relationships, citing such recent topics as birth control, safe sex and building intimacy. They also enjoyed articles by male
writers who helped them understand how men think and stories that
dealt with battling eating disorders.

One way *Cosmopolitan* is trying to meet its readership's demands   21
is with a sister publication, *Cosmopolitan's Life After College,* targeted to
recent graduates and seniors who are making the transition from
college to career. On newsstands now, the second annual issue includes articles on finding jobs in a recession, roommates and living
back at home.

The "problem" stories, as Then sees them, are those that reinforce   22
negative beauty images and take on an "as-a-woman, it's-up-to-you-to-
fix-it" attitude about relationships.

"What I worry about is that some women read them as if they're   23
gospel," says Then, who also presents seminars on body image.
"Women need to be sophisticated consumers about what they're reading as much as they are about other things."

Questions for Thinking and Discussion

1. In this article, Debbie Then says that women often have a "love-hate"
   relationship with magazines such as *Cosmopolitan, Elle,* and *Glamour.*
   Why would the women, ages 18 to 30, feel this way? Do you think
   women over 30 would feel the same way?

2. The magazines mentioned in Kato's article try to establish an image for
   women. Are there any magazines that attempt to do this for *men?* To
   what extent do they succeed? How do you think a group of college men
   would react to these magazines? Would it be the same or different from
   the way the college women in Then's study reacted to the women's
   image magazines? Why?

Look at Me Now!

ANDREA HEIMAN

HE WATCHES HIMSELF INTENTLY IN THE MIRROR, gut sucked in, sweat   1
streaming, muscles rippling, teeth clenched.

"Finally, I can fit into these size 31 jeans," he says triumphantly.   2

Meet the new breed of man.   3

He's sleek, he's slim and he's doing what women have been doing   4
for ages—openly talking about his body. He might do it under the
guise of health and fitness, but deep down, it's plain old-fashioned
vanity that drives him in his quest for the perfect physique.

"Men have gotten away with murder in the eyes of women and   5
other men in appearing to be less vain," says Dr. Barry Glassner, author
of *Bodies: Overcoming the Tyranny of Perfection,* which is out of print.

"Men are terribly vain and always have been," says Glassner,   6
chairman of the University of Southern California sociology department.

In the not-so-distant past, men could get away with a potbelly   7
and a $4 haircut. And an unsightly blemish would never keep a real
man from leaving the house.

But times are changing.   8

"Men are coming out of the closet with their mirrors," says   9
Beverly Hills psychologist Susan Krevoy.

Nowadays, not only do men spend loads of money on beauty   10
supplies and subject themselves to exotic procedures, they even obsess
about their weight.

Just check out the local gym.   11

Bob Conti, a 33-year-old lawyer, started working out after he saw   12
an extra 10 pounds of gut. He goes to the gym five days a week—if he's
being "good"—and carefully monitors his weight. He says he and his
friends talk incessantly about nutrition and different ways of working
out.

"There's a tremendous societal pressure on relatively young, sin-   13
gle men to look a certain way," he says. "We're inundated with images
in the media. I would like my life to be like a light beer ad—everyone
is in shape, tan and looks fantastic."

The number of men buying health and fitness books is also on the rise: At Crown Books in the Westwood section of Los Angeles, sales to men have risen 20 percent to 30 percent in the past year, says assistant manager Stacey Florence. These buyers are not obese but are average guys—"suits" in their 30s and 40s, and students.   14

"There are also more books for men," says Florence. "Not Arnold Schwarzenegger books, but 'gutbuster' books targeted toward everyday guys. They're more open about caring what they look like."   15

Indeed, the illusive V-shape is becoming almost as important as, well, the car they drive.   16

"The body obsession is transferring from women to men. Plus no woman wants to be seen with a man with a potbelly. It's unsightly," says designer Maggie Barry, whose clothes are made with Lycra.   17

A decade ago, men wouldn't be caught dead in her form-fitting fashions. Now they're a statement.   18

The "ideal man" these days—as portrayed in magazines and movies—is not only fit, but he's getting thinner. A spread in *People* magazine recently featured Michael Douglas, Dwight Yoakam and Luke Perry flaunting their under-30-inch waists.   19

These days, men can choose from a plethora of attractiveness-enhancing procedures, from cosmetic surgery and liposuction to hair, calf and pectoral implants; chest-hair dying; and face patterning. About 20 percent of cosmetic surgery is done on males, up from about 5 percent just 10 years ago, according to the American Academy of Cosmetic Surgery.   20

Cosmetic companies have product lines for men, and the men's grooming industry has grown to a $2.5-billion business annually. These services and products are not aimed only at a certain type of man; they are being used, if only in small measure, by everyman.   21

It's not that men haven't always cared about their looks. A man or two has been known to secretly primp for hours, sulk over a bad haircut and flex in front of the mirror.   22

But while billboards, magazines and movies have constantly bombarded women with images of how they should look, it has been only recently that men have been confronted with the same barrage.   23

"What the popular culture does is present ideal types, attractive people, that make us presume that attractive people are happy people," says sociologist Sanders, who specializes in popular culture. "In the past, that wasn't focused on men. That's changed."   24

Ten years ago, the only magazine focusing on men's appearance was *GQ*. Now there is *M, Details* and *Esquire,* as well as a number of European magazines.   25

Eating Disorders Become Equal-Opportunity Problem

The pressure to be thin has led to unhealthy obsessions and dangerous eating disorders among women who starve and purge to maintain an "ideal" weight.

And as men become more concerned with their looks, they too are suffering from these problems, experts say.

"The equivalent of the female anorexic has been the male jogger," says Susan Krevoy, a Beverly Hills psychologist who specializes in treating eating disorders.

"Today it's more acceptable for men to be into their bodies, to work out, get a trainer. Men will talk about their weight and their body, which they didn't do 10 years ago.

"There's a whole different emphasis, and although it's supposed to be about health, it often camouflages an eating disorder," she says.

But it has also become more acceptable for men to admit they have eating problems, and more male bulimics and anorexics are seeking treatment, says Murray Firestone, a Century City psychologist who specializes in eating disorders and addictions.

Because bulimia and anorexia have been considered "women's diseases," he says, men have been afraid to admit they were victims.

"Men come to me with eating disorders which have been active for years," Firestone says.

"It's not only a woman's domain now. Men are seeing that it's OK to acknowledge their [problems] and to get help."

—Andrea Heiman

"The images in the media have influenced the average guy," says 26 Vahe Shaghzo, who runs the men's division of LA Models. "Men's concern about their looks is absolutely catching up to women's."

In another relatively new development, advertisers are using 27 men's bodies to sell.

"Ultimately, we're selling sex, and women like to see men with 28 nice bodies, broad shoulders and the V-shape," Shaghzo says.

And while men have always openly objectified women's bodies, 29 women were not encouraged to do the same to men's. Instead, men were judged by their power, money and prestige.

All that changed with the women's movement and the sexual 30 revolution, says Krevoy. Only fairly recently has it been acceptable for women to openly look at men's bodies.

And as women become more financially independent, taking on traditionally "male" roles in society, psychologists say, men are more able to acknowledge that "female" side of themselves: their vanity. 31

"Men have the same neurosis women do," says Marty Weiss, manager of Sammy Dinar, a men's clothing store in Beverly Hills. 32

"When a man gets up in the morning, he wants to look good to himself and to everyone out there he meets. He wants to have people notice him for his attractiveness and grooming. . . . He wants to stand out as much as a woman." 33

Questions for Thinking and Discussion

1. This article explores how men are becoming obsessed with their body images, a trait usually attributed to women. Why do you think this change has come about? Why are men thinking more about their physical images than ever before?

2. Think about the stereotypical image of the American male with "a potbelly and a $4 haircut." How does the stereotype compare to the "new man" described in Heiman's article? Which type of man are there more of in your experience: the stereotypical man or the "new man"?

Oh Mom!

BARBARA MELTZ

ATLANTA PSYCHOLOGIST Marshall Duke tells the story of a mother 1
and her 10-year-old son who weren't getting alone. In a session with
the whole family, Duke gave everyone a handful of tokens. In the next
two days, each person was to give a token to any family member who
did something that was appreciated.

At the next session, the mother was upset because she had not 2
received any tokens from her 10-year-old son. She began to describe
all the things she had done for him that week, including laying out his
clothes.

"That's it!" the son exclaimed. 3

"That's what?" the mother asked. 4

"You put out that balloon shirt, and all the kids made fun of me. 5
They always make fun of how I dress."

Duke uses the example to highlight a fact that many parents, 6
especially those of firstborns, don't realize: Clothing is an important
nonverbal communicator that can foster or impede relationships, especially peer relationships, but even parent-child ones.

Disagreements between parent and child over clothing choices 7
have a way of escalating quickly, usually because the parent views the
child's behavior as willful and bratty. Psychologists Carol Seerfeldt and
Louise Bates Ames offer other explanations:

- A 3-year-old girl who will wear only dresses or whose socks
  must have lace ruffles may be coping with gender identity:
  She's trying to learn what it means to be a girl.
- A preschool boy who throws a tantrum when he has to wear a
  pull-over, for example, or something red may have a legitimate
  physical aversion to a fabric, style, texture or color.
- A 5-year-old girl who refuses to wear specific outfits for no real
  reason may be trying to gain a sense of independence in one
  of the few ways available to her.

- A 7-year-old who insists on wearing his raggedy baseball cap wherever he goes could be using the cap as a transitional object, to gain a sense of security.

In situations like these, it is not a good idea to insist consistently on your choice, according to Seefeldt, a professor of early childhood education at the Institute for Child Study at the University of Maryland. It could result in a child who feels his needs aren't being met, that his parents don't understand him.   8

"It can cause conflict," says Duke, who is a professor at Emory University and co-author of *Helping the Child who Doesn't Fit In* (Peachtree Publishers Ltd.). Seefeldt suggests doing as she did with her own daughter: "Tell yourself, she's the one wearing it, not you."   9

At the age of 3, 4, or 5, clothing choices usually reflect personal taste and developmental issues. By first grade, that can start to change.   10

"Children need to connect with their peers," says clothing expert and author Marilise Flusser. Research shows one of the ways they do this is by dressing alike. "This is developmentally correct," says Flusser, adding, "You need to find a way to manage it, not judge."   11

Your first grader, who never cared about what he wears, suddenly wants a specific pair of sneakers.   12

"This is not about label consciousness or status symbols, not at this age," says Flusser. "This is about another child who runs really fast and your child wants to run that fast, too. Or your child admires a girl who is reading chapter books so she wants to dress like her." Flusser's book, *Party Shoes to School and Baseball Caps to Bed: The Parent's Guide to Kids, Clothes and Independence* (Simon & Schuster) is as full of solid consumer tips as it is of psychological ones.   13

Seefeldt labels what goes on for children about this age as a survival instinct. "A child now senses that there are ideas in the world other than the ideas she has, and those ideas may be about her," she says. Dressing alike makes her feel safe.   14

In these early elementary years, clothing also may be a way of expressing a friendship. A group of boys who play together wear neon shoelaces. Girls get to school and exchange one sock, the mismatch showing the world they are best friends.   15

But by third or fourth grade, the touching, tentative gestures symbolized by clothing can become power plays and tools of meanness and exclusion, says Flusser. She urges parents and teachers to make a rule that friendship necklaces or twin dressing be reserved for after school or weekends.   16

Clothes

Controlling the Fires of Young Fashion Fever

Fashion fever and other clothes calls:

- October and November are good months for the bulk of your back-to-school shopping. Tell your child, "Let's wait and see what your friends are wearing." Your child will appreciate your thoughtfulness and you'll save yourself the aggravation of having August-bought clothing sit in the drawer.

- While hand-me-downs are a necessary and thankful reality in many families, they can make a child feel bad, especially if styles have changed. Find a way for your child to have something new now and then, even if it's something small from a discount store.

- When your child has strong opinions, one outfit that he or she chooses is probably a better investment than three that you choose.

- At age 6 or 7, children may suddenly object to certain fabrics or complain about the way something feels on their skin. This can be a very legitimate developmental sensitivity that may last for a year or so. Respect your child's wishes.

- Include your child in the planning and/or buying process. Go through her clothes together, make a list of what she needs. Discuss costs, set priorities. "You can get by on two pairs of bike pants, but you need new sneakers. You know, if you stop using the toes of your sneakers as a brake on your bike, they might last longer and you could buy something you like."

- Clothes-consciousness knows no gender.

This is the time, too, when clothing takes on proportions that can   17
be downright frightening to parents, especially economically. Does the
10-year-old need a certain brand of jeans to feel safe and secure in her
environment, to not be isolated and ostracized, or is this just an
extravagant demand by a kid who is following the crowd?

"Parents walk a thin line, needing to cue into the kid's needs,"   18
says Seefeldt.

Whatever you do, don't insist your child go it alone, don't say she   19
doesn't "need" the jeans or that she should stand up and be an individual. "There's plenty of other opportunities to teach the values of individualism," Seefeldt says.

Duke explains, "Wearing the same clothes is a way for a child to   20
say, 'I'm part of the group. I belong.' Belonging is the important part."

This is not to say that Seefeldt or Duke or anyone else advocates   21
buying $80 jeans or $100 sneakers.

When something coveted is out of the question, Ames tells par-   22
ents not to minimize or devalue it and not to get angry or make your
child feel guilty for wanting it. She is the founder and associate director
of the Gesell Institute of Human Development in New Haven, Conn.

"Recognize how important the item is to him," she advises. "Then   23
say in a perfectly nice voice, 'We can't afford it. But maybe you can
save money to buy it, or we can help your buy it, or maybe for
Christmas. . . .' "

For all the difficulty parents may have with children who are very   24
clothes-conscious, there is another whole set of problems for the
parents of children who don't care what they wear.

"Lot's of kids don't understand this clothing thing," says Flusser.   25
"This child can become an outcast, a dork, without even knowing it.
It can be painful for parents to watch."

These out-of-touch kids may need their parents to run interfer-   26
ence for them, according to Duke. Flusser tells how: "I wouldn't even
talk to your child about it. I would go on a class trip to [see what other
kids are wearing and] make sure my child's clothing isn't ammunition
for ridicule."

Clothing issues may escalate when a girl reaches pre-puberty.   27
"They're comparing themselves to the images they see, and they can't
see themselves fitting it," says Flusser. They resort to "uniforms"—
Dad's V-neck T-shirt, baggy black jeans, a pony tail, stiffly sprayed
bangs.

For the 12-year-old, these styles provide a way to hide and be   28
accepted at the same time. The developmental issue is different but for
the parent, at least, it may feel like the preschool years all over again.

Questions for Thinking and Discussion

1. Meltz quotes psychologist Marshall Duke, who says that, for children,
   clothing is an important non-verbal communicator that can create or
   destroy relationships, especially peer relationships, and even parent-
   child ones. What does Duke mean by "non-verbal communicators"?
   What does Duke's statement about clothes as non-verbal communicators have to do with people's images? To what extent is any image a
   non-verbal communicator?

2. Clothing is one source of conflict between parents and children. What other areas of conflict typically occur between parents and children, particularly in regard to the image a child is trying to project? What experiences as a child or parent can you cite in this area? What advice could you offer to both parents and children to try to resolve these areas of conflict?

The Fine Art of Changing One's Image

Loraine O'Connell

Donny Osmond is trying to shed his goody-two-shoes image. The cover of his new album, *Donny Osmond,* features a moody black-and-white of Osmond in a leather jacket, blue jeans and tousled hair. The too-nice Mormon kid who once sang "Puppy Love" has returned to the charts with "Soldier of Love," a faintly suggestive tune set to a post-disco beat.

But Osmond's not alone in trying to revamp his image.

Bryant Gumbel is struggling mightily to inject a little warmth into his frosty persona. The NBC *Today Show* host, who pilloried his *Today* colleagues—especially weatherman Willard Scott—in an internal memo that made its way into print, is working to overcome his image as arrogant and dour. In his attempts to lighten up, he even resorted last month to doing the weather forecast—with Scott sitting by and clearly relishing every moment.

One of the most infamous examples of media image massaging is Dan Rather, he of the steely glint and quick temper.

After Rather replaced Walter Cronkite as anchorman of the CBS nightly broadcast in 1981, the show's ratings began to drop. People just didn't find Rather as appealing as Uncle Walt. But when he began wearing sweaters—the result of having developed a severe cold—audience reaction changed. Apparently people found Rather more warm and fuzzy. His ratings improved, and while the upturn can't be attributed entirely to Rather's woollies, he continued wearing them long after his cold had cleared up.

Changing one's image is no easy feat, according to psychologists and image experts—but it can be done. A lot depends on how firmly entrenched a person's image is.

"The clearer our impression of someone, the more likely it is we'll use it to affect how we interpret what that person is doing," said Dr. Barry Schlenker, a social psychologist at the University of Florida. "Our identities aren't just something that exist to us. They're something we have constructed with the help and agreement of others."

Schlenker says that's why, in the case of Osmond, "if he wears a leather jacket, we say, 'Why would a nice, sweet guy like him wear that leather jacket?' "

On the other hand, lots of studies show that people *can* become   9
the roles they act.

"Most military training manuals for officers advise people to act   10
the part of an officer even if they don't feel it in their heart," said
Schlenker. "When we play a role, if we start to get feedback conforming
the new role, we start to act more and more consistently with the role
we've been playing."

The key is sincerity, Schlenker said. "If a person plays the new   11
role halfheartedly, he'll get feedback indicating he's not authentic. The
person must be convinced there's a chance he can pull it off."

Indeed, to be really effective at changing your image, you must   12
change who you are, according to Dr. John Bengston, an associate
professor of psychology at the University of Florida.

"One of the problems with changing an image is that people   13
expect certain things of us and may not see" the changes we're trying
to make, Bengston said.

The other problem is that we tend to reveal our true selves in lots   14
of ways we can't control, he said. "We are what we are, and that
emanates through so much of us that superficial changes are difficult."

Not to mention stressful. Charna Davis, health reporter at WCPX-   15
Channel 6, can attest to that.

About two years ago, Davis said, it was "strongly suggested" to   16
her by the station management that she tone down her glamorous
image. She complied, cutting her hair, changing her makeup and
wearing less distinctive clothes.

"I'm sure I could have fought it, but I figured I'd do it in good   17
faith. But it was not me." Davis believes the discomfort her new look
caused affected her on-air performance.

"When you're uncomfortable with yourself, you can't do a good   18
job. One of the things you need more than anything on the air is
confidence. I have to go on not thinking about what I look like at all."

When new management took over at Channel 6, Davis said, the   19
broadcasters were encouraged to be themselves and she happily
obliged. "Whether we like it or not, what we look like is a statement
about who we are. I'm a little unconventional; I wear clothes that are
not dress-for-success clothes. I feel I'm a lot better on the air now
because I'm being me."

TV personalities are experts on the subject, but even they take a   20
back seat to politicians and their consultants when it comes to image
metamorphosis.

"Sixty-five percent of the people get their perception of a candi-   21
date from television," said Oscar Juarez, a Republican Party political
consultant. "What can you possibly get in 30 seconds? So you mention

the candidate's name as much as possible and you use a pretty picture of the candidate and his wife and children—hopefully younger children because that makes him look younger. Then you find a dog, even if it's a stray mutt, and in the background you put an American flag."

The only way for a politician to change his image, Juarez said, is   22
to start early in a campaign, accenting the positive more effectively than the opposition can accent the negative. "That translates to an awful lot of money and advertising. You're voting for an image," he said.

Sen. Bob Graham used that tactic successfully, Juarez said. "He   23
had a liberal image" and had voted in a very liberal manner as a state senator. To counter that image, he incorporated "work days" into his campaign, spending full days trying his hand at various jobs. As a result, he developed an image of being the working man's friend, Juarez said.

Schlenker, the social psychologist, said a key factor in the success   24
of an image swap is the way it's packaged. "Nobody wants to be viewed as inconsistent. A politician never says he has changed his opinion on an issue. He says times have changed or the situation has changed, but his attitudes haven't."

True to form, Osmond—the face that launched a thousand quips   25
about wholesomeness, apple pie and Mom—has said that what we're seeing now is the way he has been all along.

"He's saying, 'It's not me that's changing; you've misperceived   26
where I was,'" Schlenker said. "The extent to which he can get away with that, we'll have to wait and see."

Questions for Thinking and Discussion

1. In O'Connell's article, she quotes Dr. Barry Schlenker as saying, "Our identities aren't just something that exist to us. They're something we have constructed with the help and agreement of others." Would you say Schlenker's point is valid? Who are some of the people who have helped you construct your own image? How did they help you?
2. What can happen when people try to change their images? Think about some people you have known who have tried to change their images. What did they do and were they successful?

Piercing Schemes

ROBERT V. CAMUTO

IT STARTED with an earring.   1

Then about four years ago, Frank Mashado, the 26-year-old son of   2
a prominent Arlington surgeon, began having other parts of his body
punctured. His nose. His tongue. His nipples. Even more private places.

"I pierce myself to treat me," said Mashado, an artist who crafts   3
ceremonial objects and who crafts ceremonial objects and who today
has 11 piercings, and displays tattooed patterns from ancient Egypt
and the Hopi Indian tribe on his arms. "I don't go out and buy clothes
that often."

The logic often used to explain body piercing is often as bizarre   4
as the trend which has managed to spread from the West Coast underground into the well-scrubbed neighborhoods of Fort Worth-Dallas.

In the last couple of years, a handful of body-piercing enterprises   5
has sprouted in tattoo parlors and other businesses across North
Texas—catering to head-banging generation X-ers, trend-conscious
yuppies and even mid-life professionals looking for a thrill.

Some of those who have a front row seat for the passing parade   6
of pop culture say body piercing, along with a resurgence in tattooing,
may provide a sense of tribal belonging in an increasingly impersonal
society.

To some it's all a mindless fad—the latest frontier of rebellion   7
fueled by MTV and rockers such as Axl Rose (who has a much publicized nipple ring) and Aerosmith (whose recent music video *Cryin'*
shows a young woman getting her navel pierced.)

"I think it's just another phase of rebellion," said Agnes Commack   8
a *Women's Wear Daily* fashion-market editor who has seen more and
more young New York models show up for fashion shoots with pierced
tongues and other body parts.

"First it was more than one earring, then it was the nose piercings,   9
then tattoos, now this," she said. "I hate to think what's going to be
next."

Tattoos were once considered a mark of bikers and sailors, but   10
that is changing. Two years ago, 11 members of a prominent Texas
Christian University sorority had dime-sized tattoos of marine mam-
mals placed on their bikini lines as an initiation rite, according to one
officer in that sorority, who spoke on the condition of anonymity.

A decade ago, body piercing was limited to what's commonly   11
referred to in California as the "leather community"—the sado-maso-
chistic subculture of whips and chains.

Nowadays, suburban kids with attitudes line up at the touring   12
music festival Lollapalooza to get navel hoops and lip studs.

Piercing is not regulated by law. Often piercers learn their trade   13
from magazines or videos. But they typically require their clients to be
18 years old, a hurdle that's pushed some trend-crazy teens to infect
themselves by trying it solo.

"For a lot of kids today it's shock value—to keep up with your   14
peers that kind of thing," said Jim Ward, editor of the San Francisco-
based publication Piercing Fans International Quarterly and the owner
of the 19-year-old chain of body jewelry shops called Gauntlet. "It's
only in the last three to five years that it's expanded significantly
outside the SM world."

In an age when all it takes is cable television to keep abreast of   15
the avant-garde—putting rings in what were once considered all the
wrong places—has even moved west of Cowtown.

The 2-year-old Rebel Tattoos, on Jacksboro Highway in Sansom   16
Park, was getting so many inquiries about body piercing that owner
Trish McElroy decided to cash in.

Her daughter, Cassie, took a four-day piercing course this sum-   17
mer in San Francisco. Down came the old Confederate Battle Flag
inside the shop and up went a tie-dyed banner and a sign with the
store's new name, Erotic Shock.

Trish McElroy is betting on the now far-off proposition that body   18
piercing will become as common as kid-packed minivans in Tarrant
County.

"Five years from now when you go to Kroger, you won't even look   19
back—it's absolutely the rage," the mother professed.

Kwin Smith, 25, of Weatherford, a sign company worker and avid   20
rock climber, drove to Jacksboro Highway on a recent Saturday afternoon to have a steel ring placed in his upper navel.

He lay down on a padded table while Cassie McElroy, wearing   21
rubber gloves, labored for minutes to get a pinch of flesh in the grips
of a pair of surgical clamps. That done, she took a surgical needle
dipped in cream and pushed it through the fold of skin.

Smith later described the sensation as similar to a medicinal shot.   22
It cost him about $50 including a piece of surgical steel jewelry and a
bottle of cleaning solution.

For his $50, Smith walked out of the shop believing he'd struck   23
a blow for his individuality.

"I have some friends who have body piercing and I think it's really   24
cool," Smith said. "It's like piercing your ear, but it's not that mainstream yet."

In Dallas, Stace Maples, a graduate of Trinity High School in   25
Euless, runs one of the area's largest piercing businesses—dubbed Skin
and Bones—set in a storefront row near Fair Park where Doc Marten
boots, shaved heads and faces studded with jewelry are the uniform of
the moment.

Maples, who plies his trade in an old dentist's chair while a stereo   26
blares such bands as Alice In Chains and the Honeymoon Killers, has
the word "Sleazy" tattooed in living color on his arm and counts 15
piercings over his body.

His clientele on a recent Saturday afternoon included a J.C. Penny   27
sales associate from Plano who had a nipple pierced and offered this as
her explanation: "It's just something I wanted to do for a long time."

"All these middle-class kids are grasping for culture," Maples   28
observed in a philosophical moment. "We have no culture anymore
except for television, MTV and the corporate garbage that's being fed
to us."

Maples' fiance, Trish Rice, sprawled on a black vinyl sofa, mocked   29
her husband-to-be.

"It's a fad," she said. "I don't want it. I have nice skin. Why destroy   30
it?"

Still, there may be an element of truth in Maples' analysis. Uni-   31
versity of Texas at Arlington sociologist Ray Eve likens body piercing
to tribal "status markers" that identify members of a group in an
otherwise impersonal society.

Indeed, some piercing enthusiasts have begun exploring what   32
they say are the tribal and even "spiritual" aspects of piercing like the
Native American rite popularized in the movie classic *A Man Called
Horse*.

One such piercing devotee is Allen Faulkner, a 24-year-old from   33
an affluent neighborhood in Dallas who sold his Harley Davidson a
year ago to open a piercing studio called Obscurities in the back of an
Oak Lawn vintage clothing store.

Faulkner who has practiced such native rituals as the chest pierc-   34
ing "Sundance," describes it as a "mind-over-matter-thing" like walking
on coals.

"I'm sober, I don't smoke or drink or do any drugs," Faulkner   35
explained. "This is a physical release to me. Some people would say it's
not sane. But I think it's sane."

Questions for Thinking and Discussion

1. Camuto offers several explanations about why people have taken to body piercing and tattooing as a means of creating a new image. Here are some of Camuto's explanations:

   People are seeking *"a sense of tribal belonging in an increasingly impersonal society."*

   "All these middle-class kids are grasping for culture. . . . We have no culture anymore except for MTV, and the corporate garbage that's being fed to us" (quote from Stace Maples, who operates a piercing business).

   Kwin Smith, a sign company worker, had his navel pierced to "[strike] a blow for his individuality."

   "I think it's just another phase of rebellion" (quote from Agnes Commack, a fashion-market editor).

   Piercing represents a way of releasing the spirit from the body.

   What do these explanations really mean? Which of them seems most accurate to you? How do you explain the fact that some of the explanations seem to contradict each other: for instance, that some people want an image of *individuality* but also an image of *tribal belonging?*

2. When you see someone who has a pierced nose, eyebrow, or lip, how do you interpret it? That is, what characteristics do you tend to associate with that person, even if you don't know him/her?

   How about a person wearing an earring? Is there a difference in the characteristics you associate with the person? How about a male wearing an earring versus a female? Is there a difference between the characteristics you associate with these two? Why do these differences in our interpretations of the images exist?

Diet? Forget it! Get the Skinny on Being Fat

JENNIFER BRIGGS-FRENCH

A PINT OF CHOCOLATE CHOCOLATE CHIP HAAGEN-DAZ is fine in a size 9   1
lap. Yet when spooned into a size 16 gullet it becomes Hog-en-daz.

The National Association to Advance Fat Acceptance would like   2
to point out that there are some serious double standards causing size
24 problems for portly people.

For National Association to Advance Fat Acceptance and some   3
other overweights, fat, be it spilling over Spandex or lumpy in lace, is
where it's at.

They don't diet. They don't mope. They are fat and fight for their   4
right to remain so despite discriminatory skinnies out there.

They are fat, happy and determined to stay that way.   5

"We are comfortable with ourselves," said Sally Smith, executive   6
director of the Sacramento-based organization with 40 chapters across
the nation, including Dallas.

"But it should be easier to be fat in our society. That's what we're   7
working toward."

Queen-size Leggs are available in almost any supermarket, but a   8
queen-size airline seat is non-existent.

Often, Smith says, airlines require fat people who desire a larger   9
seat to purchase an extra half fare, move the armrest and use two seats.

Surprisingly, airlines do not require purchase of an extra half   10
engine to carry the extra 70 pounds of body fat. (And unfortunately,
they don't also charge extra for large mouths and big heads.)

Just My Size pantyhose may fit without pinching or binding "in   11
four roomy sizes," but restaurant seats are Just One Size—with room
for the average roach rump.

"Restaurant seats can be very small for the regular size person,"   12
Smith said. "We are putting pressure on restaurants to have chairs with
no armrests. They realize fat people have money. We are an economic
force."

The National Association to Advance Fat Acceptance is a   13
"human-rights" organization, Smith said. "Our premise is that fat people desire the same things as everyone else and size discrimination is
wrong."

Smith said she went to a physician for three years who took her   14
blood pressure with a regular-size cuff, known to cause false readings
on extra-large arms. She was on blood pressure medication for three
years before going to a doctor with an extra-large cuff who found she
had no blood pressure problem at all.

"We attempt to destroy myths and stereotypes like, 'If you wanted   15
to lose it you could,' " she said.

"We try to take the blame away from being fat. Most members   16
have already chosen to accept themselves when they come to us.

"You go in for an unrelated problem, and the doctor will say,   17
'Come back when you lose 50 pounds.'

"It's not easy being fat in our society."   18

Not easy, but Smith and other members of the fat advocate group,   19
which is made up of fat men and women and "thin allies," are happy
with hefty.

"I grew up as a fat kid," said Ray Hackney, the fat advocate group's   20
Dallas chapter chairman, who weighed 96 pounds in the first grade. "I
definitely have a preference for fat females."

When he graduated from high school, Hackney, 6 feet 2 inches   21
tall, weighed 315. Today he is a slimmer 245.

"After I lost weight, I realized you're the same person whether   22
you are fat or skinny," he said. "You realize you don't have to lose
weight to gain self-respect."

Dallas members of the National Association to Advance Fat Ac-   23
ceptance range from size 18 to 48.

"You don't try to change the weather," Hackney said. "You dress   24
accordingly. The same is true of being fat."

Hackney recently went to a New Year's party in New York where   25
the average female size was 26. Bear in mind, the average average is
about an 8 to 10.

"We were having a lot more fun than the size 5s and 8s upstairs,"   26
he said.

Yet the Lean Cuisine generation knows heft and health are not a   27
traditional mix.

"The thing that concerns me is not that they said it's OK to be   28
overweight because you're still the same person inside," said a dietitian
at the Baylor Medical Center in Dallas who requested anonymity lest
he become a part of the fat fray. "What concerns me is they're saying
being overweight is not a health risk.

"Being overweight is unhealthy."   29

But some heft can't be helped.   30

"The fact is, 95 percent of all diets fail over three years and most   31
fat is caused by heredity and metabolism," Smith said.

"You just have to be the healthiest you can be, whatever your weight. There are some that feel it is healthier to reach a standard weight and keep it than yo-yo dieting."

And, some people are rather fond of billowy buttocks and thick thighs.

Eclectic R&B group Root Boy Slim and the Sex Change Band extolled the virtues of having flab enough to grab in its 1979 *Dare to be Fat.*

Dare to be fat's where it's at, sings Root Boy.

Havin' a ball with cholesterol

Come on, ya'll, fat don't matter at all.

The National Association to Advance Fat Acceptance has yet to adopt Root Boy's sentiments as the fat anthem, but they fit snugly with the fat philosophy of *Big Beautiful Woman,* a Beverly Hills total concept magazine for the large-size woman.

Fat people can be where-it's-at people is the message of *Big Beautiful Woman.* Though it provides no advice for the big, ugly women, mainstream magazines do not address unsightly skinny people either.

In addition to *Big Beautiful Woman,* there is *Radiance,* a quarterly issue-oriented publication for overweight women and *Magna,* a bimonthly with fashions and self-help for the fat guys.

The emphasis is on comfort in a 300-pound package.

Big Beautiful Woman contains fat fashion, large letters, sizable stories and portly pictures, all of them of, about or for the large-size person who is comfortable and confident.

In a refreshing twist on women's periodicals, *Big Beautiful Woman* touts not a diet one. Not a single fat-free recipe. No "Lose a pound a day the rodent's way." And mercifully, no saccharin and fruit concoctions for deadly diet daiquiris.

"Are you any smarter if you wear a size 8 dress," asks *Big Beautiful Woman* Editor in Chief Carole Shaw.

"Is your basic character any more worthwhile if you're 120 lbs., rather than 220-plus? Will the world applaud you in 100 years if you forgo that piece of cake and settle for black coffee?"

Angela Bormann, size 16, adorns the cover of the January issue with a toothy smile and peachy skin. "Interview with *Bold & Beautiful* Stylish BB Soap Star! Darlene Conley," goes the teaser on the cover.

Features such as "99 ways never to be bored in 1990!," "Fashion Now! Way-Out Western, Nautical, Fringe" and "How to survive when you drive: Gridlock, Breakdowns & Freeway Romance" provide information obviously not limited in value to the population's portly portion.

The introduction to a *Big Beautiful Woman* article about a Minne- 48
sota winter celebration considers the plump proposal, "If you were
going to sponsor a winter celebration in Minnesota, where tempera-
tures dip into deeply negative numbers, what sort of woman would
you choose to serve as hostess? An angular blonde with less than 17
percent body fat? Hell no! She'd be a blue-eyed icicle before the
flaming-red sun could set behind your Ice Palace.

"What you'd require is a woman big and beautiful. A woman with 49
a power plant to equal the elements of the frozen North. A real
Klondike Kate."

There is typical advice for women over 40 (years old, not inches 50
wide) with an emphasis on weight. It is a typical magazine with
atypical size 16 models pivoting in pearls and sashaying in sweaters.

"As you can see from this photo, I am married, and my fighting 51
weight is usually around 290 lbs. Men do like large women as evi-
denced by the fact that my husband and I just had a beautiful boy
about a week ago," writes Marilyn, a reader from San Francisco.

Much as popular culture prefers to ignore the extra-large exist- 52
ence, *Big Beautiful Woman* indirectly points out that yes, fat people even
drive, get married and wear black-lace teddies, with photos on the
latter.

Teen-age boys in shopping malls may remain compelled to mimic 53
barnyard sounds when a size 14 backside passes the Poncho's, but *Big
Beautiful Woman* readers and the National Association to Advance Fat
Acceptance members are nonplussed, labeling such adolescent animals
"insecure" and calling fat people pretty.

Or as Root Boy Slim (yes, him again) put it: 54

"*I saw a fat girl in my neighborhood, good God almighty she was* 55
lookin' good.

"*Tight ski pants, cashmere sweater. Root Boy can't think of nothin'* 56
nothin' better.

"*She's got a shape that makes me drool. Lord, I'm just a fat girl's fool.* 57
"*She weighs in at 202.* 58
"*That's fine with me, 'cause I'm portly, too."* 59

Questions for Thinking and Discussion

1. Many people who are overweight do not accept themselves as they are,
   and they are constantly trying to lose weight, often unsuccessfully.
   What could these people do to work toward accepting their own sizes

as just another dimension of who they are? Think of several reasonable suggestions for people who need to work at accepting their large sizes. How might they go about working with the suggestions?

2. What are the standards for the "ideal" male and the "ideal" female today? What things do people do to try to fit the "ideal" image?

Writing Projects

1. Write a paper analyzing your own image(s) and what you have been using to project them. These image(s) might be evident in your clothing, automobiles, language, friends, reading material, listening material, or behavior. The image(s) need not be ones that you have consciously tried to create through the years; they may be ones you have been totally unaware of until now. To help you understand more about your own image, you may need to ask some of your closest (and most honest) friends what images they think you have been projecting. You might conclude the paper by discussing whether you are pleased with the image(s) you are projecting.

2. In her article about men's images, Heiman implies that standing behind much of the image of the new man is advertising. She quotes Vahe Shaghzo, who works in modeling: "Ultimately we're selling sex. . . ." Write a paper in which you examine the role of advertising in personal image making (men's or women's, or both).

   For the paper, you might do some "research" by watching about four hours' worth of television, especially during times and programs that many younger (below age 30) people might be watching. What images are the advertisements on these programs selling viewers? Take notes on all the ads selling personal images. Then construct your paper around the kinds of personal images that advertising seems to be trying to create.

3. In her article in this chapter, Meltz speaks about how children develop images. She discusses how the way preschool children dress is a matter of "personal taste" almost entirely to please themselves. Before they are very far along in school, however, children become more conscious of others and eventually want to dress in certain ways to identify with a group.

   Write a paper exploring how this process changes (or doesn't change) when a person becomes an adult. For example, do adults ever revert to just dressing for personal taste again, as we did when we were children? Once we become adults, is personal taste ever entirely our own as it was when we were children, or is "personal taste" for adults always determined by what is considered fashionable by a group?

4. Conduct a study of some group that is trying to find a radically different image—one that is much different from most of the students on your campus. Try to get to know one or more people who are trying to project this image. Ask them questions such as the following:

   "What other images are you rejecting? What is it about these other images that you object to?"

27

"What special features make up your image? Is it your clothes? your automobile? your housing? your behavior? your friends? your language? the music you listen to? the books or magazines you read? or. . . ?"

"What do you hope to accomplish by this new image?"

"Do you expect this image to catch on with other people? Would you continue to use the image if many other people took it on, too?"

After your interview(s), write a report on your findings of this group. Do your results support anything discussed in the articles in this chapter?

2

Heroism

IN LITERATURE CLASSES IN HIGH SCHOOL OR COLLEGE, you may have read stories about heroism in works written by the Greek poet Homer. In both of Homer's works—the *Odyssey* and the *Iliad*—the main character is Ulysses, a warrior who traversed the seas in search of adventure. Or, perhaps you read about the exploits of the Teutonic warrior Beowulf, who (among performing many other deeds) slew Grendel, a most hideous monster.

Who comes to mind when *heroism* is mentioned in modern life? Many Americans immediately think of people such as Martin Luther King, Jr. and Mother Teresa. And, of course, millions of Americans find heroic qualities in sports stars, movie stars, and popular singers: Michael Jordan, Robert Redford, Madonna.

The readings in this chapter are about heroism of three different types: people who are often regarded as heroic, people who have been made into heroes falsely, and people who truly *are* heroic. As they discuss these topics, the writers of the articles seem to assume that heroes and heroines serve a central purpose: They serve as *role models,* people whom we want to be like in some way. As you read these articles, try to determine what qualities modern heroism seems to consist of.

This Year's Role Model

CHARLES LEERHSEN

THERE'S NO WAY AROUND IT; if you want to understand today's   1
teenagers, you have to discover their heroes. Or, as the philosopher
Joseph Campbell has pointed out, the people we admire are a reflection of our inner selves. Which isn't to say that pinpointing today's teen
heroes is a Herculean task. Years of research has produced a scientific
way of obtaining people's opinions about any number of things, heroes
included. Yet in preparing this report, I didn't want to go that route.

The problem with the scientific approach is that it produces   2
predictable results. I have before me a "youth survey" conducted in
1965, the golden age of the clipboard-clutching, narrow-necktied poll-
ster. Can't you just see those guys, fanning out to sock hops and science
fairs? And can't you imagine the Eddie Haskell-ish responses? Believe
me, you can. The teen heroes of 25 years ago, according to this poll,
included John F. Kennedy, Elvis Presley, James Dean and Martin Luther
King Jr. Great men. But, you've got to admit: all the usual 1965
suspects.

I wanted something less obvious, something more real. So I took   3
a trip. I visited a military academy in Indiana, an eighth grade in the
Bronx, a girls' school in Dallas, a Midwestern high school and the Pine
Ridge Indian Reservation, deep in the South Dakota Badlands. At every
school, I passed out index cards on which I asked students to write
down a few heroes, and I talked to them, in groups, about whom they
admired. When I read the cards later, I got a mild shock. The most
frequently mentioned figure among the kids I'd spoken to? Basketball
star Michael Jordan. And after that? A mishmash, but a mishmash
featuring . . . John F. Kennedy, Elvis Presley, James Dean and Martin
Luther King.

What seemed predictable in 1965 now looked strange indeed.   4
But I'm getting ahead of myself.

My tour began at the Culver Academies, in Culver, Ind. New York   5
Yankees owner George Steinbrenner went here, as did actor Hal Hol-
brook and George R. Roberts (of the Kohlberg Kravis Roberts investment firm). Culver is two institutions: a boys' military school founded
in 1894 and a girls' academy opened in 1971. Both share a reputation
for academic excellence, as well as a handsome campus with Gothic
buildings and huge, sloping lawns convenient for rolling freshmen into
nearby Lake Maxinkuchkee. Annual cost: about $18,000.

Culver is "military" only in its discipline and uniforms; the stu- 6
dents don't study war no more. Still, when asked for their heroes, the
boys came up with Ulysses S. Grant, Robert E. Lee, Douglas Mac-
Arthur, Alexander the Great, Chuck Yeager, Audie Murphy and Ser-
geant York. Mixed in with those, though, were Mother Teresa, Martin
Luther King, Houdini—and from Stephan Lower, a senior from Westfield, N.J.: Winnie the Pooh. The girls mentioned Lucille Ball, Margaret
Thatcher, Superman, Jane Goodall—and Westfield, New Jersey's own
Stephen Lower. Michael Jordan was popular with both groups, as was
James Dean. Although somewhat startled at the mention of an actor
now 24 years dead, I didn't think much of it, yet. Indiana was Dean's
home state, after all, and these kids had a sense of history and liked to
demonstrate it.

From there, it was a couple of hours' drive to Rolling Meadows 7
High School, in Rolling Meadows, Ill. A hot topic, at the time of my
visit to this big (1,600 students), clean school, located about 15 miles
north of Chicago, was the date of the Turnabout Dance (girls invite
boys). Should it be rescheduled because of a conflict with a state
tournament basketball game? It wasn't a suspenseful debate: this is an
extremely sports-minded school. Michael Jordan's picture can be found
on T shirts and classroom walls. With RMHS so near the Chicago Bulls'
home court, that's understandable. Yet the students emphasized that it
is Jordan's extracurricular activities—his charity work and anti-drug
efforts—that account for his appeal. "He knows he is a role model,"
said Lisa Soucek, 18, of Arlington Heights. "He wouldn't do anything
wrong because kids follow in his footsteps."

Just behind Jordan on the heroes list was Mike Lipnisky, the star 8
of the RMHS basketball team. I didn't know that, though, until I read
the cards. The students seemed reticent about mentioning a peer in
class—but then they were a hard bunch to get talking about *anything*.
The air at Rolling Meadows seemed thick with the kind of peer pressure that stifles expression. "Oh, some heroes *must* come to mind," I
said at one point. "Tell me whose pictures you have on your bedroom
wall." Most kids remained silent. Betsy Pappas, 17, of Mt. Prospect,
said she had a calendar featuring the Chippendale's dancers.

Next stop: the Hockaday School for girls in North Dallas. 9
Founded in 1913 by Miss Ela Hockaday, a tall, reserved woman from
Pecan Gap, Texas, this school, for grades pre-K through 12, now
occupies 100 manicured acres. Tuition and board cost about $17,000
a year. For that you get a 50,000-volume library; a NASA-esque computer center; courses in Southern lit and Japanese history; a TV studio;
10 tennis courts and a live-animal lab that, in most cities, would be a
tourist attraction. Many buildings are connected by climate-controlled

glass corridors—a reminder, perhaps, of the days when Dallas girls were deeply into bouffant management.

Today's Hockaday students tend to have a no-nonsense attitude toward heroes. Yes, quite a few did pick Dr. King, Jordan, Superman, James Dean, Anne Frank and Sinead O'Connor ("because she's not afraid to be vulnerable"). But this was one place where the traditional definition of a hero seemed outdated. "I don't have a particular hero," said Indrani Reddy, 16, of Duncanville, Texas. "I admire different characteristics in different people." Melissa Korby, 18, of Dallas agreed. "I feel the national heroes we are offered keep failing," she said. "They seem more and more corrupt." Kathleen Sealock, 17, of Dallas, said her hero was Ollie North—but only because she made $1,400 selling T shirts with his picture during the Iran-contra hearings.

Then someone mentioned James Dean, and I had to ask what the deal was. Without hesitation, the students explained: in the first place, Dean's hauntingly handsome face appears on posters sold in many shopping malls, and his movies, such as "Rebel Without a Cause," still pop up on TV. But what makes him rise among contemporary hunks is that he lived before we knew so much about our idols. "Being a total hero isn't possible in today's society," said Ronnetta Fagin, 18, of Richardson, Texas. "The media strips a person of the mystery, glory and honor that belong to a hero. We revel in finding that one ounce of dirt to smear on outstanding people."

Immaculate Conception School, on 151st Street in the South Bronx, is a long haul from Hockaday in many ways. Your humble correspondent got his primary education here. The neighborhood, not far from Yankee Stadium, has changed much since I graduated in 1963, mostly because the white middle class fled en masse and landlords burned down tenements when they ceased being good investments. Inside ICS, though, things seemed the same, except the nuns' somewhat modified habits.

The kinds of people the eighth graders at ICS saw as heroes varied widely. Even within one young mind, the range was great. I asked each student to write down two heroes. Michelle Graham, 13, said fashion model Elle MacPherson and Bart Simpson ("because I wish I could get away with treating my parents that way"); Shauneille Parker, 13, picked God and Arsenio Hall; José Centano, 15, chose Michelangelo and Larry Bird; Nicole Howel, 14, picked New York Mayor David Dinkins and Public Enemy. The two big heroes at ICS in the early '60s were John F. Kennedy and Mickey Mantle. Their names also came up in my informal survey, albeit once each.

I didn't know *what* to expect at the Red Cloud School, in Shannon County, S.D., one of the poorest counties in the nation. The alcoholism and unemployment rates among the Dakota Indians on the Pine Ridge

Reservation were, I was told, both running at about 80 percent. People familiar with Native American culture also warned me to expect reticent kids who would not make eye contact. The reality, though, was somewhat different. Red Cloud, a 101-year-old Jesuit-run institution, was more like a prep school on the Great Plains. The buildings were spotless and in excellent repair. For better or worse, the students could have blended into the crowd at any shopping mall. As for shyness, I was there 20 minutes when a boy asked me how much I made. When I mentioned to principal Chuck Cuney how typical the school seemed, he shrugged and said that "things were tougher" at the federal school, a couple miles away in the town of Pine Ridge. Red Cloud tended, he said, to get the more affluent kids, who were "connected to the world through MTV."

Some of the students cited Native American heroes: Fools Crow, Chief Red Cloud and boxing champ Virgil Hill. Michael Jordan got the most votes, though, while Axl Rose ("because he just don't care"), Donald Trump and Michael Milken also earned mentions. When I asked if the boys had any female heroes, someone shouted, "Marla Maples." Everyone laughed, and I asked how they kept up with such gossip. "Maury Povich," the class chorused, referring to the host of "A Current Affair." Everyone laughed again, and one girl said, "Hey, I put Maury Povich down as my hero." [15]

As I was leaving, I mentioned that I was headed out to see Wes Craven and asked if they knew who he was. "The guy who makes 'Nightmare on Elm Street'," one boy said. [16]

I drove back to the airport in Rapid City thinking this: if kids in the Badlands can have many of the same heroes as the girls at Hockaday, or the boys at Culver—and if many of those heroes are dead or over the hill—then heroes might be serving a different and less vital function than they used to. Thanks to TV and celebrity journalism, kids all over the country are choosing from the same menu of celebrities—and rarely with any great enthusiasm. The problem is not that fame comes, these days, to those who don't deserve it. The shortage of really inspiring heroes probably has more to do with the dearth of pure *fans*. So many kids today are so informed about pop culture—about who's straight and who's gay; who's cheating on their mate and who's cheating on their taxes; who's been to Betty Ford and who still hasn't— that it's as if they have one foot in the audience and one behind the scenes. Such familiarity must inevitably breed at least a little contempt. [17]

I got to Santa Monica the next day. Craven, as virtually everyone who meets him says, does not look like Freddy Krueger's father. The villain of the "Nightmare" series is a semidecomposed ghoul who slashes people with knives that seem to grow out of his fingers. Craven, at 50, is a well-read, serene-seeming father of two grown children, [22] and 25. The only hints of a wild inner life in his home are an Elm Street sign hanging above his kitchen sink and the autographed picture of Timothy Leary in the living room.

I sought out Craven because not only are his movies *about* teen- 19
agers, but they seem to move teens in a way that other films, including the superficially similar "Friday the 13th" offerings, do not. When I mentioned this to him, he said that, yes, that was true and he knew why. "Because Freddy does not perpetrate senseless violence," he said, "as many adults think. The only people who die because of him are those who don't face the truth. The characters who try to put them-selves to sleep in a sense—who avoid reality by using sex, drugs, eating, TV, what have you—they are the ones he slashes and pares away mercilessly." Craven took a sip of herbal tea and then went on. "I believe we are at a fairly frightening, transitional stage of history. We tried the Ozzie-and-Harriet thing in the '50s, and that didn't work. Then we tried the hippie peace-and-love thing, and that didn't work either. Then we tried the Yuppie thing, and the world got worse. So what's next? Today, there is no clear way for teenagers to go. All they have are politicians, TV preachers and cynical heavy-metal musicians telling them things that they sense are lies. No one is offering them the truth they crave so deeply.

Does Craven have any suggestions for today's teenagers? He 20
thinks, then sighs. "I'm a filmmaker," he says. "I make horror movies in which a character comes out of people's dreams and slashes away at anything that's bullshit. All I can tell you, I guess, is that I'm not surprised that Freddy Krueger is a teen hero."

Questions for Thinking and Discussion

1. Leerhsen discusses the role model-heroes he finds among students in very different schools: a military academy in Indiana, a suburban school in Illinois, a private girls' school in Texas, an inner city school in New York, and a school on the Pine Ridge Reservation in South Dakota. If he had visited your high school when you attended, would he have found the same role models as he did in the schools he visited? How would these people compare or contrast to the ones Leerhsen would find if he spoke to students at your college?

2. After his travels visiting with young Americans, Leerhsen concludes that "heroes might be serving a different and less vital function than they used to." Assuming that Leerhsen is correct in what he says, do you think this is necessarily a good or a bad thing? Why?

Why Keep Glorifying Drunks and Junkies?

BILL THOMPSON

IT WAS JUST A BRIEF ITEM ON THE SPORTS PAGE, buried among the
baseball box scores: "Sports figures in alcohol-related accidents."

Then came a list of prominent individuals in the world of sports
who had been injured—or had injured others—in motor-vehicle accidents involving alcohol.

The list included 19 names—big names such as Billy Martin,
Bill Shoemaker, Don Drysdale and Carl Lewis, and lesser-known
names such as Rob Moroso and Stacey Toran. It barely scratched
the surface in describing the massive drunken-driving problem in this
country or the problem of alcohol and drug abuse in sports.

The matter-of-fact way the list was presented in the sports section
of *USA Today*—just another statistic floating in a a sea of statistics—
seemed to say as much about the magnitude of the problem as the list
itself did.

The headline "Famous sports star arrested for drunken driving"
has become so commonplace that we barely blink when we see it.
These stories of athletes destroying themselves and others with booze
and drugs have become so routine that we now find it possible to
present them in a roundup in small type on the statistics page of the
newspaper.

Basketball star Roy Tarpley busted for DWI? What's new?

Baseball player Lenny Dykstra charged with driving under the
influence, speeding and reckless driving? Tell us something that might
surprise us.

You could probably examine any profession, any occupation,
and find an ample supply of drunks, junkies and drunken drivers.
Athletes may be no more prone to this sort of thing than anybody
else.

The problem is, athletes are high-profile individuals. They are
role models.

Athletes, like it or not, are heroes to many, many people.

But for every Nolan Ryan who is a deserving hero and role
model to be enthusiastically admired and emulated by young and old
alike, there are dozens of Tarpleys and Dykstras who are so wealthy,

spoiled and self-indulgent that they believe society's rules don't apply to them.

These over-praised, overpaid brats are coddled from the time they   12
are old enough to dribble a basketball or throw a baseball or run with a football.

They are set apart and permitted—no, encouraged—to live by   13
different standards than their peers. They are afforded special treat-ment in school, in business and in virtually every aspect of their lives.

It never occurs to them that they should obey the same laws as   14
other people or even that they should observe the simple rules of common decency that dictate the behavior of mere mortals.

It is tragic, of course, that these misguided souls seem so bent on   15
the destruction of themselves and everyone who suffers the bad fortune of crossing their path—literally and figuratively.

But equally distressing is the wasted opportunity that these ath-   16
letes represent. Just imagine what a positive force they could be if only they would choose to accept the responsibilities that should go along with the fame and fortune they enjoy.

Just imagine how many young people might be spared the night-   17
mare of alcohol and drug abuse if Roy Tarpley were to present himself to the public as an clean-living, law-abiding citizen instead of a low-life recidivist who spends more time at the police station than he spends on the basketball court.

Just imagine how many lives might be saved from drunken driv-   18
ers if football player Tommy Kramer spent his time campaigning against alcohol abuse instead of getting himself arrested for driving while intoxicated.

Athletes receive far more attention than they deserve, far more   19
money than they're worth and far more adulation than they could earn in a hundred lifetimes. It's time they started giving something back to society.

If they don't want to, it's time society started telling them to take   20
a hike.

Questions for Thinking and Discussion

1. What seems to bother Thompson in this article is that some of our notable role models have failed us. Have your personal role models ever let you down? If so, what were the situations?

2. Thompson is very harsh in his criticism of professional athletes. He makes the following generalization:

   Athletes receive far more attention than they deserve, far more money than they're worth and far more adulation than they could earn in a hundred lifetimes.

   What is your opinion of this statement?

Where's the Magic?

SALLY JENKINS

THIS IS ABOUT SEX, DEATH AND THE DIFFERENCES between men and women—subjects that produce fits, innuendos false and true, heart-break and an absence of reasonable discussion. This is about Earvin Johnson. The reaction of women to the news about Johnson is more complicated than that of men. Just eavesdrop on a gathering of women in a restaurant or stop a few on the street. Johnson's disclosures about his having contracted the AIDS virus and having had sex with count-less women provoke a response that wanders between rue and anger. Johnson has not been a hero to women. He has been a hazard. If indeed he was infected with HIV through heterosexual contact, he has been their victim and, potentially, their victimizer.

Earvin Johnson can't pinpoint the time or the place or, regrettably, the woman who infected him. He simply says, as Warren Beatty did in the movie *Shampoo,* that he did them all. One of them made him a victim. The number of those who could become victims grows expo-nentially from there.

I do not pretend to reason on this subject. It defies that. I can only ruminate.

Johnson made sport of women.

Women gave him the AIDS virus.

There is no female equivalent to Johnson, because women gener-ally don't display the blind devotion to role models that men do. What possible parallel could there be? Something dreadful befalling Jane Pauley? Perhaps the closest to Johnson would be Chris Evert, who during her tennis career seemed never to have said or done the wrong thing.

It is a fact that a woman's sexual adventures and accomplishments are not viewed by either gender as a matter for congratulations. If she's had a lot of sexual partners, it's viewed as a matter for counseling. If Jackie Joyner-Kersee announced that she had had sex with more men than she could count and had contracted HIV from one of them, she would not be regarded as a heroine. She would be regarded as a tramp. Yet the pervasive feeling among men about Johnson seems to be that he was entitled to be promiscuous and that his bravery in the face of his affliction has made him even more of a larger-than-life figure than he was before.

I think there is a lot to be admired about Johnson. I found his   8
athleticism sublime, and I view what has happened to him as a tragedy
of the highest order. That is why I feel sorrow as well as rue and anger.
But if I had a daughter who had dated him, my sense of tragedy would
be far more acute.

To me, Johnson is no model of courage, considering the scores of   9
women he slept with. I suspect that all but a few of them regard having
had sex with him as a deadly error in judgment, just as he now regards
his having had sex with them. I don't doubt that a lot of the women
Johnson slept with were as much seducers as victims. But perhaps he
should have though better of them than they thought of themselves.
Often, this is what constitutes a gentleman.

Instead, Johnson says he did his best to "accommodate" as   10
many women as possible. Given that female-to-male transmission
of AIDS virus is still relatively rare, Johnson hit long odds when he
was stricken by the virus through heterosexual contact, but his promiscuity was such that his chances of coming into contact with an
infected woman rose considerably. He now implies that women are
something like radiation: A little bit is O.K., but overexposure can kill
you. "It doesn't matter how beautiful the woman might be or how
tempting she might sound on the telephone," he wrote in last week's
SI. "I know that we are pursued by women so much that it is easy to
be weak. Maybe by getting the virus I'll make it easier for you guys to
be strong."

I do not hear enough concern for his sexual partners in John-   11
son's statement, particularly given that AIDS is transmitted far more
frequently from males to females than from females to males. I do
not hear Johnson admit that he may have done considerable pursuing
himself. I do not hear a pronounced enough sense of responsibility.

I have a friend, Nancy, who lives in Los Angeles. She is tolerant   12
about sexual matters, as might be expected of one who was young and
single in the 1970s and '80s. She read that Wilt Chamberlain had slept
with, by his approximation, 20,000 women. "He ought to be in jail,"
she said.

In the age of AIDS, even if a man had unsafe sex with "only 2,000   13
women, the numbers grow astonishingly. Let's say those 2,000 women
each slept with five men afterward. The number of those exposed to
the possibility of infection begins with a group large enough to popu-
late a zip code, then grows to a state-sized one, then to one the size of
a small nation. That is truly what is meant when it is said that, these
days, you do not just sleep with one person, you sleep with everybody
that person ever slept with.

Women must deal with Johnson's irresponsibility in other less   14
obvious ways. Another of my friends, Rachel, lives in Florida with her
husband and three children, one of them a nine-year-old boy. She
provides sexual information to her children on what she laughingly
calls a "need-to-know" basis. The other day she had to explain to her
son that Johnson is probably doomed, and then she had to stumble
through an explanation of how a condom is used.

"How does this affect women?" she is asked. She answers her   15
voice wandering between rue and anger, "Well, we're the ones who
have to explain it to the kids."

Questions for Thinking and Discussion

1. Considering the time that has now passed since Johnson disclosed his
   HIV-positive status, do you think most Americans would agree with
   Jenkins' assertion that "Johnson is no model of courage. . . ." In other
   words, how well do you think Johnson's heroism is holding up today?

2. Jenkins' article brings up the issue of how heroes as role models differ
   for men and women. For instance, Jenkins claims that "women generally don't display the blind devotion to role models that men do." She
   also believes that men's heroes live by different standards than do
   women's heroes. How accurate do you think Jenkins' statements are
   about the different characteristics of men's and women's heroes?

Model or Mortal?

STEVE CAMPBELL

TRY NOT TO GET MIXED UP in the blur of mixed messages.   1

Be like Mike—which, as all men, women, children, and space   2
invaders know, does not rhyme with Nike.

Just do it.   3

Be like Mike, drink like him, eat like him, dress like him, soar   4
through the air like him.

Wear the same shoes that Michael Jordan wears, Charles Barkley   5
wears, David Robinson wears, Bo Jackson wears, Jim Courier wears.

Then again, you might want to walk in the shoes of Shaquille   6
O'Neal, who also has a soft drink guaranteed to quench your thirst.

Of course, you can buy that soft drink where Troy Aikman shops.   7

Oh, and don't forget to use the same pain reliever, wear the same   8
boots, eat the same fast food, as Nolan Ryan.

Follow the leaders to a store near you.   9

Follow them, but how far? What happens when Air Jordan be-   10
comes Air-out-some-dirty-laundry Jordan, accused of running up
enough gambling debts to pay the salary of a utility infielder or three?
What happens when an athlete put on a pedestal falls from grace? Does
fault lie with the athlete, the pedestal or the people who insist on
putting the athlete on the pedestal in the first place?

The superstars come into our living rooms day and night, selling   11
products and themselves, and they get paid handsomely for it. The
average player in the major-league baseball and the National Basketball
Association makes more than $1.2 million a year; the average National
Football League player just under $500,000 last season.

Without these kids' games played by grown men, barrooms   12
would get quieter and office water-cooler small talk would get smaller,
and call-in shows would go the route of the eight-track tape.

Is the entertainment and escapism they provide enough? Or   13
should strings—besides higher tax rates—come attached to the pay-
checks? Should they, by virtue of their visibility and economic where-

withal, serve as examples to the rest of the world? Should they give something back and, gulp, serve as role models?

In an ideal world, athletes would embrace the responsibility of serving as role models. There is a corps of athletes, however, who don't consider themselves obligated to set an example.   14

Role models or rolling-in-dough models?   15

"Do you want to know the truth, or do you want me to say the right thing?" Dallas Cowboys Pro Bowl offensive lineman Nate Newton said. "Do you want to know the truth of what I feel and what most athletes feel?"   16

Charles Barkley makes his feelings loud and clear in a Nike ad that first aired at the start of the NBA playoffs. Instead of pumping the shoe, Barkley assailed the notion that his other worldly basketball talents translated into deeper obligations: 17

> I'm not a role model. I'm not paid to be a role model. I'm paid to wreak havoc on a basketball court. Parents should be role models. Just because I can dunk a basketball doesn't mean I should raise your kids.   18

Barkley touched a nerve with athletes and fans.   19

"What Charles Barkley says," Newton says, "is what a lot of athletes wish they had the guts to say."   20

Fran Anderson runs the East Side Boys and Girls Club in Fort Worth. On a typical summer day, some 200 kids will stream in and out of the club.   21

"A lot of kids, given their choice, will have their parents be role models first," Anderson said. "They'll idolize a sports figure or what-ever, but when you really come down to it what a person says or does makes a big difference in the way the child grows up. Nine times out of 10, they may idolize Michael Jackson or whatever, but they're not going to put that gold glove on. They'll do pretty much what Mom and Dad does."   22

Anderson, in fact, doubts many kids pay much attention when Jordan runs into difficulties off the court.   23

"All they know is he's cool," Anderson said. "He's cool with the shoes. He's making the big bucks, selling the cola, the T-shirts, what-ever he's selling. I don't think it really makes a difference to the younger kids. I don't think they understand. Even adults.   24

"We just had a debate, me and a bunch of friends of mine, and nobody basically cared that Michael Jordan was gambling on his own time. Because if I were to gamble, in say, dominoes, and lose $20, nobody cares. But if Michael Jordan gambles and loses $1 million,   25 everybody is like, 'Oh, my God, Michael Jordan is gambling.' But to him $20 and $1 million may be the same thing."

Aikman, the Dallas Cowboys' Super Bowl MVP quarterback, has used his visibility to form the Troy Aikman Foundation to help disadvantaged children. Since starting his foundation last October, Aikman has raised more than $250,000. With the help of a seven-member board, Aikman plans to channel that money directly to individual children—or groups—whose needs slip through the cracks of established programs or charities.

"I don't completely agree with Charles," Aikman said. "Obviously, we don't choose to be role models. It's part of the business. I think we do have a responsibility to be role models and serve as good examples. On the other hand, I get tired of parents complaining about players who aren't good examples.

"When I grew up, I looked up to a lot of athletes and respected what they could do. But I knew the difference between right and wrong. I knew that if they did something bad, that didn't mean I should do it. That came from my parents. It's up to parents to instill in their children the difference between right and wrong."

Newton agrees.

He describes his off-the-field obligations this way: "To my family. My wife and child. Then to my mother and father, sisters and brothers. *If* I want to. A little deeper than that, what I'm trying to say is, I don't owe anybody anything just because I play sports and society decides to hype it up.

"You're a role model, whether you want to be or not. How you want to be is up to you. I do what I do out of the goodness of my heart. I do what I do because of the way I was raised by my parents. The only people who squeal about that commercial are the people who want the athletes to raise their kid.

"When my parents raised me, there wasn't any Larry Little, or Dr. J, or George McGinnis, or World B. Free [as role models]. There wasn't anybody like that. My parents used positive models like Dr. Martin Luther King, people like that. My father would go back to the Bible, or black history, when he wanted to give me positive role models.

"I read newspapers. I listen to talk shows. I really do feel feel sorry for those people who feel that athletes have to raise their kids. Some athletes don't even like kids. What are going to tell that man? He doesn't even like kids or have kids. He doesn't want kids. You're going to tell him he has got to be a role model? No, no, no."

If Newton had his way, he would clear the Air. Sure, Richard Esquinas trashed Jordan in *Michael & Me: Our Gambling Addiction* . . .

My Cry for Help. Sure, Esquinas alleges that he won $1.25 million worth of golf bets from Jordan in a 10-day period. Sure. Jordan admits to running up a $300,000 tab.

On the other hand, this is the same Jordan who generally watches   35
his Ps and Qs to the point that advertisers pay him more than $30 million a year to pitch their products. This is also the same Jordan who donated $100,000 last winter to help Chicago schools fund their extracurricular programs.

"Michael Jordan—what do you think his kids are going through?"   36
Newton said. "His kids are the ones who are going to have to suffer from this when they go to school. If you think he's such a good role model, if you want him to be a good role model, why do you burn him so bad so that his kids have to go to school and suffer?

"A kid went from not being able to make a basketball team to   37
making a basketball team the best in the world, to bringing a shoe company off bankruptcy to buying a pair of $70 shoes with Air Jordan on them, and all of the sudden he has to be a role model. You're still buying the product from Nike. Why doesn't Nike have to be the role model? You're upset because you bought a shoe for $70, right? Not just the shoe. You want somebody to raise your kid, too.

"That ain't right. What we need to try and realize is if we're going   38
to base America on our professional athletes, then we're going in the wrong direction."

It shouldn't be necessary to remind people that athletes, even   39
those with the best of intentions, have their frailties.

Babe Ruth was a drinker and womanizer of legendary propor-   40
tions. Wilt Chamberlain claimed to have slept with 20,000 women. Pete Rose gambled his way out of the Hall of Fame. Steve Howe seemingly goes into drug rehab as often as Michael Caine churns out movies. Roy Tarpley is serving out a two-year suspension for violating the NBA drug policy. Politician breaks campaign promise. Dog bites man.

"Because of the position we're in, we're automatically looked up   41
to by kids." the Texas Rangers' Ryan said. "I look at it from the standpoint of, if I'm going to have an influence—whether it's my own kids or somebody else's kids—then I want it to be a positive influence. So that's what I try to do.

"I read Bo Jackson's article saying we shouldn't be raising other   42
people's kids. Well, we're not raising other people's kids. That's not what asked of role models. It's just that if kids look up to you and you're in a position to be an influence on them, why not be a positive influence? Is that asking too much?

Ryan said he hasn't been out of the glare of the spotlight "since the first no-hitters." The first two of his seven no-hitters came in 1973.

"I think the more exposure we get, the more we are under a magnifying glass," Ryan said. "Our actions are scrutinized much closer. That's true of politicians, entertainers, musicians, everybody. There's so much media attention now that everybody has a tendency to rebel to it. They're saying, 'Hey, I don't have to fulfill my role. This isn't my role. This isn't what I'm paid for.'

"It gets old. It gets tiresome. I would love to be out of the public eye a lot of times. But that just comes with the territory. So my attitude about that is, that's part of the job and I'm going to do the best I can. When I walk away from it, when I'm no longer in it any longer, I'd like to look back and say, 'Hey, I tried to do the best job I could—on and off the field.

"People are so into themselves and what they're doing that their attitude is, 'I'm not worried about other people.' Well, what kind of attitude is that? If everybody has that attitude, how is anything positive going to get accomplished?"

Questions for Thinking and Discussion

1. The last part of Campbell's article is made up of arguments on the issue of whether athletes should serve as role models. In this part of his article, Campbell quotes Nate Newton and Nolan Ryan, whose views on this issue conflict. Summarize the arguments of Newton and Ryan. Which, to you, is most convincing?
2. Assume that Newton and Ryan were debating the issue of athletes as role models with Lyon, whose article appears earlier in this chapter. What would Lyon say to Newton's and Ryan's arguments? Which of the two would Lyon be more apt to agree with? Why?

Here, Kids, Is a Real Role Model

Bill Lyon

We YEARN FOR THEM TO DO FOR US what we are incapable of doing   1
ourselves.

Please, we entreat, show us the way.   2

So we demand from our sports demigods more than they have to   3
give. We demand that they also serve us as role models. Invariably, we
are let down.

For it turns out that they stumble and muddle through life as   4
ineptly as we.

But every rare once in a while we are privileged. Perhaps once   5
a generation there happens along one who transcends sport, one
to whom a parent can point and say to his children: "Him. Be like
him."

There is one such in our midst now. He looks patrician, profes-   6
sional. His cheetah's body, withered by the plague of time, is below 150
pounds. Still, as always, Arthur Ashe is rushing the net, stretching to
return the unreturnable, tracking down the irretrievable, conceding
nothing.

For this, and more, he has been selected Sportsman of the Year   7
by *Sports Illustrated*.

He has long since retired, of course. But from professional sport   8
only, and not, most resoundingly, from living. It is what makes him the
perfect choice.

It is that time of year, the time to choose which sweaty brow the   9
laurel wreath shall frame. But whose? Who towered over SportsWorld
in 1992?

Th iceman Lemieux? The boxer Bowe? The batter Bonds? The   10
levitator Jordan? Some Olympian? Who?

He was under our very nose all along, and he has been identified   11
by a magazine that will take its annual brickbat barrage for devoting
most of an issue to lissome females in partial dress lolling about some
sun-splattered beach. But if anyone can appreciate that irony, it is
Arthur Ashe.

He has shown us yet again how to grapple with terrible adversity.   12

"It's like barriers just don't exist for Arthur," a friend said. He   13
intended it as admiration.

But of course, barriers are all that Arthur Ashe has ever known.   14
Barriers of inequality and injustice, of bigotry and intolerance, of

medical calamities. He played the whitest of sports and ascended to its summit. He has survived three heart attacks, partial paralysis, two by-pass operations and brain surgery. He has to ingest almost 30 pills daily.

He has survived four years of living with AIDS and 49 years of   15
living with the persecution of color, and somehow he has remained graceful, thoughtful, serious, productive.

Somehow he has always managed to make those who attacked   16
him look petty and small and ignorant. What has always struck you about Arthur Ashe is that while he must have been consumed with anger, he never gave in to it.

For all the injustices and inequities he has had to endure, he has   17
never seemed to waste his passion or his time complaining about his lot in life. Instead, he just tried to change it.

First he entertained us. Since, he has educated and enlightened   18
us.

He expresses regret for years of wasted energy on lost causes, and   19
yet that always is the redemptive side of man, the willingness to commit to a lost cause if only because of conviction. Lost is not what matters, believing it to be right is.

Arthur Ashe believes he contracted AIDS from a blood transfu-   20
sion during heart surgery. He was forced to reveal his condition last April because a misguided and intrusive newspaper threatened to print his condition.

So he came to this battle reluctantly, but as is his habit, once in   21
it he immediately rushed to the net.

Now there is a sense of urgency. So much to do, so little time.   22

It is said that those stricken by AIDS feel an odd sense of libera-   23
tion, that they feel loosened from the normal social constraints, free to do and say things with a candor and without an inhibition that they might have felt before.

Not that he ever backed down.   24

Arthur Ashe has established an AIDS foundation. And he heads   25
the Safe Passage Foundation, for inner city youngsters. And he can be found on a panel on racism one day, at an AIDS seminar the next, always with the same quiet dignity and strength, the same elegance and eloquence.

In public he is approached warily, awkwardly. He understands   26
the uneasiness.

"People don't always know what to say," he said, smiling. "We [he   27
and his wife, Jeanne] try to put them at ease."

Another irony. For so many years he made so many uneasy with   28
the graceful, unhurried way he deflected their prejudice. First he ruffled them, now he reassures them.

It is customary, when selecting athletes to honor at calendar's end,   29
to choose from among those bashing balls or bashing one another,
those altering scoreboards, those pushing back the envelope of human
velocity.

But this is a departure. This is someone removed from the arena,   30
but someone to emulate and to applaud.

This is one of sports' shining moments.   31

(*Editor's note:* Arthur Ashe died of AIDS shortly after this article appeared.)

Questions for Thinking and Discussion

1. Lyon believes the late Arthur Ashe was a true role model because he
   not only served as an entertainer but "he has educated and enlightened
   us." Do you see *entertaining, educating,* and *enlightening* as the key
   qualities that a heroic person must have? What other characteristics
   would you add to this list?

2. Lyon's article seems to be an answer to Thompson's and Jenkins' negative views of professional athletes. Although Ashe had tremendous
   barriers to overcome, he didn't resort to drugs and alcohol or promiscuous sex. Instead, as Lyon tells us, Ashe seems to have risen above it
   all. What do you think causes a person to become heroic like Arthur
   Ashe as opposed to being a "drunk" or a "junkie"?

Writing Projects

1. Who is your personal role model? Write a biographical paper about this person. If the person is famous, do a little library research to find out what you can about him or her. If the person is not famous, try to collect and recall as much as you can about him/her. As you prepare your biographical sketch, center on this question:

   What is it about this person that makes him/her heroic?

2. Select three prominent Americans who are widely regarded as being heroic. These people may be from any area of American life: sports, politics, entertainment, education, business, and so on. As you think about these people, try to account for just what it is that makes them so heroic. Is it how they act? What they say? What they look like?

   Write a paper entitled "Heroic Characteristics of Three Modern Americans," which centers on why these people are so heroic.

3. Working with a team of five other students, survey twenty-five students from your own campus to discover who your fellow students' role models are. Your survey questionnaires ought to ask students not only who their heroic-role models are, but also why. You might use Leerhsen's article as your springboard, discussing how your findings resemble or differ from his.

4. Thompson assumes in this article that a professional athlete automatically has special status as a role model. As Campbell's however, many professional athletes say that they don't see themselves as role models anymore than members of any other profession do. They say, in other words, that it is unfair to expect exemplary behavior from them since, after all, "being a role model" isn't written into their contracts.

   Write a paper in which you argue for or against professional athletes as role models.

3

Stereotypes

SINCE THE CIVIL RIGHTS MOVEMENT FIRST RECEIVED ATTENTION IN THE 1960s, many Americans have been aware of the problems involved with thinking that certain groups of people automatically have certain qualities—for instance, that Italian-Americans have tendencies to be gangsters or that African-Americans have superior athletic abilities. As you are probably well aware, this tendency to think of certain groups as always having certain traits or behaviors is called *stereotyping.*

The examples of stereotypes that most often come to mind involve ethnic and racial minorities; however, the 1990s have also made us quite aware of other stereotypes that people have—for instance, of the two genders, male and female. The readings in this chapter explore both well-known and uncommon stereotypes. The first three explore how inaccurate many stereotypes of men and women can be, and the final three are about other stereotyped groups: overweight people, elderly people, and young people.

You've Come a Long Way, Bubba

ORLANDO SENTINEL

ADVERTISERS, BEWARE! Ladies, get thee to the nearest swooning   1
couch!

According to *Men's Health* magazine survey, real men can do   2
anything women can do. (OK, truth to tell, they're at least closing the
gap.)

Men now do three hours of housework per week compared to 1.1   3
hours per week in the 1960s, according to the survey. Men also
comprise 35 percent of supermarket customers, double the percentage
of 15 years ago.

And 60 percent of men witness or participate in their children's   4
births, which is about 40 percent below the participation rate for
women. But, hey, who's counting?

"The stereotype of the American male . . . who is oblivious to   5
differences between one brand of soup or cereal and another, who
never buys anything but beer, razor blades and motor oil is outdated,"
says Michael Lafavore, executive editor of *Men's Health.*

This is the sort of news that makes a man's chest swell and a   6
woman's heave in anticipation.

More than that, it makes a woman chuckle, much as the class   7
clown does when the teacher's pet gets caught flipping peas at the
cafeteria ceiling. It's the chuckle that says, "Heh-heh-heh, now
yooooouuuuu'll see."

What does all this mean? Advertising, of course.   8

Wherever there are statistics, dollars can't be far behind. And   9
it can't be long, if it hasn't started already, before television advertisers turn their humiliating, patronizing cross hairs on the male
market.

Women have long been accustomed to being portrayed in the   10
media as imbeciles. Remember the woman who, while cheerfully
cleaning a toilet, was only mildly surprised when a large bald man
emerged from the bowl?

He swelled like an inflating balloon and popped out of the toilet   11
to give her a lecture on cleanliness and hygiene. And, by golly, she
listened. Attentively! As if this were the most fascinating bit of information she'd ever heard, with the possible exception of what she'd
heard just minutes before about *ring around the collar.*

And now, fellas, it's your turn. Your turn to look like bumbling 12
idiots who fairly salivate over a New, Improved cleanser.

It used to be commercials aimed at men were about deodorant, 13
razors, lawn mowers, power tools and beer—the stuff men of brawn
and steel needed to know about. Me Tarzan and all that.

But things changed in the jungle. Jane went hunting, so Tarzan— 14
no doubt fighting a headache—went shopping.

"A man might experience a hunterlike feeling when he's shop- 15
ping," says one interpreter. "Like the primordial male coming home
with the catch."

Just don't catch him squeezing the Charmin. 16

Questions for Thinking and Discussion

1. Similar to the article before it in this chapter, this one claims that
   modern males are breaking out of old stereotypes to meet the times.
   Look again at the article before this one. Together these two make up
   two authors' profile of what modern men are like. How accurately does
   their description depict the males in your classes at college? To what
   extent might the views of these authors also be a stereotype?

2. A major point made in this article is that men (as women have been in
   the past) are now the target of new advertising that stereotypes them.
   Which current ads do you think stereotype men? How effective do you
   think these ads are? Which ones work, despite the stereotypes? Which
   ones don't work?

Here Comes the New and Improved Dad

ASSOCIATED PRESS

SIX MEN SIT CROSS-LEGGED on a white carpeted floor. They are in the airy studio of a cedar house that hugs the flanks of the Sierra Nevada, and they are talking quietly and seriously about important things. 1

Big things. Things that could change the world. 2

Not once, in two hours, do the mention the war in Bosnia, President Clinton, the price of gold, "Jurassic Park," Charles Barkley, all-terrain vehicles or the San Francisco Giants. 3

No, for two full hours and then some, they talk about fatherhood. 4

Actually, they talk about more than that. They talk about their children, their fathers, their wives and themselves. They talk about after-school soccer, about homework, about who cooks and who fixes the car. They talk about the struggle to balance work and family, about how much discipline is too much discipline. They wonder whether their children can be their pals. 5

They talk about things that men don't usually talk about. 6

Or do they? 7

There's a new man loping about the planet, or so it would appear from reading the literature. Psychologists talk about the "New Fatherhood," whose adherents universally ascribe to the following adage: When a man is dying, he never says, "I wish I'd spent more time at the office." 8

No, the new dad is the one you see with a toddler at the playground, or standing up at the PTA meeting, or rolling Junior through the aisles of the supermarket. He's the one who misses days at work because a child is home sick; who dashes out the office door at the digital crack of 5 to make it to the day care center on time. 9

"Something has changed," says Jerrold Shapiro, a psychologist in Los Altos who has written two books on fatherhood. "Whether men have been enticed or cajoled, the fact is that we're around our kids a lot more." 10

"And," he adds, "when you're around your kids, you get to like it." 11

The evidence is both anecdotal and scientific. For instance, *Redbook* magazine recently conducted a random, national telephone poll of 420 fathers, with a margin of error of plus or minus 4.8 percent: 12

—96 percent said they changed their babies' diapers. Two thirds   13
of them thought their own fathers had skipped diaper duty.

—86 percent took their children to the doctor. Only half as many   14
thought their fathers had done so.

—75 percent had left work to take care of their kids. Fewer than   15
one-quarter thought their dads had done that.

And nearly seven out of 10 of the modern dads said they'd like   16
the opportunity to stay home and care for their children while their
wives worked. The pollsters didn't bother to ask about the previous
generation. The questions simply wouldn't apply.

Under the influence of the much-maligned men's movement,   17
books about fatherhood have been hopping off the presses in the past
few years. Besides Shapiro's books, the most recent of which is "The
Measure of a Man: Becoming the Father You Wish Your Father Had
Been," they include such titles as "Letters to My Son: Reflections on
Becoming a Man," and "Man Enough: Fathers, Sons, and the Search for
Masculinity."

Certainly, the men gathered at Troy Rampy's house, perched in   18
the forested hills above Nevada City, have thought about it.

"There's a much more participatory parenting going on than there   19
was when I grew up," says John Daly, a 48-year-old, tousle-haired real
estate agent who speaks with the clarity and precision implied by his
steel blue eyes.

"We fathers now are much more a part of the process than we   20
were. Wives are working, fathers are working, and we have to share in
the household duties. Probably most men and women will admit that
women are still doing more of the household stuff, but I think the
fathers are much more involved in the kids' lives. . . . We're really
taking on a lot more responsibility for the child-rearing."

It's true, as Daly says, that men haven't exactly shoved their wives   21
out of the kitchen, laundry room or nursery.

"Our attitudes have changed," says Ron Levant, a psychologist in   22
Brookline, Mass., who is co-chair of the Society for the Psychological
Study of Men and Masculinity. "Our behavior has changed, but not that
much."

Questions for Thinking and Discussion

1. This article maintains that present day American fathers are different
   from what fathers used to be. In other words, modern fathers are

breaking old stereotypes. Compare two or three generations of men in your family. Are the younger fathers more like those described in the article? Or, do the older ones also have some of these "new" traits?

2. The article is largely about benefits to men of breaking out of the stereotypical father role and becoming more involved in their families. After all, we are told that men "get to like it" when they spend time around their children. However, the article doesn't really say how *anyone else* might benefit from having a father who is more involved in the home. What might these benefits be? For wives? For children? Who is likely to benefit most?

Too Pretty, Too Heavy—It's All Discrimination

CAROL KLEIMAN

THERE'S AN OLD FORM OF SEX DISCRIMINATION IN THE WORKPLACE that's   1
getting new attention these days: It's one in which women's careers are
imperiled because of their looks.

Ann Hopkins, formerly a consultant in the Washington, D.C.,   2
office of Price Waterhouse, a large accounting firm, was denied a
partnership because she "needed to learn to dress more femininely."

And Teresa Fischette, a Continental Airlines ticket agent at Bos-   3
ton's Logan Airport, was fired when she refused to comply with the
company's new appearance standards requiring female employees who
deal with the public to wear foundation makeup and lipstick.

In contrast, Nancy Fadhl, a police officer in Oakland, Calif., was   4
fired because she was too well-groomed and looked "too much like a
lady."

Fischette, who was rehired after media attention focused on her   5
firing, said her situation was not unique. "I'm sorry to say that there's
still quite a lot of emphasis on looks, when the important thing is your
competence," she said.

If some women are not beautiful enough to keep their jobs and   6
others are too beautiful to keep them, how can you win?

"You can't," said Naomi Wolf of New York, author of *The Beauty*   7
Myth: How Images of Beauty Are Used Against Women (Morrow, $21.95).
"Standards of beauty hold women in place as a cheap, docile but
literate labor pool upon which our service and information-processing
economy depends."

Beauty standards, said Wolf, are applied not only in the so-called   8
"display" professions, such as Fischette's, in which women deal directly
with the public, but in all jobs. Wolf suggests that a double standard
for the appearance of employed women compared to men acts as a
"control" on women, "keeping them from asking for more money or
better jobs." Only in two professions—modeling and prostitution—do
women earn more than men, Wolf said.

The author experienced how looks are used to dominate women: 9
A 1986 Rhodes Scholar, Wolf was accused by a male scholar of winning
the coveted award only because of her looks; he made the accusation

after she argued persuasively against subscribing to pornographic magazines, and against him, in a class discussion. She came up with the term "The Beauty Myth" to describe the mercurial appearance standards "that undermine women's confidence and impede their economic progress."

"Many women have three full-time jobs," said Wolf, who earned   10
her undergraduate degree at Yale University and her doctorate in English literature from Oxford University. "They work in paid employment, do housework—and also spend hours doing beauty maintenance."

But she urges women to fight back: "We have to stop blaming   11
ourselves when faced with beauty discrimination," Wolf said. "If someone uses our appearance against us, call it what it is—job discrimination—and make it illegal."

That's exactly what American Airlines' female flight attendants   12
did in a successful battle over the airlines' weight standards. The airline and the Association of Professional Flight Attendants announced the settlement last March of a 17-year-old lawsuit concerning permissible weight of female flight attendants.

Discrimination because of weight is one of the most prevalent and   13
painful prejudices employed women face, according to a psychotherapist who specializes in eating disorders.

"Studies show that you are less likely to be considered a job   14
candidate if you are overweight, and if you do get the job, instead of focusing on being successful in your career, you have to work hard to get within 'normal' weight standards," said Diana Beliard, who practices in Evanston and Chicago. She has a doctorate in clinical psychology from Northwestern University.

"The peculiar thing," said the therapist, "is that there is an ever-   15
changing standard of what women need to look like: It keeps getting slimmer and slimmer. The net effect is that women strive desperately to meet weight standards that are completely arbitrary."

Beliard said that she had a "mild" weight problem in high school.   16
"Efforts to deal with it led to my gaining weight," she said. "Now my weight is fine and I have no need to think about it."

The therapist said she works on self-esteem when counseling   17
overweight women. "They've been disempowered at work and feel something is wrong with them," she said. "That puts them at a disadvantage in job negotiations. It's important to help women understand that weight problems are not due to some kind of moral weakness but to understandable causes."

She said the "emphasis on looks is is one of the major oppressions   18
employed women experience. Women should be judged on their abil-

ity and not have to spend time worrying about their appearance. When they do, both the women and their employers lose."

Questions for Thinking and Discussion

1. Kleiman draws on the expertise of Naomi Wolf, author of *The Beauty Myth: How Images of Beauty are Used Against Women.* When Wolf uses the term the "beauty myth" exactly what does she mean? In what way can this myth "undermine women's confidence and impede their economic progress"?

2. Though Kleiman doesn't use the word *stereotype* in her article, in what sense is stereotyping of women involved in the problems of beauty she discusses? What exact stereotypes of women seem to be responsible for the discrimination she talks about?

Why So Many Ridicule
the Overweight

Natalie Angier

On the unsavory spectrum of bigotry, some slurs are considered worse than others. Insults to a person's race, ethnicity or religion rank as completely unacceptable. Making fun of a woman for being female or a gay person for being homosexual may be somewhat taboo, but it is certainly frowned upon. Children are taught not to point at a handicapped person, and only the most callous would jeer at a down-and-out drunk.

But a fat person is fair game. People who would never publicly confess to racism have no qualms about expressing revulsion for the obese. And that just may may be because the fat threaten the thin down to the deepest levels of the psyche.

The reaction of Americans to a fat person, particularly one who is more than 25 to 35 percent above the so-called ideal weight, is so intense and so overwhelmingly negative that some scientists are exploring it as a window on the raw material of human nature.

Uncomfortable Symbol

Researchers who study the psychology of body image, and those who are struggling to foster greater tolerance of fatness in our culture, said many people of normal weight fear the fat person because obesity embodies in the most graphic way possible the terrible potential they see lurking in themselves. For many, a fat person variously symbolizes loss of control, a reversion to infantile desires, failure, self-loathing, sloth, passivity and gluttony.

Such ingrained attitudes must be confronted if fat people are ever to gain acceptance, the researchers say. With new scientific evidence showing how often obesity has a genetic or physiological basis beyond a person's control, they said, the time has come to dispel society's fear of fat.

But that will take some doing.

"The fat person represents the part of us that has gone to seed, has morally disintegrated," said Dr. Susan C. Wooley, director of the eating disorders clinic at the University of Cincinnati. "It's the only physical trait I can think of which, although it's talked about in terms of appearance, is associated with so many things other than appearance."

And while many people manage to keep their anxieties and insecurities tucked safely inside, beyond the scrutiny of others, some see the fat as their own neuroses made flesh, forcing them to confront their own imperfections.

ACCEPTABLE LOATHING

So despite growing evidence that weight is more a matter of genes than calories, fat people are still condemned as permitting themselves to get fat.

"We're running out of people that we're allowed to hate, and to feel superior to," said Dr. Wooley. "Fatness is the one thing left that seems to be a person's fault—which it isn't."

In a culture that exalts hard work, vigorous exercise and delayed gratification, the fat person seems particularly offensive.

"The history of this country was influenced by the Puritans, and people are supposed to be in control, stoic, self-denying," said Dr. Esther Rothblum, a psychologist at the University of Vermont. "When somebody looks hedonistic or self-indulgent, there's a tremendous animosity toward that person."

The recent conservative political climate may even have exaggerated the Puritanical impulses. "People are supposed to be responsible for their own behavior and station in life," said Dr. Kelly Brownell, an obesity researcher at the Yale University Medical School. "There's a tendency today to blame a person for being sick or different."

It seems unlikely that the prevailing social winds will blow differently under President-elect Bill Clinton. Indeed, when Mr. Clinton began gaining weight on the campaign trail, some saw it as a character flaw, and criticism of his weight was so scathing that he soon began a rigid program of diet and regular jogging.

People harbor all sorts of peculiar misconceptions and prejudices about fat people, said William Fabrey, founder of the National Association to Advance Fat Acceptance. "People are real wary that if a fat person sits next the them, the person will be smelly," he said. "There's also a feeling that a fat person is violating territorial limits. They're larger than their allotted space."

Because obesity also gives a body a more womanly look, fat men are often viewed as effeminate. "Fat is inconsistent with masculinity," said Dr. Wooley. "It's associated with physical weakness."

Feeling Moral Superiority

Interestingly, a fat person is no likelier to be tolerant of another   17
fat person than is somebody slender, and often is even more scathing.
Adele Rosenthal, a librarian in New York who is about 70 pounds
overweight, admits that she feels disgusted when she sees another fat
person eating, and that she feels morally superior to somebody who is
fatter than she.

"I still have this strong belief that I'm in control, and that I can   18
pull that control again at any point," she said. "I know I get fat when
I overeat and eat things I should avoid, so another fat person seems
lazy and self-indulgent to me."

Dr. Rothblum and others said the tide may at last be turning, as   19
ever more people rebel against the tyrannical demands toward eternal
slenderness, as the population ages and thickens, and as excessive thinness becomes associated, not with athletic prowess, but with disease.

"The AIDS epidemic is changing people's minds," said Dr. Roth-   20
blum. "Whenever you have a disease that makes people thin, suddenly
thinness is seen as suspicious."

Questions for Thinking and Discussion

1. Angier discusses a number of ideas that she sees associated with
   people's stereotypes of overweight people:

   "... a fat person variously symbolizes loss of control, a reversion to
   infantile desires, failure, self-loathing, sloth, passivity, and gluttony"

   "When somebody looks hedonistic or self-indulgent, there's a tremendous
   animosity toward that person" (quotation from Dr. Esther Rothblum)

   "There's ... a feeling that a fat person is violating territorial limits.
   They're larger than their allotted space" (quotation from William Fabrey)

   "Fat is inconsistent with masculinity. It's associated with physical weakness" (quotation from Dr. Susan Wooley).

   What does Angier mean in each of these cases? How widespread do
   you think that these attitudes are toward overweight people?

2. In Angier's article, Dr. Wooley says that "We're running out of people
   that we're allowed to hate, and to feel superior to." What does Dr.
   Wooley mean by this statement? What does the statement have to do
   with overweight people? How do stereotyping and prejudice relate to
   people's need to feel superior to someone? Is this a characteristic of
   human nature? If it is, is there any way to eliminate stereotyping?

Against All Odds, I'm Just Fine

BRAD WACKERLIN

WHAT TROUBLED TIMES THE AMERICAN TEENAGER LIVES IN! Ads for Nike   1
shoes urge us to "Just do it!" while the White House tells us to "Just
say no." The baby boomers have watched their babies grow into teens
and history has repeated itself: the punk teens of the '80s have taken
the place of the hippie teens of the '60s. Once again, the generation
gap has widened and the adults have finally remembered to remember
that teenagers are just no good. They have even coined a name for their
persecution of adolescents: "teen-bashing."

If what is being printed in the newspapers, viewed on television   2
and repeated by adults is correct, it is against all odds that I am able
to write this article. Adults say the average teenager can't write complete sentences and has trouble spelling big words. Their surveys
report that I can't find Canada on a map. According to their statistics,
my favorite hobbies are sexual intercourse and recreational drug use.
It's amazing that I've found time to write this; from what they say, my
time is spent committing violent crimes or just hanging out with a
gang. In fact, it is even more amazing that I'm here at all, when you
consider that the music I listen to is supposedly "warping" my mind
and influencing me to commit suicide.

Nonetheless, here I am. I write this article to show that a teenager   3
can survive in today's society. Actually, I'm doing quite well. I haven't
fathered any children, I'm not addicted to any drugs, I've never wor-
shiped Satan and I don't have a police record. I can even find Canada
on a map along with its capital, Ottawa. I guess my family and friends
have been supportive of me, for I've never been tempted to become
one of those teenage runaways I'm always reading about. Call me a
rebel, but I've stayed in school and (can it be true?!) I enjoy it. This
month, I graduate from high school and join other graduates as the
newest generation of adults. I'm looking forward to four years of
college and becoming a productive member of society. I may not be
America's stereotypical teen, but that only proves there is something
wrong with our society's preconceived image of today's teenager.

My only goal in writing this article is to point out the "bum rap"   4
today's teenager faces. I feel the stereotypical teen is, in fact, a minority.
The true majority are the teenagers who, day in and day out, prepare
themselves for the future and work at becoming responsible adults.
Our time is coming. Soon we will be the adults passing judgment on

63

the teenagers of tomorrow. Hopefully, by then, we will have realized that support and encouragement have a far more positive effect on teenagers than does "bashing" them.

Questions for Thinking and Discussion

1. The stereotyping that Wackerlin discusses in this article is also a very different kind from what we normally hear spoken about in the mass media: one generation stereotyping another. How accurate do you think Wackerlin's claim that "the generation gap has widened and the adults have finally remembered to remember that teenagers are just no good"?

2. Wackerlin goes so far as to call the stereotyping of the young "teen-bashing." Though he doesn't discuss it, what do you suppose causes people to "bash" young people? To what extent might some of the articles in the "Generation X" chapter (chapter four) of this book be examples of this "bashing"?

Give a Dog a Bad Name

PAT MCNEILL

"MAN AGED 90 INJURED IN FIGHT" ran a headline in the *Guardian* 1
recently. The story told of an "altercation" in an old people's home
when one man had "wandered" into another's room. Other residents
had been questioned by the police who were making enquiries. But,
said the police, "due to their age not all (the residents) could remember
the incident."

How many labels and stereotypes can you spot in this story? First, 2
the story would never have reached the national press had the combat-
ants been in their twenties. The specifying of the injured man's age in
the headline demonstrates that this is where the story's news value lies.
Presumably we are expected to smile patronisingly as we imagine the
men concerned going for each other with their walking-frames:
"Naughty old things!"

Then there are the assumptions made in the police statement. If 3
some of the witnesses to the incident could not recall it, this was almost
certainly due not to their age but to memory loss associated with brain
failure and suffered by only a minority of elderly people. Ageing is not,
in itself, a cause of memory loss. It is equally possible that some of the
residents could remember the incident but, like people of all ages on
such occasions, chose not to get involved.

Such an explanation would not, however, occur to anyone whose 4
assumptions about elderly people, and especially those in residential
care, are that they are no longer capable of ordinary human behavior,
including subterfuge. This is the essence of labelling. People who have
been labelled may act in the same ways as other people do or as they
themselves did before the label was applied but, because of the label,
the meaning imputed to their actions by others changes.

This can be well illustrated via the example of mental illness. In 5
the classic study carried out by Rosenhan (1973), he arranged for
eight people to gain admission to mental hospitals in the US by
claiming that they were hearing voices in their heads, a classic symp-
tom of schizophrenia. Once admitted, these "pseudo-patients" ceased
to complain about their voices and behaved as normally as was possible in the circumstances of the hospital routine. Rosenhan wanted to
see how long it would take for their deception to be spotted by medical
staff.

In fact, none was detected. All were eventually discharged as   6
schizophrenics "in remission." Their case notes revealed how their very
ordinary life histories had been given whole new meanings in the light
of the known fact of their schizophrenia, and how their "sane" behavior
while in hospital had been interpreted by staff as evidence to confirm
their illness rather than as rational actions. For example, keeping
research notes had been recorded as "engaging in writing behaviour."

It is unlikely that Rosenhan's experiment would work so readily   7
today, not least because of the impact of studies like this on the training
of psychiatric staff. But it remains true that "once a person is designated
abnormal, all his other behaviours and characteristics are coloured by
that label." It may even be that the individual comes to accept the label
and to act accordingly, the so-called "self-fulfilling prophecy."

Labels are a central element in the process of stereotyping. The   8
term "stereotype" is usually used to refer to a disparaging or negative
view of a whole group of people which identifies one characteristic,
oversimplifies, distorts and exaggerates it and generalises it to every
member of the group. This certainly underlies the conception of elderly people embodied in the news item that prompted this article.

Negative stereotypes are the basis of systematic prejudices such   9
as sexism, racism and ageism, and they are very resistant to change in
the face evidence. What happens is that evidence supporting the
stereotype is emphasised, while contrary evidence is ignored or belit-
tled. There may be a grain of truth in the stereotype and one individual
confirming it is taken as evidence for the whole group.

Thus the racist who believes that all young black males are a   10
threat to law and order will always draw attention to those instances
where a young black man is convicted of a criminal offence and will
ignore the evidence that the great majority are no less law abiding than
whites of the same age. A common variation of this kind of illogicality
is the person who says something like: "All blacks are scroungers. Oh,
except my friend John; he's different."

Negative stereotyping both reinforces the group solidarity of   11
those who practise it and enables them, in their own eyes, to legitimate
their claim to superior status. It therefore constitutes a central element
in most ideologies, including occupational ideologies.

However, not all stereotypes are negative and it is a mistake to   12
condemn all stereotyping as being wrong in principle. It can be argued
that is a necessary element in the ordering of experience. We simply
have to classify people into types if we are to cope with the huge range
and complex variety of individuals with whom we interact every day.
We have to be able to think, at least at first meeting, "this person is one

of that type" if we are to have any idea of how to initiate interaction with them.

It should also be stressed that people are not just passive victims of labelling and stereotyping. Many people actively resist their labels, and there are even occasions when it may appear to be of short-term advantage to play up to and exploit a stereotype, such as that of the helpless male in the supermarket who gets motherly females to find the items on his shopping-list, or the female student who plays the "scatty girl" act in an attempt to divert her male teacher's wrath, or the elderly person who "cannot remember what happened". 13

The problem with such manipulation of stereotypes is that where the manipulator is in the weaker position, there is then the risk that the act may become reality. 14

Questions for Thinking and Discussion

1. This article is a sociological explanation for what stereotyping is and what it does. According to McNeill, stereotyping can actually serve a positive purpose. What is it? What distinguishes this kind of stereotyping from what McNeill calls "negative stereotyping"? What does the process of using "labels" have to do with stereotyping?

2. In the first part of the article, McNeill is talking about the same thing that Wackerlin talked about, except that the stereotyping is of older generations by younger ones. To what extent do you see this kind of stereotyping happening around you daily?

Writing Projects

1. Because of the way that stereotyping works, nearly everyone has been stereotyped at some time. What sorts of stereotypes have people held of you, of members of your family, or of friends of yours? Write a paper explaining the stereotypes that have affected you.

2. Your reading in this chapter should have given you some new insights into stereotypes. Drawing on examples you find in the readings in this chapter, write a paper in which you summarize the wide variety of forms that stereotyping might take today.

3. After reading articles in this chapter by Angier, McNeill, and Wackerlin, write a paper in which you uncover some new stereotypes—ones that aren't talked about very much. For instance, your paper might cover stereotypes that people have of football players, cheerleaders, left-handed people, automobile mechanics, college professors, lawyers, or doctors. In whatever stereotyped people you cover in your paper, you might also show how actual people you have known don't fit these stereotypes.

4. In the article about stereotyping of the elderly, McNeill discusses the positive side of stereotyping:

   > [N]ot all stereotypes are negative and it is a mistake to condemn all stereotyping as being wrong in principle. It can be argued that it is a necessary element in the ordering of experience. We simply have to classify people into types if we are to cope with the huge range and complex variety of individuals with whom we interact every day. We have to be able to think, at least at a first meeting, "this person is one of that type" if we are to have any idea of how to initiate interaction with them.

   Using this passage as your basis and drawing on personal observations for contents, write a paper about good and bad stereotyping. Your paper might center on one of these questions:

   > What are some situations in which people have to stereotype others in order to get along?

   > Where is the line dividing harmful stereotyping from necessary stereotyping?

4

Generation X

THROUGHOUT THIS CENTURY, newspapers and magazines have been trying to tell us what young people are like: what they think, what their goals and values are, why they behave as they do. Through the years, analyses have been made of the so-called "Lost Generation" (youth in the 1920s), the World War II generation, the 50s generation, and the so-called "Baby Boomers" of the 1960s.

This chapter contains readings that profile the current generation of young Americans (in their late teens to late twenties)—sometimes called "Generation X." No doubt many of you are members of this age group; even if you aren't, you probably have children, relatives, or acquaintances who are. As you read these articles, try to get a whole picture of young Americans, at least as the writers see them. What characteristics do they find? Do the descriptions in these articles represent the young people you see around you, or are they only speaking about one segment of the population of young Americans? Think about people you know who do fit what these writers are saying—and people who don't.

Busters and Boomers: Caught in the Middle

Susan Mitchell

Pity the poor middle children outflanked on both sides by older
and younger siblings. They struggle to attain a sense of self while being
compared to big brother or ignored in favor of baby sister.

Today's young adults—ages 16 to 27—are demographic middle
children, sandwiched between a big boom and a little boom. The
seemingly anonymous "Generation X," because of the adversity they've
faced, may turn out to be the most pragmatic of the lot.

Almost 76 million babies were born in the United States between
1946 and 1964, averaging 4 million per year. Between 1965 and 1976,
41 million babies were born, averaging 3.4 million per year. Since
1977, 56 million babies have been born, averaging 3.7 million per
year. It wasn't surprising that America is preoccupied with the twin
peaks of the boom and boomlet.

Because of this, though, many business leaders and others hold
misperceptions about the baby bust that isolate them from these young
adults. First, they often believe this generation is cynical and unrespon-
sive. Second they believe it is simply a younger version of the Baby
Boom. In fact, each generation demands its own kind of outreach. Baby
Boomers, who now dominate the nation's advertising and marketing
departments, may have forgotten that business adapted to them in the
1960s. Now it is their turn to make a leap in content and style to
address today's youth.

Lukas Barr and Sean Gullette are Harvard-graduate baby busters
struggling to fill a void with *Blast*, a magazine for young adults. Many
efforts to reach this generation are simply "Baby Boomer sensibilities
repackaged in a style that attempts to appeal to twentysomethings," Mr.
Barr says. He adds that young adults easily see through such efforts.

"You have to suspend you own experiences and take a look at
what's happening nowadays," says Stuart Himmelfarb, a vice-president
with The Roper Organization, a polling group.

Young adults are not unknowable or unreachable. They simply
aren't all grownup yet. In many ways the baby-bust character has not
fully evolved or solidified. Author Douglas Coupland's "Generation X"
describes a group that does not have a clear identity. The labels

"twentysomethings" and "13th generation" (counting back to the founding fathers) are innocuous and imply nothing about character.

Perhaps worst of all, the label "baby busters" itself implies that 8 the group is a bust and not worth bothering with. One trait of young adults is already crystal clear: They resent Baby Boomers. In the eyes of young adults, Boomers had a party and didn't clean up the mess.

Surprisingly, many Americans are oblivious to the latest genera- 9 tion gap, perhaps because Boomer marketers fail to realize that they are no longer the younger generation. Many still cherish the mistaken hope that an appeal to Boomers will also attract younger adults.

Reared by dual-income or single parents, busters are more likely 10 than their elders to accept differences in race, ethnicity, national origin, family structure and lifestyle. Growing up in an age of AIDS, divorce, latchkey kids, national economic decline and rising violence, they are well aware that stability is hard to find and that danger is just around the corner.

Though many Boomers, especially younger ones, are financially 11 strapped, they are still optimistic that they will do as well as or better than their parents did. A college education was seemingly a ticket to affluence for Boomers. But is it leaving the younger busters with student loans to repay and limited employment opportunities. One in five people who graduated from college between 1984 and 1990 has a job that does not require a college education, according to the Bureau of Labor Statistics.

Despite the lack of peer competition that a smaller generation is 12 expected to bring, the immediate future does not look brighter. There will be fewer openings in jobs requiring a college degree during the 1990s than there were in the 1980s. But the number of college gradu- ates will continue to grow. This could leave as many as 30 percent of college graduates underemployed or without jobs.

Prospects are even grimmer for young adults without a college 13 education. High school graduates entering the job market today face stiffer competition, even for lower-paying jobs.

Although they wear "retro" fashions from the 1960s and may 14 know who the Beatles were, young adults don't identify with the rebellious change-the-world mentality of that era. Twentysomethingers are irreverent about issues they don't think affect them personally. As a result, they are more conservative than Boomers in some ways—but more liberal in others.

Almost half of people ages 18 to 24 identify themselves as inde- 15 pendents rather than Democrats or Republicans compared to the 38 percent of all Americans, according to the Times Mirror Center for People & the Press, a surveying and polling group.

But a lack of party affiliation does not mean that busters lack   16
principles or commitment. Media sophisticates from an early age, they
are less than impressed with pundits and talking heads on news shows.

One-third of young people get at least some of their political   17
information from comedy shows such as *Arsenio Hall* and *Saturday
Night Live*, according to a 1992 survey by the Times Mirror Center.
Many young adults object to what they see as "slick packaging of
politicians," according to Mr. Gullett of *Blast* magazine. They distrust
hype and "spin" wherever they see it, from product advertising to
political campaigns.

The least-packaged 1992 presidential candidate, Ross Perot, gar-   18
nered a slightly higher share of votes from people younger than 30 than
from any other age group. Perhaps they simply expect less from the
government, but people age 18 to 24 are less likely than older adults
to believe the United States needs new leaders in Washington, according to Times Mirror.

They are also less critical of federal bureaucracy. Only half agree   19
completely that "when something is run by the government, it is
usually inefficient and wasteful," compared to 65 percent to 76 percent
of older Americans.

People younger than 25 also have higher opinions about the   20
positive influence of business executives and of Congress than do other
age groups. On social issues, young adults are often more liberal than
their elders, including Baby Boomers. They are less likely than others
to believe in banning books from public school libraries or firing
teachers because they are homosexual.

They are more likely to feel that the women's movement has had   21
a good influence on America. They also accept interracial dating more
readily. And 49 percent of people ages 18 to 24 approve of giving
preferential treatment to minorities to improve their situation, compared to about 33 percent of Boomers.

Although their incomes are lower than those of Boomers, young   22
adults can still be a lucrative market. Census data show that young
adults are delaying marriage and children even longer than the Boomers did. As a result, they may have more discretionary income and
more time to spend it. Young people are a key market for products that
Boomers discarded when they acquired homes and children, according
to a national survey for *Mademoiselle* magazine by the Roper Organization. Female busters are the primary consumers of cosmetics and
fashionable clothing.

Because they are buying fun stuff for themselves, young women   23
enjoy shopping far more than Boomer women do, surveys show. Young
adults indulge themselves in other ways too. Thirty-eight percent of

young women go to the movies each month, according to the *Mademoiselle* survey, compared to 19 percent of Boomer women. People younger than 25 devote a larger than average share of their spending dollars to eating out, alcoholic beverages, clothing and electronic items such as televisions and stereos, according to the Bureau of Labor Statistics. The Roper Organization's Mr. Himmelfarb says that if you want to appeal to this group, "it is very important to associate yourself with causes and with positive activities."

A discussion of AIDS, environmental dangers or drug abuse is likely to galvanize young people, especially college students. The price of ignoring young adults can be very high. Calling it a "teeny-bopper network," 67-year old George Bush refused to appear on MTV until late in the presidential campaign.   24

But Baby Boomer Bill Clinton courted youth by appearing on the network last summer and fielding viewer questions. Young adults favored Mr. Clinton in the election. Even more important is that Democrats have claimed the first votes of Generation X. The big payoff may come in 1996.   25

Questions for Thinking and Discussion

1. In this article, Mitchell attempts to identify some characteristics of the so-called "baby-busters." If you are a member of the age group she is writing about, to what extent do statements such as the following apply to you personally or to friends or relatives who are in this age group?

   "[Baby busters] are aware that stability is hard to find and that danger is just around the corner."

   "[Baby busters are] more likely than their elders to accept differences in race, ethnicity, natural origin, family structure, and lifestyle."

   "[Baby busters] resent Baby Boomers."

2. Mitchell argues that the immediate economic future does not look very good for young people, even college graduates. She predicts that eventually "as many as 30 percent of college graduates" may be underemployed or unemployed. However, despite these potentially troublesome economic times, Mitchell portrays baby busters as being big spenders who are dependent on fashion and entertainment for satisfaction.

   How accurately does Mitchell represent the values of young people? If she is correct, how can this seeming contradiction be explained: spending money without the financial means to do it?

The One Who Has the Most Toys When He Dies, Wins

PAUL CHANCE

THAT BUMPER STICKER COULD EASILY BE THE MOTTO of today's college   1
freshmen. It represents values that are a far cry from those of students
two decades ago, when conservative social critics lambasted college
students for being naïve, idealistic intellectuals. What business did
students have picketing, campaigning for candidates, burning draft
cards, protesting injustice? If they would spend less time filling their
heads with literature, philosophy and the social sciences, the critics
complained, and more time on practical matters such as making a
living, they and the country would be better off.

Those critics stand silent today, in awe perhaps at the extent to   2
which college students are heeding their advice. Today's freshmen seem
concerned with little other than the practical matter of making a living.
They are pragmatic and materialistic to a fault, or so it seems from the
latest survey by the Cooperative Institutional Research Program
(CIRP), an affiliate of the University of California, Los Angeles. Every
fall since 1966, CIRP has surveyed a representative sample of 300,000
of the nation's college freshmen. A comparison of answers given in
1966 with these given in 1986 reveals some striking—some will say
disturbing—trends.

Contrary to popular opinion, students have not become mark-   3
edly more conservative over the years: They still want arms reduction,
less military spending, a clean environment, a fair shake for minorities
and women. But they think government should take care of these
matters while they busy themselves with the task of getting on in life.

Getting on means, according to CIRP pollsters Alexander W. Astin   4
and Kenneth C. Green, accumulating money, power and status. Money
seems to be especially important. In 1986, more than 70 percent of
college freshmen said that a major reason for attending college was "to
be able to make more money," and a like number of students said that
to "be very well-off financially" was an essential or very important goal.
These figures are up nearly a third in the past 10 years.

Today's materialism is reflected in the choice of majors and in   5
career plans. Psychology has held its own as a major, but other traditional liberal-arts majors such as foreign languages, history and phi-

losophy have lost so much ground that Astin and Green worry that they may disappear from some campuses entirely. The number of freshmen planning to major in business, however, has nearly doubled over the past two decades, from about 14 percent to slightly less than 27 percent.

It seems clear that the appeal of business is the promise of high   6
starting salaries and the prospect of event greater wealth later on. And students want to get rich quickly, with a minimum of academic preparation. Any career that requires schooling beyond the bachelor's degree is shunned. This is true not only of professions that are not very lucrative, such as research and college teaching, but of well-paid professions, such as medicine and law. Students have evidently decided that the potential income of these fields does not warrant the extra years of training. In the business jargon these students like so well, becoming a physician, lawyer, social worker, teacher or scientist is not "cost-effective." The fact that these and other fields offer nonmaterial rewards seems not to be a part of the formula for career choice.

Astin and Green also suggest that students are steering clear of   7
the arts and sciences because these majors and career choices require high-level verbal and critical thinking skills, skills that have declined markedly since 1966. Student choices therefore reflect insight into their weaknesses. But Astin and Green believe that a radical change in values has taken place. Twenty years ago more than 80 percent of freshmen said that developing a meaningful philosophy of life was an important or essential goal. Today only about 41 percent of freshmen consider that goal worthy. Astin and Green note that it could be that making a lot of money precludes the need for a philosophy of life: "It may be that some students view making a lot of money as a kind of 'philosophy of life' in itself."

Questions for Thinking and Discussion

1. In this article, Chance reports on the results of a survey study at UCLA that tries to examine values, behaviors, and goals of young people today. Just as you did with Mitchell's article, think about yourself or baby buster-age people you know. Are there any ways that Chance seems to be talking about modern young people as you know them? In what ways is he accurate?

2. In Chance's article, he discusses how Alexander Astin and Kenneth Green's survey shows that today's college freshmen are "concerned with

little other than the practical matter of making a living." Astin and Green conclude that, for many of today's freshmen, making money seems to be a "philosophy of life" in itself.

What is a "philosophy of life"? What do you think Astin and Green mean by saying that making money becomes a "philosophy of life" itself? If making money is a philosophy for young people, what effects do you think there might be on individuals? On society?

U.S. Youths' Ethics Alarming, Study Says

REUTERS

A PRIVATE INSTITUTE HAS ISSUED AN ALARMING REPORT on the ethics of   1
American youths, saying many young people admitted to lying, cheating and stealing.

"The study reveals that a disturbingly high proportion of young   2
people regularly engage in dishonest and irresponsible behavior.

"They lie, cheat and steal at work, at school and in their personal   3
relationships," said Michael Josephson, president of the Josephson
Institute for the Advancement of Ethics.

Mr. Josephson, founder of the Los Angeles institute, which pro-   4
motes ethical behavior, disclosed the results of a two-year study on
ethics Friday at a meeting of the Commonwealth Club of California.

The institute questioned almost 9,000 young people and adults   5
during 1991 and 1992 in what it said was thought to be the most
comprehensive survey of American ethical attitudes and behaviors ever
undertaken.

Although there was no way of proving that young people's ethics   6
today are worse than in the past, "they are bad enough to cause grave
concern," said Mr. Josephson, a former law professor.

Among the study's findings: 7

- 33 percent of high school students surveyed and 16 percent of
  college students admitted that they had stolen something from
  a store within the past year.
- Sixty-one percent of the high school students and 32 percent
  of college students admitted that they cheated on an exam in
  the past year.
- More than one-third of the high school students said they
  would lie on a resume or job application to get a job.
- Twenty-one percent of college students said they would falsify
  a report if it was necessary to keep their job.

"Far too many young people have abandoned traditional ethi-   8
cal values in favor of self-absorbed, win-at-any-cost attitudes that

77

threaten to unravel the moral fabric of American society," Mr. Josephson said.

Questions for Thinking and Discussion

1. This article reports on a study of the ethics of young Americans. Michael Josephson, head of the research group that carried out the study, thinks that ethics have declined because good values have been pushed out by bad ones: Young people have "abandoned traditional ethical values in favor of self-absorbed, win-at-any-cost attitudes."

   What other reasons might account for an ethical low point? In what ways might the findings of this study be related to the other characteristics of modern young people, discussed in articles by Mitchell, Chance, and Bozzi?

2. In your experiences with young people, what instances have you witnessed of the kinds of dishonesty that are discussed in the article: cheating on examinations, lying on job applications or resumes, and falsification of facts on a report? Based on these experiences, how much concern should all of us have about the values of the young?

Generation X

KIRSTEN COLE

DO YOU REMEMBER SEEING STAR WARS on the big screen? Was one of   1
you favorite childhood games Atari? Did you spend your teenage years
wanting your MTV?

A "yes" answer to one or more of those questions may mean you   2
are one of 44 million people between the ages of 18 and 29 and a
member of Generation X.

The generation following the baby boom is slowly creeping into   3
the spotlight. As the boomers age, advertisers, marketers and media
have begun to recognize and pay attention to this new group, which
has been saddled with such titles as "baby busters," the "bland generation," "13ers," "twentysomethings," "slackers," the "repair generation,"
"post-boomers," "Xers," and the "shadow generation."

This generation represents a $125 billion market. But thanks to   4
its one commonality, diversity, everyone—including the media, advertisers and just about everybody else—are having a hard time defining
Generation X.

Heidi Shields, 25, of Chicago, fits many media definitions of   5
an Xer. She graduated from college in 1991 with a degree in graphic
arts.

"When I started college, computer graphic people were in de-   6
mand," she said. "When I got out of college, the market was completely
saturated. There had been cutbacks in the field, so people with 20
years experience were back in the market. It made sense, but I thought,
'it's our turn.' "

So, like an estimated 58 percent of all unmarried singles age 20   7
to 24, Shields moved back home and began a two-year search for a job
in her field.

Also, like many of her contemporaries, she took several jobs,   8
none career-related, just to pay the bills and save a little money.

"I knew it was going to be hard, but I didn't think it would take   9
two years," Shields said, "I searched endlessly for a job in the Peoria
area (where she was from). I would have liked to stay in Peoria but I
was scared to be too far out of school without any experience."

Shields ended up working four jobs, including bar tending and   10
painting sweatshirts with her sister, to save up enough money to move
to Chicago.

Shields was able to find a job in computer graphics in Chicago. [11] Although she doesn't plan on staying with the company for a long time, she sees it as a stepping stone.

"I want something more challenging. This job is not very crea- [12] tive," Shields said, "but, I am definitely getting experience. Ultimately, I would like to do freelance graphics for people."

"I may be living check to check right now, but I am not at the [13] total bottom. I am trying to stay optimistic for sure."

Shields falls in the middle of the generation, whereas Tom Sar- [14] geant, 28, accountant supervisor for Resource Marketing, which is a division of R & B Productions, falls at the tail end.

Sargeant, who found work almost immediately out of college, had [15] a different outlook on employment than Shields. Although he didn't know for sure if the money he was spending on college would be worth it, he was banking on it.

"I figured it would ultimately pay off. I looked at college as an [16] investment," he said. "My expectations haven't changed that drastically after college. I maintain the attitude the harder you work, the more money you make."

Some people claim baby busters are cynical about boomers. [17] According to an article in U.S. News and World Report (Feb. 22, 1993), busters see boomers as "insufferably self-righteous yuppies who sold out their principles, placed work over family and money over community."

Sargeant, however, said there shouldn't be an "us against them [18] philosophy."

"All we've talked about is baby boomers, so many people, so [19] many years," he said. "Now, another generation wants the spotlight."

Twenty-four-year-old Eric Blankenburg agreed with Sargeant that [20] baby boomers are not all to blame.

"Things were not perfect when they were born," he said. "It has [21] progressively gone down hill and unfortunately things will get worse."

"Baby boomers say we are rebels or hooligans. I think we are [22] exactly the opposite. Like people my age, 99 percent vote and honestly care about the future. Society needs to look at us as the future," he added. "They should work with us instead of against us."

Ellen Clore, 24, is not so convinced by people her age. [23]

"Some are and some aren't more aware and active," she said. "I [24] think the majority are apathetic, with a few that are very concerned. They don't watch the news or read the paper."

"Aspirations were not as high for the baby boomers. We (busters) [25] have greater expectations, but they are harder to reach because it is more competitive," she added. "Back then, a high school diploma was equivalent to our college degree. Now we need to attend graduate school to get a good job."

Blankenburg, like Shields, discovered a degree doesn't automatically guarantee someone a job. 26

"I wanted the best job out of college. I thought after I graduated I could have any job I wanted and be making $35,000 a year," he said. "A week before graduation I said 'great a degree, the key to the world.' After graduation, reality hit me. It's not like that (receiving the dream job) and it still is not two years later." 27

Blankenburg, who works for Multi-Ad, did end up moving back home with his parents for several months. However, he did find work before they enforced a rent rule. Things have improved, but he is still a ways from the income level of his dreams. 28

He said he is living a lot check to check, even though living expenses are lower, due to a roommate. However, he blames this on the attitude, "the more you have, the more you spend." 29

"Among friends my age, it's typical to live like this. They are not doctors and lawyers," he said. "It is harder to make money for our generation." 30

"I know our parents worked hard and climbed the ladder to be successful. It is time for us to take out ladders and start climbing. It may be longer, but we need to climb it just the same." 31

Clore, who is currently working at the Peoria Civic Center as a temporary executive assistant, was another Xer who discovered ways of cutting expenses, including living with her parents. 32

"I used to have a roommate and we split most everything," she said. "I didn't have car payments, so I had lower expenses. I worked in the suburbs of Chicago and took the train to work, which was cheaper." 33

Clore, who attended graduate school, also experienced a reality check after graduation. 34

"I really did believe the money spent on college would be worth it," she said. "I went to a private school, spent a lot of money and now have a lot of debt. I didn't make nearly as much money as I thought I would, but I will probably step up the ladder with my extra education." 35

Observing the struggle of peers has created somewhat of a pessimistic attitude at the lower end of Xers. Steve Szymke, 18, expects there is going to be a struggle after graduating from Bradley University. 36

"I see my friends that don't have jobs," said Szymke, who dreams of directing films one day. "In the movie industry, it's a real struggle to get above water. But, I have a definite advantage over those who don't have a degree. A person also needs the extra edge of graduate school." 37

"I am sure there will be a rude awakening for a lot of us, but now   38
we sit around at Lums and think we know everything. We pretend we
are solving the world's problems."

Contrary to Clore's concern about the involvement of Xers,   39
Szymke votes and also reads, not fluffy material, but "Time." He does
agree that attitudes have changed.

"In the '60s kids cared about political things. Now, kids are into   40
activism and have stances on abortion, environmental issues and religion," he said. "Our political involvement is nowhere near the '60s
involvement."

Szymke is also aware that money isn't a bumper crop.   41

"My first semester of college I would spend a dollar here and   42
another one there," he said. "I figured out quickly that it adds up. And
although my dad is helping quite a bit with college, I still have to pay
for my graduate work."

Reportedly, three quarters of college professors say students are   43
very unprepared in basic skills. Szymke, a sophomore at Bradley
University, doesn't dispute that fact.

"I was lucky when I went to Dunlap, but there were some stu-   44
dents from California at Bradley who studied in public schools," he
said. "They are really bad and don't know how to study. They also don't
know how to take tests."

Though there are common links in attitude, like the group's bleak   45
economic and financial future, the common denominator, for the
group, as Sargeant said, is diversity. That may explain the term "Generation X."

"There is no given for "X." It's a variable. It's not an acronym," he   46
said. "You can't put the same values in place of the variable for everyone."

"I think we are lost," Szymke said. "There are so many variables   47
and things are so uncertain. Maybe X means exploration."

"I think we associate with material things rather than an eco-   48
nomic situation. We were asked to categorize Generation X in an art
class. They asked people if they remembered seeing "Star Wars" on the
big screen," he added. "If you said yes, they said, 'Well, then you're a
member of Generation X.' Look at MTV, too, its the channel for 18–27
year olds."

And if Generation X is recognized as the Atari and MTV genera-   49
tion, then what's in store for the next generation?

"We'll probably have the Nintendo generation next," Szymke   50
said, laughing.

Questions for Thinking and Discussion

1. As you read Cole's article, what ideas did you find that had been discussed in the previous six articles in this section? Jot some brainstorm notes to yourself about what characteristics these writers seem to be finding in American youth today.

2. Near the end of this article, one of the young people Cole quotes indicates that he sees his generation as "lost." What do you suppose he means by a "lost generation"? Do you agree with his assessment?

Young Beyond Their Years

KENNETH L. WOODWARD

Sandy and Marvin Miller have three children, ages 19 to 25, and are wondering when they will grow up. Though the younger of the two come and go, all three consider their parents' lavish house in Encino, Calif., home. Each child's bedroom is equipped with a stereo and color TV set. "Our kids were spoiled rotten," Sandy admits.

Jason, the youngest, is enrolled in college. Last summer his parents promised to buy him a Jeep—if he got a job. But Jason "just fooled around," his mother complains, and now Jason is upset because they won't give him the car.

Mia, 22, also attends college. Like her brother, she has never had to work except for pocket money. The Millers hit the roof, though, when Mia's recent college bill included hundreds of dollars in parking tickets on her Mustang convertible. "She's so used to having us pay for everything, she has absolutely no sense of values," her mother says.

But the real problem is Todd, the oldest child. With a loan from his parents, Todd started a limousine business from the family home. His parents have given him till the year's end to move out and even have offered him the money to buy a house. But Todd refuses to budge. He pays no rent and gets his clothes laundered free by the family maid. "I grew up here," he argues. "You're throwing me out of my own house." "I don't want to throw them out in the street," Sandy Miller says of her children. "But they've got to take responsibility and stand on their own two feet. They've got to grow up."

SOMETHING HAPPENED ON THE WAY to the 21st century: American 1 youth, in a sharp reversal of historical trends, are taking longer to grow up. As the 20th century winds down, more young Americans are enrolled in college, but fewer are graduating—they are taking longer to get their degrees. They take longer to establish careers, too, and longer yet to marry. Many, unable or unwilling to pay for housing, return to the nest—or are slow to leave it. They postpone choices and spurn long-term commitments. Life's on hold; adulthood can wait.

Experts on the family say they've never seen anything like it. 2 "Young people are growing up with much less commitment of any kind," says Rutgers University sociologist David Popenoe, author of "Disturbing the Nest," a comprehensive new study of family life. "Never before has it been so hard to leave the period of youth."

It wasn't supposed to be this way, or so some experts initially   3
thought. Surveying the vaunted "youth revolt" of the '60s, anthropologist Margaret Mead concluded that the young had become "pioneers" of a brave new future for which their elders could no longer serve as trustworthy models. But pioneers, it turned out, were not headed toward adulthood. What was happening, observed psychologist Kenneth Keniston, was "the emergence on a mass scale of a previously unrecognized stage of life," which he labeled "youth." By 1972 sociologist James S. Coleman had discerned the regressive character of burgeoning new youth culture: locked into a world of their own creation, with their own music and money and a license to do as they wished, the young saw no reason to abandon this "pleasing surrogate for maturity." The age of extended adolescence had arrived. And it shows no signs of going away.

Adolescence is a period of intense self-absorption—a time for   4
finding out who you are and the sort of person you can and ought to become. Adulthood, on the other hand, implies the development of character, competence and commitment, qualities essential for self-discipline, cooperation and taking care of others. By these standards, young Americans entering the 21st century are far less mature than their ancestors were at the beginning of the 20th. The difference is evident in all areas of youthful development: sex, love, marriage, education and work.

Physically, today's youth are maturing earlier than previous gen-   5
erations, but emotionally they are taking much longer to develop adult attachments. They are marrying later than their parents did—partly for economic reasons—and many college graduates are postponing marriage beyond age 30. But unlike earlier generations, they live in a permissive society that tolerates teenage sex. According to a 1986 Harris survey, 57 percent of today's adolescent boys and girls have had sex before age 18. By the time they reach their mid-20s, many no longer regard sexual relationships as a matter of values or commitment. "Most of us got one-night stands out of our system in college," writes Nancy Smith, 25, in a recent essay for The Washington Post on her generation's struggle with adulthood. "Sex outside a relationship is not so much a matter of right or wrong as: Is it really worth the hassle?"

Uninhibited adolescent sex, however does have serious social   6
consequences. One is unwanted pregnancies: currently, more than one American child in five is born out of wedlock, 40 percent of them to teenagers. Another result is a soaring abortion rate. More than two

thirds of all abortions are performed on single women under the age of 27. "In this age group you see many young women who have had multiple abortions," says psychoanalyst Glen Gabbard of the Menniger Clinic. "The ease with which they choose to abort reflects a disturbing sense of self-absorption and an alarming indifference to the moral gravity of their actions and an inability to make commitments."

Another striking feature of extended adolescence is the unprecedented rise in cohabitation—in effect, the commitment not to be committed. Today half of all men and women in their 30s cohabited before marriage, many of them on the assumption that it is better to look—deeply—before they leap. But studies now demonstrate that couples who cohabit before marriage are more likely to divorce than those who do not. "It's a relationship that attracts those, mainly men, who are looking for an easy out," observes sociologist Glen Elder of the University of North Carolina, "and it is uncertain what, if anything, it contributes to marriage." 7

Along with these changes in sexual mores, marriage itself has ceased to reflect permanent commitment. Angela Chiklakis of Boston married in her mid-20s and divorced at 30 because her husband no longer appealed to her. Besides, Angela explains, she felt she was "becoming an old fogy." At 34, Angela is lanky, beautiful and looks ten years younger than her married agemates back home in Somerville, Mass. "They don't look good." Angela observes of her friends. "Their bodies have changed. I know they envy me." Angela cuts hair in a beauty salon and is still unattached. "Whatever I have is mine," she says. "I'm not trapped into saving for a kid's education." 8

To be sure, most young Americans still expect to marry and have children. But unlike their parents, the prospect fills them with dread. They have grown accustomed to keeping their options open. There are so many choices to make—in relationships, careers and consumer goods—that they hate to limit their freedom. They sense that marriage requires compromise, negotiation and discipline—habits the youth culture does not encourage. "Some of us look at it as giving up," writes Nancy Smith. "That is, giving up the search, the quest for the better job, the better city, partner, life. Settling down means this is as good as it gets, this is all I want." 9

Like love, work, too, has become an opportunity for immediate gratification, rather than for long-term growth and commitment. In the '70s, Coleman and other American sociologists warned that the young were becoming expert consumers long before they were learning how to produce. These experts urged society to provide challenging part-time jobs under responsible mentors so that the young could learn the value of meaningful work, thrift and responsibility for others. By the 10

'80s, three out of four high-school seniors were working an average of 18 hours a week and often taking home more than $200 a month. But their jobs—often in fast-food chains—were rarely challenging and earnings were immediately spent on cars, clothing, stereos and other artifacts of the adolescent good life. Indeed, researchers at the University of Michigan find that less than 11 percent of high-school seniors save all or most of their earnings for college or other long-range purposes.

In short, teenage employment has only intensified the adolescent drive for immediate gratification. Instead of learning how to delay desires, students are indulging what University of Michigan researcher Jerald Bachman calls "premature affluence." The problem, says Bachman, is that these adolescents tend to get accustomed to an unrealistic level of discretionary income which is impossible to maintain at college, unless they have extravagant parents. "And if they don't go to school," he observes, "they will have to continue to live at home if they hope to keep up their personal spending habits."   11

For many college students, higher education provides a slower transition to adulthood than the passage their parents experienced. Since the mid-'60s, when university officials abolished *in loco parentis* rules as inappropriate for "young adults," campuses have come to resemble giant youth preserves where students are relatively free to do as they wish. Inevitably, many 17-year-olds lack the intellectual or emotional maturity to achieve in this laissez-faire atmosphere. As the decline in SAT scores suggests, many incoming freshmen are already handicapped by poor secondary schooling. By 1988, according to an annual survey by Alexander Astin of UCLA's Higher Education Research Institute, 43 percent of all students who entered a four-year college or university in 1984 had flunked at least one course, and over 30 percent had taken special courses to strengthen basic reading, study or other scholastic skills. Even professors at elite schools see a difference. "A third of my students are illiterate," says Robert Bellah, a distinguished professor of sociology at the University of California, Berkeley. "By that I mean they are unable to understand a complex sentence, or write one that makes much sense."   12

There are, unfortunately, no SATs to measure maturity, no tests to determine how a student handles frustration, resolves conflicting choices or develops intellectual interests in people, events and ideas that are older than yesterday. These are qualities of character that are best developed at home, and the absence of these values in the young, many experts believe, reflects a lack of parental concern. "The irony is that we have the best group of educated parents in history doing the least for their own kids," says historian Maris Vinovskis of the Univer-   13 sity of Michigan. In contrast, Urie Bronfenbrenner, professor of human development at Cornell University, points to the extraordinary academic success of Asian students, especially the children of impoverished and linguistically handicapped boat people. "They're walking away with the fellowships," Bronfenbrenner observes. "Why? Because they come from cultures which have strong family systems where the notions of activity, responsibility and work are values."

Other experts point to the influence of television, with its ability   14
to provide instant, incessant and intellectually passive diversion, as a major cause of protracted immaturity. Students of the '80s represent the first generation to have lived from birth with television as a constant companion, and in millions of college dorms, the TV set flickers constantly. Today's students are also the first to have entered adolescence in the era of earphone electronics, which allows them to remain constantly plugged into the youth culture's mass-produced musical narcotic.

"America's young have become literally attached to the TV, the   15
stereo and the radio," observes psychologist David Klimek, a specialist in maturation in Ann Arbor, Mich. "And if you take those away, they go through more loss and despair than if you took away their parents." As Klimek sees it, endless hours of watching the tube and listening to music has bred a passive population of college students. "This may sound trite," he says, "but the ability to grow from passive to active is a major passage from childhood to adulthood."

Evidence of this passivity can be found in the changing vision   16
that students have of life after college. For the past 23 years UCLA's Astin has been surveying trends in the "life goals" of some 250,000 full-time college freshmen. In the early '70s, the most cherished value was "developing a meaningful philosophy of life." By 1989 that value had dropped to ninth, far behind the first choice—"being well-off financially."

What this means, says Astin, is that fewer students are using   17
higher education to find out who they are, the sort of human beings they ought to be or even the kinds of careers that are worthy of pursuit. Involvement in extracurricular activities is down, and with it the quality of educational experience. "Students today limit learning to the classroom," Astin observes, "and the fast-trackers are setting the pace. They're defining themselves according to external things—money, power, status—and choosing courses that will get them these things. They're terribly preoccupied with their bodies but they they've lost touch with mental disciplines."

Of course, there are young Americans who defy the norm. They   18
work hard and arrive at adulthood ready to nurture the next genera-

tion. But for the majority, the passage through adolescence will remain a slow one well into the 21st century. A sharp recession might force some to grow up faster, but economics is not the most important reason why the young take longer to mature. Ultimately, it's a question of cultural values. What the young see enshrined in the media and malls of America are, after all, the values adults put there: consumerism, narcissism and the instant gratification of desire. When those change, so will American youth.

Questions for Thinking and Discussion

1. If you know young people who are lured by the appeal of perpetual youth, what do you suppose their goals are? What are their motives? To what extent do you regard their situations as negatively as Woodward does?

2. Near the end of his article, Woodward finds a major reason for the lure of perpetual youth:

   "What the young see enshrined in the media and malls of America are, after all, the values adults put there: consumerism, narcissism and the instant gratification of desire. When those change, so will American youth."

   What do you think Woodward means by this criticism? Try to think of specific examples of "consumerism, narcissism, and the instant gratification of desire." How optimistic or pessimistic are you that these values will change in American youth, as Woodward says they must?

Writing Projects

1. The writers of the articles in this chapter have attempted to depict Generation X. If you are a member of this generation, write a paper about whether you fit the descriptions of Generation X in these readings.

2. Most of the portrayals of young Americans in these five articles have been negative. Write a paper in which you take the *other* direction, examining the positive characteristics of Generation X. This paper could be based on your own observations, but you might also interview people who work with young people (professors, counselors, ministers) to get a broader view of the positive side of Generation X.

3. How well do the descriptions of Generation X outlined in these readings fit students at your college? Prepare a paper that explores this question by putting together a list of ten supposed Generation X characteristics from readings in this chapter and then using them for interviews of twenty Generation X members on your campus. On the whole do your findings suggest that the writers are really capturing some features of this generation, or are they merely stereotyping the young?

4. Write a paper entitled "Coping with the Problems of Our Generation" to present to an audience made up of members of Generation X. Your paper should select about five primary problems outlined in the articles in this chapter and then suggest ways in which individuals can best respond to them.

5

Crime and Violence

OPINION POLL AFTER OPINION POLL IN THE 1990s shows that one of the primary concerns of Americans is crime, especially violent crime. The results of these polls reflect American citizens' frustrations that things seem to be getting worse and their fears that they might be victims of crimes themselves, even as innocent bystanders.

The readings in this chapter take a brief look at violent crime in America from a variety of viewpoints. As you read the articles, look for statistics that dramatize the sheer numbers of crimes that occur in America. These statistics also show who is most likely to be affected by that crime. Look also in the articles for discussions of the ways that children are often victimized by violent crime. Note speculations by the writers as to the reasons for violent crimes. Finally, read the articles to find ways that the writers debate solutions, especially the controversial notion of controlling guns.

4,200 Teens Fatally Shot in '90, Study Shows

CHRISTOPHER CONNELL

FIREARMS KILLED NEARLY 4,200 TEEN-AGERS IN 1990, and firearms are now involved in one in every four deaths among people ages 15 to 24, the government reported yesterday.

Health and Human Services Secretary Donna E. Shalala called the statistics "frightening and intolerable."

Only motor vehicle accidents kill more teen-agers and young adults than firearms, the National Center for Health Statistics reported.

Thirty-nine percent more deaths occurred from firearms than from natural causes.

The firearms homicide and suicide rates for young men were five to 10 times higher than for females.

Among all 15- to 19-year-olds, there were 4,173 firearms deaths in 1990, an increase of nearly 600 over the year before and 1,675 more than in 1985.

The rate for black males in that age group has soared from 37 deaths per 100,000 in 1985 to 105 per 100,000 in 1990; among white males, it nearly doubled from five deaths per 100,000 to almost 10.

"These are the data behind all the stories we've been reading every day," said Lois A. Fingerhut, the author of the study on *Firearm Mortality Among Children, Youth and Young Adults 1–34 Years of Age.*

Shalala, in a statement, decried "the waste of young lives. As a society, we need to do a better job of understanding why this is happening and what we can do to turn these numbers around."

Richard Aborn, president of the Center to Prevent Handgun Violence, said the United States had rushed to the aid of children starving in a far-off land, but "where is the intervention needed to save the children who are dying needlessly right here in the U.S.A.?"

Aborn also heads Handgun Control Inc., which is lobbying for tighter restrictions on gun sales.

Paul Blackman, research coordinator for the National Rifle Association, said, "There may have even been a tiny increase in the number of innocents killed, but for the most part the dramatic rise over the past five years has been among persons who are up to no good who are killed by other persons who are up to no good.

"Those who do their homework, go to church on Sunday, have   13
proper family upbringing aren't being shot in any particularly different
numbers. . . . The rise is among those involved in drug trafficking and
other criminal activity."

Questions for Thinking and Discussion

1. A question lurking beneath the surface of what all the writers in this
   section are dealing with is *why crime should be on the increase.* Health
   and Human Services Secretary Shalala, quoted in Connell's article,
   says that "we need to do a better job of understanding why this is
   happening . . ." From your previous thinking and reading on this
   subject, why do you think violent crime has increased in America?

2. Paul Blackman, a representative of the National Rifle Association
   (NRA), does not seem concerned about the statistics given in this
   article. He believes violent crime isn't really affecting people who play
   by the rules: "do their homework, go to church on Sunday, have proper
   family upbringing. . . ." However, even if innocent bystander crimes
   don't happen very often, one could still argue that any violent crime is
   a problem that affects Americans. To what extent would this be true?

Guns Are Death for Our Children

Carolyn Poirot

THERE WAS NOTHING MORE SPECIAL that a 10-year-old tomboy could do in the 1950s than tag along on her father's hunting trips on crisp, quiet Saturday mornings in the early fall. 1

Sunflowers 8 feet tall attracted the dove while thick mesquite and salt cedar hid the cottontails along the creek bed that ran through my grandfather's dairy farm in Archer County [TX]. 2

You had to wait until after the first frost to shoot rabbits. I never knew why. But dove season started when school did. And, in my memory, the first dove hunt in September was always a celebration, marking completion of the first week of school. 3

I seldom got to carry a gun; I always carried an old gunnysack that had once held chicken feed. But I loved the smell of gunpowder from the spent shotgun shells that I picked up for reloading later and put in the sack along with the birds and rabbits. And I loved just being with my father. 4

With such good childhood memories, why am I so opposed to guns today—especially where children are concerned? 5

On the average, 11 U.S. children and adolescents now die daily as a result of firearm injuries. 6

In the mid-1980s, there were 3,000 firearm-related deaths among those 19 years old and younger. By 1989, the number had risen to almost 4,000. 7

National Safety Week is Sept. 19–26, and gun safety seemed like a good place to start, until I realized there may not be any such thing—at least not where children are concerned. 8

There is no evidence that children of any age can be reliably educated to be gun safe. Lack of experience, judgment and self-control can always lead to dangerous experimentation. 9

Homicidal and suicidal thoughts are directly related to impulsive, confused behavior, and access to a gun creates a lethal situation, the American Academy of Pediatrics said earlier this year in a policy statement calling for a ban on deadly handguns, air guns and assault weapons. 10

Most people purchase handguns to protect themselves and their families from criminals, but studies show a gun in the home is more likely to kill a family member or friend than an intruder—43 times more likely, according to one study, cited by the pediatricians. 11

A common misconception is that teen homicides are largely   12
related to crime, gang activity or premeditated assault. In fact, the
majority of shootings are committed by friends or relatives usually
because of an argument, according to the Centers for Disease Control.

"Due to the emphasis our society places on firearms, guns hold a   13
unique fascination for American children," said Dr. Alfredo Santesteban, a Bedford pediatrician, who has written extensively on children's
safety issues.

"It is only natural for your child to be curious about something he   14
sees used by heroes and villains alike in books, movies and on television," he said. "And, if you allow your child to play with toy guns, it
will be difficult for him to distinguish between a toy and the real thing."

A recent survey of 266 unintentional shootings by the Center to   15
Prevent Handgun Violence revealed that more than half of all weapons
involved in domestic accidents were found by children in bedrooms—
on dressers, closet shelves and nightstands, between mattresses and
under beds and pillows—and in living rooms on coffee tables and
between sofa cushions, Santesteban noted.

Among 1- to 9-year-olds, the causes of shootings are divided—   16
half are unintentional and half are homicides, Santesteban said. Reports also indicate that of all children hospitalized because of firearm
injuries, about 12 percent die, and many who survive are permanently
disabled.

"The surest method of protecting your child from the threat of   17
improperly used firearms is to completely remove handguns from your
home and from any environment in which a child might play," the
doctor said.

The AAP recommends: 18

- Regulation and reduction of the destructive power of handgun
  ammunition,
- Reduction of the romanticization of gun use in the popular
  media, which influences violence and gun use by children,
- Reduction of the number of privately owned handguns and
  restrictions on handgun ownership,
- Identification of high-risk adolescents (teen-age males, alcohol, drug-prone or drug-addicted individuals) to provide them
  with age-appropriate services,
- Development of community-based coalitions of professionals,
  parents, schools, police, media and advocacy groups to address issues of public education, legislation, protective inter-
  ventions and social action.

Questions for Thinking and Discussion

1. In this article, Poirot offers us a set of suggestions for reducing handgun violence, especially when it involves children. In the last paragraph of the article, she quotes five solutions proposed by the American Association of Pediatrics. Reread these solutions and respond to them critically. How workable do you think they are?

2. The statistics in this article give a somewhat different view of the problem than offered by Blackman, the NRA spokesman, quoted in Connell's article. What statistics in this article suggest that innocent bystanders *do* get caught in handgun crossfire? Whose article do you believe?

"Bang, Bang, You're Dead" Isn't a Game

CLARENCE PAGE

LIKE OTHER MIDDLE-CLASS CHICAGOANS, Arwilda Burton was shocked 1
by the news that seven bodies had been found in the meat locker of a
chicken and pasta restaurant franchise.

In numbers, it was the equivalent of Chicago's legendary St. 2
Valentine's Day Massacre. But this time it was in Palatine, one of the
suburbs to which Chicagoans have fled in great numbers to escape
urban violence, and two of the victims this time were teen-agers.

So Arwilda Burton was shocked, like other middle-class Chicago- 3
ans, but she says she also felt the twinges of an additional emotion:

"Empathy," she said. "I understand what the children of that 4
community are going through."

Burton, a social worker, counsels children at the Jenner Elemen- 5
tary School, which services Chicago's crime-plagued Cabrini-Green
public housing complex, about 20 miles and a world away from
Palatine.

Cabrini-Green made national news last year when Dantrell Davis 6
became its third child in 1992 to be fatally shot in sniper cross-fire.

While teams of social workers, psychologists and other grief 7
counselors descended on Palatine High School, which the two slain
teens attended, Arwilda Burton helps grade school children at Jenner
School deal with similar shocks every week.

One little boy, who lost his brother to gang-related gunfire, loses 8
sleep at night contemplating revenge against the youth accused of the
slaying. A small girl copes with the loss of a mother whose body was
found in a drainage ditch. Another tries to deal with the violent death
of a grandmother and an uncle.

"They are not children as I used to know children," says Burton. 9
"They are not carefree."

The equivalent of the St. Valentine's Day Massacre is happening 10
in Chicago every couple of days in one neighborhood or another. The
residents of the high-crime neighborhoods never get used to the violence that churns all around them. But the rest of us seem to get a little
too easily accustomed to hearing about or, for that matter, to caring
about it.

It is hard to comprehend the massive numbers of handgun-   11
related deaths in America (22,000 Americans over the last two years
alone). But a glimpse into the world of Arwilda Burton should cause
us to stop, for a moment, to consider a horrible new development: the
appearance and growth of young children on the list of casualties.

But what can we do about it? We might not be able to stop all   12
such violence but we can at least close gaping holes in the laws that
control the sale and distribution of guns in America, where the homicide rate dwarfs that of the rest of the industrialized—and civilized—
world.

The National Rifle Association, which never saw a gun-control   13
law it liked, argues that we don't need new gun-control laws. Instead,
they say we need only to enforce existing laws with tougher sentences
for anyone who uses a gun to break the law.

But that blame-the-users approach is a cop-out, since existing   14
laws leave gaping loopholes for gun makers, dealers and distributors
to make a killing, figuratively and literally, by making and selling guns
to unlawful or irresponsible people.

In "The Story of a Gun," an eye-opening examination of today's   15
gun trade in the January *Atlantic magazine,* writer Erik Larson describes
how "a none-of-my-business attitude permeates the firearms distribution chain from production to final sale, allowing gunmakers and gun
marketers to promote the killing power of their weapons while dis-
avowing any responsibility for their use in crime."

Larson, who says he does not oppose guns, not even handguns,   16
in the hands of responsible owners, describes how mass killers like
Nicholas Elliot, 16, who shot up Atlantic Shores Christian School, in
Virginia Beach, Va., in 1988, acquired their weapons through federally
licensed dealers, using a means "that existing federal gun-trade regulations do much to encourage."

Yet, what happens when lawmakers try to impose even the slight-   17
est impediment on the gun flow? The NRA goes, well, ballistic, un-
leashing massive amounts of campaign donations, then calling in the
IOUs, stopping reform in its tracks.

Virginia Gov. Doug Wilder, whose state may be the biggest single   18
supplier of guns trafficked up and down the Eastern seaboard, has
proposed limiting gun purchases to one per month per individual.
It's a modest proposal, yet the NRA vows to fight it. Wilder, a vet-
eran of many legislative battles, expects "the biggest fight I've ever
encountered."

Amazing. Sometimes I wonder how those who knowingly supply   19
heavy weapons and silencers to kids, gangsters and crackpots manage

to sleep with themselves at night. But I wonder even more how the rest of us can sleep with ourselves at night, knowing that we could put a pinch on the traffic, yet we do nothing. Apathy is killing us.

Questions for Thinking and Discussion

1. Like Poirot, Page is concerned with the effects of violent crime on children. He worries that the NRA consistently blocks attempts to create gun control laws. According to Page, whenever lawmakers talk seriously about gun controls, the NRA "goes . . . ballistic," eventually "stopping reform in its tracks." Page also presents some of the NRA's positions. What are these positions? Has Page represented them accurately? What do you think of these positions?

2. By contrast, Page wants to control guns. What reasons does he give to defend this position? Compare Page's position with that of the NRA, which he presents in the article. If you were a lawmaker, what compromises would you suggest that could bridge the gap between the two?

Federal Programs Just Intensify the "Who, Me?" Factor

MIKE ROYKO

WHEN THE WORRIED TALK IS ABOUT SCHOOLS, the answers are always
money and new programs. The politicians talk about the money, where
it will come from and how it will be spread around. The educational
experts talk about programs and how they will be implemented.
Where would they be without programs to implement? 1

When the worried talk is about crime, the answers are always
stricter gun control laws and, of course, the implementation of a vast
array of new drug programs. 2

When the worried talk is about troubled families, the answers are
new federal social service programs. Even now the White House is
talking about new multibillion-dollar "family preservation" programs
that will send out hordes of social workers to bring broken families
together. Assuming, of course, that these programs are properly implemented. 3

And now that we have a Democratic president and a Democratic
Congress, there will be a blizzard of new programs. But there is
something missing in the talk about the problems and the programs
that are intended to solve these problems. 4

It is what I call the "Who, me?" factor. As in, "It is your responsibility," followed by, "Who, me?" 5

Start with the schools. The problem isn't money. We spend vast
sums on schools. Nor is it a lack of programs. We have more educational programs than can be implemented in the next 100 years. 6

Where there are problem schools, the biggest source of the problem is the parent. The kind of parent who, when told that she or he is
responsible for her or his children, says: "Who, me?" 7

Show me the worst school districts in Chicago, Detroit, New
York, Los Angeles, and I will show you parents who should not be
raising a Chia Pet, much less a child. 8

These are the places where the illegitimacy rates are jaw-
dropping, where ignorance and illiteracy are handed down from generation to generation like family heirlooms. 9

What kind of program do we implement to persuade some dense
teen-age girl that she should not couple with some street-swagger 10

boyfriend? What program, if implemented, will make the young man understand that if he fathers children, it is his responsibility to live with those children and try to support them?

The same applies to crime. Strict gun laws will make only a tiny   11
dent in that problem. Thickheaded as the gun lobby can be, it is right about one thing: The grocer killers and drug dealers aren't deterred by registration or cooling-off laws. They don't shop at sporting marts with the skeet-shooting crowd. Their gun suppliers deal out of car trunks or abandoned buildings.

And we can trace the rise in violent crime to the same source of   12
the school ailments. The parts of the cities that produce the illegitimate illiterates are giving us the greatest number of trigger-happy young felons. You don't have to know how to parse a sentence, much less read one, to point a gun at a convenience store clerk or deliver a load of crack.

So now we are going to get a Family Preservation Act and more   13
programs for social workers to implement. If it does some good, which I doubt, fine.

But what we need as much as a Family Preservation Act is a   14
Family Prevention Act. There's not much point in trying to preserve families that weren't families in the first place. If you go to a family court in a big city, what you see is some stupefied young woman, her physically or mentally abused kids and a slack-jawed boyfriend sitting in a back row. Since when has that been a family? And what is there to preserve? If the kids survive the abuse and neglect, they'll be the next generation of social misfits and menaces.

And when they are told that they are responsible for their own   15
actions and for those of their children, they will look blank and say: "Who, me?"

If President Clinton intends to create public works jobs, then I   16
suggest he do it this way: Round up the young fathers who breed and walk away. Give them a choice: Work and use the paycheck to support your family or go to jail.

If he wants to reform welfare, then apply the same standards we   17
do in our fishing and hunting laws. There is a limit. And what would be wrong with telling a woman: "Two is your limit, and you have reached it. Any more than that, you support them yourself."

Is that hard-hearted and insensitive? Maybe. But for several dec-   18
ades, we have been good-hearted, bleeding-hearted and ultrasensitive. And what has it given us? The highest rates of illegitimacy, illiteracy, homicide and chronic dependency of any developed country.

And at the rate we're going, it is only going to get worse, not   19
better.

So the social engineers and program implementers should start   20
taking a new approach. Which used to be the old approach.

When someone says: "Who, me?" the answer should be, "Yes,   21
you, and don't do it again."

Questions for Thinking and Discussion

1. Royko believes that problems in schools and the violence in the streets
   both stem from the same source: "The parts of the cities that produce
   the illegitimate illiterates are giving us the greatest number of trigger-
   happy young felons." Do you believe that, as he suggests, if education
   were more widespread, violence would be less likely to occur? Why or
   why not?
2. How would you characterize Royko's solutions to the problems of
   violence in America? What does he mean by the idea of trying to
   prevent the American family from happening rather than *preserving* it,
   as political figures want to do? What do you think of this argument?

Violence, A Problem in Our Society Today

RODERICK RICHARDSON

ON MY FIRST RETURN TO MY HOMETOWN since my sophomore year in   1
school, I witnessed a killing. No one should be subjected to this
experience. Unfortunately, killing is now a sad reality of today's changing world.

It started as a routine night on the town with friends and relatives   2
gathered together at the only hangout in town, but no one imagined
that the night would end like it did.

Just before closing time, two African-American men got in an   3
argument outside. The crowd did not take the argument seriously,
though, since the two men knew each other and had just had one too
many beers. But the atmosphere changed dramatically when one man
took a knife out of his car.

Both men struck blows, but only one was armed. In a matter of   4
seconds, blood stained the sand on the ground, and a once innocent
night was ruined. As the suspect fled, the victim was still standing,
pacing back and forth, looking down at his body as if he was wondering what had just happened to him.

Then he saw his blood and realized that the cuts were not flesh   5
wounds. He stopped, whispered "I'm bleeding!" and fell to the ground,
never to rise again.

The morning after, I still had a picture in my mind of the body   6
lying on the ground. At that time, I was not only trying to figure out
an answer to this crime, but I was also looking for a general reason for
violence in America.

In order to find an answer, I thought of all the excuses that the   7
public and media would give for this kind of violence:

Was he killed because of a song the killer had heard on a cassette?

Was he killed because of a movie or television show the killer
saw?

Was he killed because society pushed the killer to his edge and
that was his way of letting out his frustrations?

Was he killed because of racism?

Was he killed because of drugs or alcohol?

The first three answers have nothing to do with this particular   8
crime or any violent act, as far as I am concerned. Whatever violence
that occurred was the decision of the killer only. Anyone who has to
blame someone or something else for a mistake like this is, in my
opinion, a very weak person.

And, though racism is the cause of a high percentage of America's   9
violence, it has nothing to do with America's problem of black-on-
black crimes such as this one.

And, though alcohol and other drugs can alter the mind, drugs   10
cannot tell anyone to destroy human life.

The fact is that none of these theories has discussed the simple   11
fact of human nature. Two people were having a disagreement. Neither
of them had the sense or courage to back off and walk away.

Their pride and ego prevented them from walking away. If they   12
had backed down, then they would have lost their respect and dignity.

So, they continue to taunt each other until it gets out of hand. A   13
man's life is gone because of a psychological game of "chicken."

That's my view of violence. If we look too far outside ourselves   14
for a reason, then our hope for peace is lost.

Questions for Thinking and Discussion

1. In this article, Richardson gives a rather chilling first-hand account of
   what it is like to witness a violent crime. Have you ever witnessed any
   crime, violent or otherwise? Did you respond to it the next day in a
   manner similar to the way Richardson did? That is, did an image of the
   crime linger in your memory the way that a picture of "the body lying
   on the ground" lingered in Richardson's memory?

2. Richardson cites a number of explanations for violent crimes such as
   the one he witnessed. However, he dismisses them all, saying that if
   "we look too far outside ourselves for a reason, then our hope for peace
   is lost." What do you think of his conclusion? Has Richardson cut to
   the heart of the problem, or, in dismissing most other explanations for
   the crime, has he oversimplified it?

Writing Projects

1. If you have ever experienced a violent crime (or if you know someone who has), write a paper addressed to other students who have never experienced such a crime. One objective of such a paper would be to educate your reader by describing the event as vividly as you can. Another objective would be to teach your readers about ways that they might avoid being victims of such a crime themselves.

2. Several of the writers in this chapter are interested in whether innocent bystanders are often the victims of violent crime. To study how innocent bystanders are the victims, do some research by watching five television news broadcasts during the next week. Count up the number of news stories that tell about innocent victims of crime.

    Then, write a paper in which you discuss what you have found, comparing your results with those of your classmates. According to these TV broadcasts, who are most often the victims of crimes? Do your results seem to support Blackman's idea, (in Connell's article) that people who "do their homework, go to church on Sunday, [and] have proper family upbringing" are not the victims of violent crime?

3. Write a paper that summarizes the solutions to violent crime proposed by Poirot, Page, Royko, and Richardson. Identify each writer's solutions and explain how they are similar to or different from each other. At the end of your paper, explain which of the writers' solutions you think is the best.

4. Royko identifies the major reason for the existence of violent crime to be the families that criminals have grown up in. Richardson, by contrast, believes that the reasons for violent crime lie within the individual. Write a paper in which you, first, explain further Royko's and Richardson's reasons for crime and, second, discuss which of these two reasons you think is most accurate.

6

Relationships

IT IS EASY TO THINK that love and romance are so much a part of the human experience that they have been the same for as long as human beings have existed. The truth is, however, that the way people carry on mating relationships, or "courtship," actually differs a great deal among cultures and over time. For instance, mating has occurred in such diverse ways as arrangements by families, political alliances, and even capture. Beginning in the Middle Ages, the Jewish matchmaker—the *skadkans*—had a major role in bringing together partners for marriage. In his book *Love and Courtship in America,* Paul McPharlin describes how, in many areas of rural America during the last half of the nineteenth century, several events became stages in the ritual of courtship: the buggy ride, the picnic, the cornhusking, the afternoon at a bathing beach, and the quilting bee.

Most of these elements of courtship seem strange to us in the 1990s. Most modern Americans who are seeking mates do so through dating, but even dating has changed over the last thirty years. This chapter introduces a variety of issues related to courtship in the 1990s and beyond. It includes a humorous article predicting what dating will be like in the next century and two articles offering suggestions for improving dating. The last three readings in the chapter are a bit more serious; they involve a modern version of the *skadkans*, the question of interracial dating, and the possibility of rejecting dating entirely.

The Dating Game

Merrill Markoe

THE NEXT CENTURY WILL BE a time of many informational break- 1
throughs. Most notably, the battle between the sexes will take on a new
complexion because it will be scientifically documented that men and
women are completely different species of animals (not unlike, say,
hyenas and pumas, although there will be a lot of heated arguments
about who gets to be the pumas).

Once everyone accepts that we're speaking different languages, a 2
computer system will be developed that allows instantaneous in-
tersexual communication to occur. For the first time, certain simple
but formerly bewildering transactions will become clear. At the end of
an evening out, when the single man of the future says to his date, "I
had a nice time. I'll call you" (I predict that men will still be using this
line), the woman to whom he is speaking will immediately hear in her
headset: "What he means is that while he thinks you are attractive, he's
concerned that you already have expectations of him that he will never
be able to meet. He's associating you with his needy, castrating mother
because she had the same hair color as yours."

By this time, sex and dating will be so dangerous (owing to 3
the numerous rampant communicable diseases and personality disorders) that they will be attempted only by the kind of thrill seekers
who now do things like bungee jumping, sky surfing and eating at
Denny's. By the year 2020, in fact, "casual dating" will be a popular
arena sport. People too terrified to pursue something so hazardous
themselves will witness actual live human beings who, for big money
stakes, will eat dinner with and then perhaps (if dinner goes well)
become intimate with people they are attracted to but basically know
nothing about.

Because the average person will be far too cautious to risk even a 4
single totally worthless encounter, we will see the transformation of the
medical clinic into a kind of after-hours meeting place where nervous
but lonely people will be able to undergo a battery of health tests and,
while awaiting the results, stop by the bar to enjoy a trendy snack with
others who may have the same ailment. (I predict that honey-roasted

songbirds will be the snack of choice by then because they will turn out to be the last remaining edible creature that is domestically plentiful, low in fat and still has not been made into a trendy snack item.)

All of this escalating terror will, oddly, increase the number of marriages taking place, even though we will see the divorce rate rise from 1 in 2 marriages to 2 in 2. These alarming statistics will cause the birth of a new nuptial tradition. Savvy couples will create the most intimate bond two people can share by agreeing to get married and divorced simultaneously. At that point, they will possess so much file data about each other that they will negotiate in advance the terms of every day they plan to spend together, deciding what annoying habits they are willing to tolerate and, more important, what personal details each one will permit the other to use either in court or in the eventual tell-all book. "Looking at me cross-eyed" could emerge as the most common charge of misconduct in the personal nuisance suits that will clog the legal system.

Playing right into that will be the amount of specific evidence people will have accumulated about each other as "compulsive video documentation" becomes the most common new addiction. By the year 2010, TV networks will decide to give all video-equipment owners a shot at their own show as long as they promise to supply footage that is extremely disturbing. Recorded evidence of violence and malicious mayhem will draw such astronomical sums that criminals contemplating an illegal activity will consult with movie developers during the important planning stages of the crime. They will thus make sure that the approach they are taking with regard to plot and details is the one that will have the best eventual effect on sales figures and marketing potential.

This blurring of the line between life and entertainment will culminate in a scandal when a giant underground facility is discovered in the Midwest that is being used as a breeding lab by desperate talk-show producers who have been completely out of new guests since the mid-1990s. It will be discovered that the producers have been assembling affable humanoids from the fat, tissue, bone, and spare parts of celebrities who have undergone a lot of plastic surgery, training the "guests" to cultivate zany or inappropriate hobbies and schooling them in how to tell 10 different 15-minute anecdotes about themselves. This will constitute their entire life-span, after which they will be melted down and reworked for an additional booking.

Yes, it's going to be a bold new world, full of brand new dysfunctions, addictions and disorders: a million new things to worry about! But that's progress.

Questions for Thinking and Discussion

1. Markoe's article is a humorous look at dating in the future. Much of what she says, though, focuses on the problems men and women have communicating with each other. Why do you think men and women very often have a breakdown in communication? Have you ever misinterpreted what someone of the opposite sex said or meant? Have you ever been misinterpreted? What was the situation in which this happened?

2. In your own opinion, what do you think dating in the future will be like? What are some changes you might project? Which of the rules of dating do you think will stay the same? Which are most likely to change? Why?

Fear of Failure

DAVE BARRY

As a mature adult, I feel an obligation to help the younger genera- 1
tion, just as the mother fish guards her unhatched eggs, keeping her
lonely vigil day after day, never leaving her post, not even to go to the
bathroom, until her tiny babies emerge and she is able, at last, to eat
them.

But today I want to talk about dating. This subject was raised in 2
a letter to me from a young person named Eric Knott, who writes:

"I have got a big problem. There's this girl in my English class 3
who is really good-looking. However, I don't think she knows I exist.
I want to ask her out, but I'm afraid she will say no, and I will be the
freak of the week. What should I do?"

Eric, You have sent your question to the right mature adult, 4
because as a young person I spent a lot of time thinking about this very
problem. Starting in about eighth grade, my time was divided as
follows:

Academic pursuits: 2 percent. 5

Zits: 16 percent. 6

Trying to Figure Out How to Ask Girls Out: 82 percent. 7

The most sensible way to ask a girl out is to walk directly up 8
to her on foot and say, "So, you want to go out? Or what?" I never
did this. I knew, as Eric Knott knows, that there was always the
possibility that the girl would say no, thereby leaving me with no
viable option but to leave Harold C. Crittenden Junior High School
forever and go into the woods and become a bark-eating hermit whose
only companions would be the gentle and understanding woodland
creatures.

"Hey, ZITFACE!" the woodland creatures would shriek in cute 9
little Chip 'n' Dale voices while raining acorns down upon my head.
"You wanna DATE? HAHAHAHAHAHA."

So the first rule of dating is: Never risk direct contact with the girl 10
in question. Your role model should be the nuclear submarine, gliding
silently beneath the ocean surface, tracking an enemy target that does
not even begin to suspect that the submarine would like to date it. I
spent the vast majority of 1960 keeping a girl named Judy under

112

surveillance, maintaining a minimum distance of 50 lockers to avoid the danger that I might somehow get into a conversation with her, which could have led to disaster:

Judy: Hi. 11

Me: Hi. 12

Judy: Just in case you have ever thought about having a date with 13 me, the answer is no.

Woodland creatures: HAHAHAHAHAHA. 14

The only problem with the nuclear-submarine technique is 15 that it's difficult to get a date with a girl who has never, technically, been asked. This is why you need Phil Grant. Phil was a friend of mine who had the ability to talk to girls. It was a mysterious superhuman power he had, comparable to X-ray vision. So, after several thousand hours of intense discussion and planning with me, Phil approached a girl he knew named Nancy, who approached a girl named Sandy, who was a direct personal friend of Judy's and who passed the word back to Phil via Nancy that Judy would be willing to go on a date with me.

Thus it was, that, finally, Judy and I went on an actual date, to 16 see a movie in White Plains, N.Y. If I were to sum up the romantic ambience of this date in four words, those four words would be: "My mother was driving."

After what seemed like several years we got to the movie theater, 17 where my mother went off to sit in the Parents and Lepers Section. The movie was called *North to Alaska,* but I can tell you nothing else about it because I spent the whole time wondering whether it would be necessary to amputate my right arm, which was not getting any blood flow as a result of being perched for two hours like a petrified snake on the back of Judy's seat exactly one molecule away from physical contact.

So it was definitely a fun first date, featuring all the relaxed 18 spontaneity of a real-estate closing, and in later years I did regain some feeling in my arm. My point, Eric Knott, is that the key to successful dating is self-confidence. I bet that good-looking girl in your English class would LOVE to go out with you. But YOU have to make the first move. So just do it! Pick up that phone! Call Phil Grant.

Questions for Thinking and Discussion

1. Dave Barry, a humorist, is able to look back at his own dating experiences and see some of the "dating crises" he went through as a junior

high student. As a young teenager, what do you remember about your own dating experiences? Were they positive, negative, or both?

2. What kinds of advice would you give to someone who wants to date but is afraid to ask anyone out? Is there some sort of systematic plan you might suggest for someone to try?

Creative Dating

DON OLDENBURG

THE WORST EVENING OUT DAVID COLEMAN EVER HEARD OF was a young   1
woman who went on a blind date only to get stuck at the top of a
carnival roller coaster. For a long time. Upside down. The guy vomited
on her. And she didn't even like him.

Mostly Coleman talks about positive experiences. But the 30-   2
year-old director of student activities at Xavier University in Cincinnati
likes to keep dating in perspective. So the horror stories aren't only for
amusement; they establish a basis for comparison that makes all those
uneventful nights on the town not seem such a waste. And social lives
that aren't wasted are what he tries to help college students and other
young adults create for themselves.

"I try to get them to think of ways to enjoy each other's company   3
other than drugs, alcohol, and sex—the three biggest things that so
stereotypically come to mind when you hear the word dating," says
Coleman.

Six years ago, with Xavier students moping around his office one   4
evening trying to think of something to do besides go to a bar,
Coleman recognized that most of them either weren't dating at all,
or their social life wasn't what they wanted it to be—sort of a micro-
cosm of what he's found in many young adults off the college campus
as well. Deciding to do something about it, he designed a 90-minute
workshop called Creative Dating, sort of a cross between a pep talk
and a brainstorming session, meant to boost confidence and provide
ideas for dates that won't leave anyone hanging upside down with
disgust.

Since then, Coleman has conducted the workshop nearly 100   5
times, for groups that average about 100 participants, but that have
been as large as the 750 students who once showed up at Indiana State
University. With a big dose of common sense about dating and a list of
almost 250 "creative dating options" from past workshops, he has
crisscrossed the continental United States spreading a message about
romance in all the right places.

"It has blossomed to something I never could have predicted,"   6
says Coleman, who will visit a Virginia campus this spring. He attributes the success of the workshop to its upbeat and refreshing approach
to how people can interact, but has no doubt that troubles today in the

115

dating scene—AIDS and other diseases, and date rape, among them— are driving people to reconsider what their social lives are all about.

"It is almost Phil-Donahue-like what I do," he explains. "I get   7 them to communicate with each other. I give members of the audience a chance to stand up and talk about the best or worst dates they ever had. People are anxious to talk about dating; it is a very stressful thing if it is handled improperly. I try to give people options and confidence. . . . Then they can put themselves in a position to win."

Unfortunately, says Coleman, people generally aren't innovative   8 when it comes to dating. The most typical of first or second dates—a movie followed by dinner at a restaurant—can stack the cards against comfortable interaction between two strangers. "At a movie you don't communicate at all, and afterward at dinner you have to force conversation with each other," he says. "One thing I stress is that, for the first couple of dates especially, if you can focus on a kind of date that takes the attention off yourselves, it's better.

"Go spend some time with those pets at the humane society, or   9 go to a nursing home and visit with the elderly. The action of doing that takes the pressure off and people feel good about doing it."

Coleman adds that expensive dates aren't necessary. "If people   10 were more creative and had a more diverse view of what dating could be, they would spend less money," he says.

Here's a sampling of dating ideas from the workshop: 11

- Make your own video together.
- Climb trees together.
- Take a self-defense course.
- Go stargazing.
- Visit significant places for one another and explain why.
- Cosponsor a Tupperware party.
- Test-drive a new car.
- Go to a ballet or creative dance production.
- Take a walk in a graveyard (preferably in the daytime).
- Visit a nearby college campus.
- Look at each other's baby pictures.
- Get up early and watch the sun rise.
- Make homemade ice cream and invite friends to bring toppings.
- Go to the airport and watch planes land and take off.
- Make tapes of favorite music.

- Visit another city.
- Go to a pick-your-own orchard and pick fruit.
- Rearrange your rooms.
- Run together in the rain.
- Visit flea markets.
- Go to an art gallery.
- Have a picnic indoors.
- Take photographs of the season.
- Cook dinner for each other.
- Go for a drive in the country.

"I've been asked more and more to do this for people in their thirties and older, and for married couples," says Coleman. "I suggest to couples that they put every one of these dates on separate cards, get a fish bowl, and when they're feeling in a rut, pull one at a time out until they find one they want to do." 12

Coleman says he and his wife of seven years have tried out some of the ideas themselves. "Every once in a while we steal one," he says. "Once, we did the 'visit significant places for each other' one, which is really a great chance for people in a non-threatening way to learn about each other." 13

That time, his wife drove him to a park near Wittenberg University, in Springfield, Ohio, where she used to spend a lot of time as an undergraduate. But, mostly, he admits, they stay closer to their home in the appropriately named Cincinnati suburb of Loveland, and chuckle at the worst date descriptions that come out of his latest workshop. "My wife," confesses Coleman, "calls me The Dating Doctor of Loveland." 14

Questions for Thinking and Discussion

1. In this article about the "creative dating" workshops held by David Coleman of Xavier University, how do your experiences on your own campus support Coleman's claims that most [students] either weren't dating at all, or their social life wasn't what they wanted it to be. . . ." If there is any truth to this as a whole, what might be the reasons for it? Are the reasons a matter of how the students perceive their situation, or do they really have lousy social lives?

2. Near the end of the article, Oldenburg lists twenty-five of Coleman's "dating ideas." Evaluate how good you think these suggestions would be for people you know. Which seem to you to be the best? Which are the worst? Why? Compare Coleman's dating ideas with those given by Barry in the article before this one. Whose suggestions do you find to be better?

With This Headhunter, $10K
Defines a Spouse

DEIRDRE FANNING

"A LOT OF EXECUTIVES DON'T HAVE TIME for a personal life," said   1
Robert M. Davis, an executive recruiter in Philadelphia. "Executives are
also picky about relationships. They want people form the same background as themselves."

The voluble Mr. Davis said he had fixed up friends for years   2
before he decided last year to start a matrimonial search service that
caters specifically to executives. Mr. Davis promises that within a year
of paying his $10,000 fee, clients will be provided with 10 potential
spousal candidates. And so far, he claims to have made a number of
successful matches.

"I do the exact same things I do when I'm doing executive   3
recruiting," he said. "I draw up a profile of the perfect candidate based
on what the client tells me, and then I go out and look for all the
possible candidates. In executive recruiting, I try to mirror the company and the candidate. I do the same with the matrimonial service."

Actually, matrimonial service is a bit of a misnomer, since Mr.   4
Davis really only guarantees a committed relationship. But then a lot
of things about Mr. Davis are not quite what they seem.

He claims to have been a guest on such television shows as "Good   5
Morning America" and "Today," yet officials at those shows say they
have never heard of him.

He sends around a press packet on himself containing, among   6
other things, a gushing profile from what at first appears to be a
popular national magazine. But despite its identical typeset and the
"People Weekly" logo across the top of the page, the article was never
published in the Time Warner weekly. Mr. Davis now concedes that it
appeared in a little-known Temple University Journalism School publication called "Philadelphia People." He could not, he said, explain the
People Weekly logo.

The Philadelphia Inquirer described Mr. Davis's habit of embel-   7
lishing his credentials in an article last February. Yet many executives
in the Philadelphia area seem to have no qualms about trusting Mr.
Davis with the delicate matter of romance. Several have tapped his
services with, they say, satisfying results. Few of them would talk on

the record, for fear of being ridiculed by colleagues for having conducted a love search.

But discussions with them have suggested several reasons why   8
such otherwise resourceful people would resort to paying an outside
consultant to find a soul mate.

"I went through a divorce a few years ago," said John Burns, a   9
partner at Computer Specialty Products Inc., a Philadelphia computer
supply company. "Afterward, I did the bar scene and the personal ads
but I found the people there were tremendous liars." Mr. Burns met his
wife-to-be, a hospital administrator, through Mr. Davis and plans to
marry in the spring.

Mr. Davis had done some executive recruiting work for Mr.   10
Burns, who said he was impressed by the headhunter's contacts. "He
knows a lot of people," Mr. Burns said. "I travel a lot and spend too
much time working to find a spouse. I knew with Bob that he would
screen the people and get only quality-type people."

This emphasis on quality seems to be a preoccupation with the   11
executives. "I have a master's degree in engineering," said one. "Being
an engineer, I'm very logical. I don't believe that the earth moves and
bells chime: I believe it all comes down to having the same interests.
Also, I'm looking for intelligence, personality and looks. You don't
meet quality in singles bars."

To scope out potential "quality," Mr. Davis first takes a client to   12
his local health club's juice bar, where the two sit at a table and
people-watch. "I say to them, point out what kind of person turns you
on, so I can get an idea of the type of profile they're looking for,"
explained Mr. Davis. "An executive woman, for example, probably
doesn't want a man with a jellybelly."

Once the physical profile has been established, Mr. Davis takes to   13
the phones to scout out potential candidates, then sets up a conference
call with the interested parties and himself. "This way, if something is
turning either party off, I can see what's really happening," he explained. The next step is a date and then, well, the rest is up to the
client.

"It's not a cheap service," said another Philadelphia engineer who   14
has just hired Mr. Davis. "But then neither are the alternatives, like
video dating or personal ads. I work too much now to be able to find
someone on my own, so I'm giving this a try."

In most cases, these executives blamed the hectic pace of their   15
work schedule for their lack of success in finding a mate on their own.
But another reason may be that these business men and women seem
to approach romance and companionship much as they would a business project. "Bob finally found me my current steady girlfriend after I

had gone through a couple of candidates," said the executive with the master's degree in engineering. "The others fit my criteria but they weren't particularly special."

Another of Mr. Davis's clients can't explain why she is single. "I'm 16 reasonably attractive, divorced with no kids," said the client, a vice president at a Philadelphia vending machine manufacturer. "On paper, I'm fine. But that doesn't seem to account for much these days."

Mr. Davis attributes their difficulty in part to the narrow field of 17 choices. "These are all overachievers," he said. "They have excelled academically, and survived in a corporate culture. Yet this fast-track environment makes them only want to meet people like themselves."

Questions for Thinking and Discussion

1. Fanning introduces us to what amounts to the modern version of the *skadkans*—the matchmaker. What advantages do you see to this system? What disadvantages do you see? Which do you think predominate: The advantages or disadvantages? Would you personally use the services of this mating "headhunter," if you had the money? Why or why not?

2. Robert Davis, the executive mating recruiter featured in this article, gives a little insight into the people who are eager to pay for his services:

   "These are all overachievers. . . . They have excelled academically and survived in a corporate culture. Yet this fast-track environment makes them only want to meet people like themselves."

   Do you think that Davis' "recruitment" system is a good thing for people such as this? Or, do you think there might be better ways for them to find mates? What method would you suggest to this type of person for finding a mate?

Interracial Relationships

INGRID WATSON

YEARS AGO WHEN AMERICA WAS DIVIDED by racial tensions and segregation, interracial relationships were considered taboo.

Times have progressed since then. In today's society, interracial dating has been more acceptable, though racial conflicts still exist.

People who date or marry someone of a racial or ethnic group different from their own sometimes encounter disapproval from society, peers or family members.

For young people, who experience more culturally diverse settings such as school and other activities, going out with someone "different" may not be a big deal.

"They tend to look at other students as just other students," said Quincy Moore, president of the Association of Multicultural Counselling and Development.

Often, objections come from parents.

"I, quite frankly, don't see a lot of problems except where parents are concerned," said Becky Martinez, counselor at Jefferson Middle in Grand Prairie. "I've been in schools before where black and white relationships produced a lot of problems with parents, but not with the kids."

WHEN PROBLEMS ARISE

The relationship between a Hispanic boy and white girl produced more than a problem last year in Frisco, a town 35 miles north of Dallas. It resulted in death.

Krissi Lynn Caldwell, 17, and Robert Anthony Gonzales, 16, recently were found guilty of plotting to kill Krissi's parents because they opposed the teens' involvement. Krissi's mother was shot to death and her father critically wounded last March.

In January, Robert was sentenced to 75 years in prison. Two months earlier, Krissi was sentenced to life in prison. Each teen awaits another trial in connection with that crime.

Most conflicts with parents are not that extreme. When Maria Olguin and Victor Carr began dating almost two years ago, her parents objected. His didn't. Maria is Hispanic. Victor is African-American. Both attend Diamond Hill-Jarvis High in Fort Worth.

"My parents, at first, didn't like it," said Maria, a 15-year-old freshman. "I think they think I would be better off with a Mexican."

Initially, Maria and her parents fought over the subject, she said.   13
Now the battles have ceased.

OFF LIMITS

Some teens, like some parents, consider interracial dating off   14
limits.

"I wouldn't date someone from another race because society as a   15
whole hasn't accepted interracial relationships," said Kenitra Walton,
15-year-old sophomore at Trimble Tech High.

"If I were to date a guy that went to my school that was a   16
Hispanic, I would get a lot of criticism and jokes about having 'jungle
fever,' " said Kenitra, an African-American.

"The criticism and peer pressure are enough to bring your self-   17
esteem down and end the relationship," she said.

Hollie Armstrong, junior at Weatherford High, witnessed how   18
much society can create stress for interracial couples. When her family
lived in Midland two years ago, her sister, who is white, dated an
African-American.

Hollie's parents didn't like that. Neither did some folks in the   19
community.

"We got death threats," said 16-year-old Hollie, who disagrees   20
with the disapproval. "I think that if two people are happy, it's no one's
business."

A BETTER MATCH

Race or ethnic background likely is not a problem when two   21
people are close in age, have similar interests and come from similar
kinds of homes.

Martinez, the school counselor, said youths in interracial relation-   22
ships who face objections should look closely at their situations and
listen. There will be obstacles. If they decide the relationships are
important and strong enough, they should hang in there.

How do you feel about dating someone from another race?

Here's what *Class Acts* readers had to say in response to the
viewpoint question, "What are your feelings about dating someone
of another race?"

"I really don't think it's right. I know people say if you love
them, nothing will keep you apart. You have to think about
your children . . . I have seen a lot of mixed children, and most

of them aren't pretty. I have seen how other children make fun of them.

"Plus, the children might get confused distinguishing what race they are. How do you tell a kid, 'You are both black and white?' "

Jesse Lopez, 16
Trimble Tech

"It's cool with me. I don't think it matters because you should look at someone by what they say, judge them by how they act and how they treat you. I think it's kind of ignorant when you don't."

Tiffany Lathorp, 16
Weatherford High

"I think that somebody should have their own right to choose who they date, when they date and how they date."

Dianna Black, 10
Pope Elementary

"I'm a product of my parents' interracial relationship, so anybody who can stand going through what people have to go through when that happens, I think they're pretty brave. I'm all for it."

Tiffany Thomas, 17
Sam Houston High

"My feelings are to do what you want to. God may have made our skin colors different, but we are all made the same on the inside."

Tennille Craven, 15
Trimble Tech

"I don't approve of interracial relationships . . . I don't have anything against other races, just interracial relationships."

Troy Brown, 15
Azie High

"Interracial relationships are OK if you really love a person and if you really think they're right for you."

Christina Singletary, 11
Monnig Middle

"I feel that interracial relationships are out of the question. If God had planned on us interdating with other races then he would have made us all one race. I'm not putting anybody down, but that's just how I feel."

Amber Horton, 13
Bedford Junior High

"I feel that I would not be comfortable, but I'm not going to tell anyone else what to do. If it makes someone else happy, by all means, they should do it."

Kristin Lankford, 18
Martin High

Questions for Thinking and Discussion

1. What do you think about interracial dating? Which of the students quoted do you most agree with and why? In looking at the students' quotes, could you discover profiles for the people who accept interracial dating and for those who do not? Think about their value systems, where they grew up, etc.

2. It seems that people who are in more diverse cultural situations do not see interracial relationships as a big problem. Where, in modern American society, can you find the most culturally diverse settings? What are the benefits of experiencing cultural diversity?

Being Alone Doesn't Have to Mean Being Lonely

Karen S. Peterson

Do you think you can't be happy unless you have a mate? Then you're a "love junkie," says psychiatrist David Burns, author of *Intimate Connections* (Signet, $5.99). 1

Your thinking is incorrect and destructive. It's not the fact you are single that's the problem, it's the way you *think* about singlehood. You can change that perception—and your life—whether you've never married, or have lost a spouse to death or divorce. 2

Burns, whose books on changing negative thinking have sold more than 2 million copies, shares some of his views on being yourself, developed in *Feeling Good: The New Mood Therapy,* to be reissued in June by Avon at $5.99. 3

Q. **Why do we think we need somebody to be happy?** 4

A. We hear it all the time. So much is based on romance and how wonderful things will be if somebody loves you. That acts as a self-fulfilling prophecy. Then whenever you are alone, you mope, stare at walls, eat peanut butter and jelly sandwiches and say this isn't any fun. 5

And there may be some evolutionary forces at work—a species that needs to form relationships, create families. But that has a potentially destructive side, if you count on other people to make you feel fulfilled. And it isn't true that having somebody means you won't be lonely. I see married people all the time who are lonely. 6

Q. **But don't we need love?** 7

The idea you can be happy alone can be really frightening. It seems like a cold thought. 8

But the difference between thinking you *need* love to survive and *wanting* love is one of the most important distinctions in your life. The best way to get over being a love junkie is what I call a cost-benefit analysis. Literally list advantages and disadvantages of believing you *need* love to live. One advantage might be "This attitude will make me work very hard to find someone." A disadvantage: "When I don't have someone, I feel depressed." 9

Then list the advantages and disadvantages of *wanting* someone in your life, and compare the lists. Your revised belief might be, "It can be desirable to have a loving relationship, but it's not a need like oxygen. In the meantime, I can survive happily on my own." 10

And there is a paradox here. The more you act like you must have love to survive, the more you are likely to drive it away. Others pick up on your neediness. The more independent you are, the more secure you will be in your feelings. Then you don't suck the blood from the other person.

Q. **What other techniques can you use?**

A. You can test your belief that you will be miserable if you are alone by making a "pleasure predicting sheet." Schedule something positive, rewarding things to do during the week, some by yourself, some with others. They might be jogging, making a nice meal for yourself, going to dinner, even cleaning up your desk.

Then list how enjoyable you expect the activity will be on a scale of 1 to 100. And then record how pleasurable it actually was after you do it. Many times you'll see that the things you did with others turn out to be much less exciting than expected, and the activities by yourself, far more rewarding.

Q. **How is feeling lonely the result of distorted thinking?**

A. Loneliness is a mind set. I see it over and over. When people feel lonely and depressed, they use thoughts that persecute themselves. And these thoughts are illogical and wrong, even though they seem very logical to them.

You need to talk back to these constant negative thoughts. Let's say you're in a restaurant by yourself and it strikes you people must think you are a loser if you're alone.

First of all, you can't tell what others think. You're labeling yourself a loser, and there is no such thing as a "loser." You're using emotional reasoning; you believe because you *think* people are down on you that they actually are. And you're making a type of "should" statement—"I should have a partner"—and because you don't, you feel guilty.

And write out that cost-benefit analysis when you get home. What are the advantages of telling yourself you are a loser? The disadvantages?

But before, right then in the restaurant, write out the rational responses to your distorted thinking. You don't have any idea what others are thinking and so on. That type of written list is very powerful.

Questions for Thinking and Discussion

1. Many Americans are remaining single longer than ever before. Why do you think people are waiting so long to settle down, either in marriage or in a relationship with someone significant?

2. Do you think people need a mate to be happy? Do you know of any social situations that require the presence of a mate? Why do people believe they need a mate? Could these needs be met in other ways?

Writing Projects

1. Prepare a paper entitled "My Philosophy of Dating in the 1990s." As material for this project, draw on your own experiences and insights, as well as on readings by Barry, Oldenburg, and Peterson. Develop what you see as a solid set of strategies for meeting a mate and enjoying a good relationship. You may also want to identify pitfalls to avoid in dating as well as suggestions for success.

2. How have dating customs changed through the years? Write a paper based on an interview with a parent or grandparent who can describe the typical customs when he/she first began courtship. Your paper should explain the ways that courtship in that earlier era differed from courtship in the 1990s.

3. As an extension of Writing Project #2, do some library research and prepare a report for your classmates on some of the practices in courtship that have been common in other cultures and other times. You might look for books such as William Fielding's *Strange Customs of Courtship and Marriage* (1960). Eventually, even though you find differences between our own traditions of courtship and the ones you discuss, try also to find similarities.

4. One source that we often don't consider that helps give us our ideas about dating is popular music. What are the predominant pictures of dating and romance that we get from listening to various types of modern music?

   Write a paper that explores this question. Focus your paper on one kind of music (for instance, 1990s rock, earlier rock, rap, rhythm and blues, country, etc.). Then listen to one or two CDs; in particular, look at the way the videos accompanying the songs promote an idea of what romantic relationships are like. Are the pictures generally positive? Are they ever negative?

7

Women in Education

In his book *A History of Women's Education in the United States*, Thomas Woody reports on the case of Lucinda Foote, a young woman who wanted to attend Yale University in 1783. Even though she was thoroughly qualified, Lucinda was denied admission simply because she was a woman. Cases such as Lucinda's were common early in American history, but this kind of obvious exclusion of women doesn't exist in the 1990s. In fact, in many colleges in the United States, more women are enrolled than men. In addition, women today major in fields such as engineering, medicine, and law as well as in fields traditionally thought of as "women's professions" such as teaching and nursing. Nevertheless, being a woman in educational settings is still not easy. Often women are excluded in more subtle ways because of biases and stereotypes about their abilities.

The articles in this chapter explore some reasons for biases against women in education. The writers of the articles focus on ways that modern education—elementary, high school, and college—treats women. The information in these articles comes from a variety of recent studies, especially one by the American Association of University Women (AAUW). As you read the articles in this chapter, look for problems that women in education experience today: for instance, lack of self-esteem by young women, biases against them based on gender, and special problems in mathematics and science. Also, as you read, look for and evaluate solutions given by the writers.

Wide Gender Gap Found in Schools

MARY JORDAN

THE MOST COMPREHENSIVE REPORT to assess the gender gap in American schools found widespread bias against girls in tests, textbooks and teaching practices—findings that set off an immediate controversy among educators.

"The bias that exists in how girls are taught is no longer blatant, but they experience it on a daily basis," said Sharon Schuster, president of the American Association of University Women (AAUW), which commissioned the report.

The Education Department, which last month proposed eliminating the only federal program aimed at promoting education equity for girls, said the new report lacked perspective and hard data and maintained yesterday that gender-equity programs were no longer needed.

"You have to look at the larger context, at all the great strides women have made," said Diane S. Ravitch, assistant secretary for educational research and improvement at the Education Department. "This is a period of history in which there have been the most dramatic strides for women."

Ravitch cited statistics showing the percentage of female high school graduates enrolling in college is now larger than males and that the number of women who become lawyers, doctors and other professionals is rapidly increasing.

In 1970, 5 million college students were male and 3.5 million were female, a vastly different composition than in 1989, when 7.3 million were female and 6.5 million male. Likewise, Ravitch noted that only 8 percent of medical degrees were awarded to women in 1970, but 33 percent went to women in 1989.

"But quantity does not make quality," countered Mary Lou Leipheimer, co-chair of the National Coalition of Girls' Schools, who endorses the AAUW report, which is to be released today.

Leipheimer, who runs the Foxcroft School for girls in Middleburg, recited the other side of the statistical battleground: lagging pay for women compared with men, and underrepresentation of women in leadership roles in education. Women earn 69 cents on the dollar compared with equally educated men, according to a Labor Department analysis. And, while the overwhelming number of public elementary and high school teachers are women, more than 95 percent of the nation's school superintendents are men and 72 percent of its principals are men.

However, much of what the report "How Schools Shortchange Girls" focuses on is more difficult to quantify: little encouragement for girls to pursue math and science, few female role models in textbooks, and subtle teacher practices, such as calling on boys more often or gearing school and play activities more to the males.

The report by the Wellesley College Center for Research on Women is largely a compilation of existing studies by well-known researchers at Harvard, American and other universities and is believed to be the most thorough documentation of the gender gap in American schools.

Research by Myra and David Sadker, professors at American University, shows that boys in elementary and middle school called out answers eight times more often than girls. When boys called out, teachers listened. But when girls called out, they were told to "raise your hand if you want to speak."

Even when boys did not answer, teachers were more likely to encourage them to give an answer or an opinion than they were to encourage girls, the researchers found.

The study, noting the disparity between males and females in standardized math and science tests, said teachers often steered more boys than girls to those fields.

From 1978 to 1988, female scores on the SAT increased 11 points while male scores increased by four points. However, males still outscored females 498 to 455.

In science, the gap is wider, and some studies indicate it might be increasing. On the 1988 SAT achievement test in physics, males averaged a 611 score out of 800, 56 points higher than females' average score of 555.

The scores are noteworthy because girls often received better grades than boys, leading some researchers to suggest bias in the tests, which often determine college admittance and scholarships.

Several studies have suggested that teachers encourage male students to work with laboratory equipment, especially in the more complex sciences. For instance, one study found that 51 percent of boys in the third grade had used a microscope, compared with 37 percent of girls. In 11th grade, an electricity meter had been used by 49 percent of males but by only 17 percent of females.

The study also shows that vocational educational programs are often geared to males despite the fact that 45 percent of the work force is female. It also showed that since the early 1970s, the participation of girls in interscholastic athletics has increased dramatically, but that boys still participate in them at twice the rate.

The report, timed to be released at the AAUW National Educa- 19 tion Summit on Girls, is drawing the attention of many of the most influential education groups in the nation, including the head of the largest teachers union.

The report says some progress has been made since the enact- 20 ment of Title IX, the landmark 1972 legislation banning sex discrimination in federally funded education programs. Yet, it says stereotypical images still appear in textbooks, the overwhelming number of authors and role models studied in class are male, and problems confronting women, including sexism, the higher rate of suicide among women, and eating disorders are often all but ignored in the curriculum.

"I think you can look at any situation and see the progress or see 21 the way we have to go," said Susan McGee Bailey, director of the Wellesley research center. "But I think it's dangerous to say that because one-third of our medical students are now women" the struggle for gender equality is over. "There is a great deal more to be done."

Questions for Thinking and Discussion

1. This article, which discusses at length the AAUW report, offers two different explanations of what the report means. One side (represented by Diane Ravitch) disagrees with the results of the study; Ravitch believes that women have already made enormous strides in education. The other side (represented by Susan McGee Bailey) is that "there is a great deal more to be done." Which side do you agree with? Why?

2. In your own educational experiences, how prevalent are these problems that the AAUW report points to:

   . . . stereotypical images still appear in textbooks, the overwhelming number of authors and role models studied in class are male, and problems confronting women, including sexism, the higher rate of suicide among women, and eating disorders are often all but ignored in the curriculum.

U. Can't Ignore It

SHEILA TAYLOR

SOME YOUNG WOMEN FRIENDS WERE ENRAGED after their campus newspaper published lyrics from a fraternity song book.

The songs weren't *The Sweetheart of Sigma Chi* or any of the romantic—OK, sappy—tributes that brought girlish tears to my own eyes once upon a time. No, these promoted rape, violence, sexism at its most despicable. In a word, misogyny.

The women, sorority members who'd been asked by the newspaper to respond, were advised by their national office not to comment. To respond would dignify the situation, giving credence to the absurd.

The women asked me what I thought they should do. Ignore it came to my mind, too. You're about to start exams, then spring break; you're all busy. Let it ride. Besides, when male schoolmates make obscene remarks to and of their female classmates, you're supposed to ignore them. To do otherwise only encourages them, we're told. Ignore *it,* and it will go away. Ignore *it* and it will be like it never happened. *Act as though it never happened.* Now there's a phrase that sets my locks acurl.

Teen-age girls and college women have ignored *it,* and "it" hasn't gone away, not among the school set. A study by the American Association of University Women, "Short-changing Girls, Short-changing America," shows that both sexes up to age 9 have strong self-images; then at adolescence, self-esteem in both drops. Emerging from adolescents, boys have recovered the self-esteem in much higher percentages than girls.

Reasons are myriad; one factor likely is that girls have already been treated as sex objects; their bodies remarked upon derogatorily at an age when body-image is particularly impressionable on the total self-image.

One teen-age girl recently took legal action against Duluth (Minnesota) Central High School because her complaints of vulgar graffiti, which humiliated her daily, were ignored for a year and a half. She was paid $15,000 in settlement.

Any woman personally acquainted with the U.S. school system, private or public, knows sexism flourishes, even into the 1990s. The more enlightened schools fight it in official ways, but much of the sexism comes from attitudes that can't be governed.

Where does it come from, this hostility? I think of those fraternity men, for instance, products of homes much like my own. I think of my son, his friends, my daughter's boyfriends. Their parents, I'm sure, are well-intentioned, like me, like you, and of similar values. They'd no doubt be stunned at how far beyond "boys will be boys" behavior their sons have stepped, just as I would, if mine were involved.

The New York Times report of the Duluth case also said that in the California Legislature, a bill was introduced to make sexual harassment grounds for suspension or expulsion, and two recent court rulings have held schools liable for damages in sexual harassment cases.

I'm aware of the complications of deciding whether adolescent behavior is a result of illegality or simple immaturity. But 16-year-olds are considered old enough to understand and follow driving laws, to understand and follow labor laws. They're plenty old enough to understand what sexual harassment and discrimination are, too, and to be held accountable.

I don't think you should ignore this, I told the young women. Tell the reporter what you've told me. Write the fraternity presidents and tell them the same thing and that you're not going to socialize with those fraternities. Write the presidents of other campus organizations, too, and tell them what you're doing and ask for support, and tell every university official you can think of.

You, we, can ignore *it* till the cows come home, but that's not going to make it go away.

Questions for Thinking and Discussion

1. Taylor analyzes (paragraphs five and six) the changes that occur in women from childhood to late adolescence. She says that before adolescence women generally have "strong self-images." Then, like men, they lose some of that self-esteem during adolescence but are slower than males to regain it after adolescence. If you are a woman, how accurate is Taylor's analysis of the changes in your self-esteem up to this point in your life?

2. Taylor's article reports on the case of a teenaged girl in Duluth, Minnesota, who was the victim in school of "vulgar graffiti," which we assume to have been written by her male schoolmates. As Taylor tells us, the case ended up in court in a sexual harassment case that was settled for $15,000. Taylor then discusses the sexism that "flourishes, even into the 1990s" in the U.S. school systems. How are sexism and sexual harassment alike or different? Are both always present at the same time? Should both be punishable by law?

How Do You Teach a Girl to Value Herself?

DEBBIE M. PRICE

LAST SPRING, MARY, a freshman at a local high school, called to talk. 1
A girl at her school had committed suicide.

"I know why she did it," Mary said. "There is a lot of pressure at 2
that school. I used to say that suicide is stupid, but this month, I've
thought a lot about it."

Mary and I talked for a long time. She told me that when the 3
principal announced the girl's death, some students laughed. The girl,
Mary said, did not fit in.

Mary said she knew what it was like not to fit in. At her old school 4
in Arizona, she wore sleeveless shirts and short skirts to class. Mary
dressed that way her first day at the new school, and one of the popular
girls asked her if she were a slut.

Mary changed her wardrobe, but the hateful label stuck. 5

"I try to dress up as much as I can because everything I wear, they 6
say something about it," Mary said. "I stay up late, late at night trying
to find something to wear."

Mary's mother is raising three children alone. She can't afford 7
the $70 jeans that the high school fashion standards demand. She
tries to tell Mary that life will not always be like high school, that
the nerds with the tape on their glasses may become physicists and
the popular jocks can end up pumping gas. But the reassurances go
only so far to deflect the sniggering and snide remarks.

"Sometimes I sit in my room and cry and think 'what am I doing 8
so wrong?'" Mary said. "I feel so worthless."

I was thinking about Mary recently because folks from Gloria 9
Steinem to child psychologists are talking about an epidemic of low
self-esteem among women and girls. Low self-esteem is not new, but
it's only recently that the experts have named it and started measuring
it. And looking at the damage that it does.

Studies by the American Association of University Women last 10
year found that girls entering high school have much lower self-
esteem than boys. A majority of boys and girls started out in elementary school feeling pretty good about themselves, but by the time
they reached high school, fewer than a third of the girls seemed self-

confident and positive. Almost half the boys, meanwhile, retained their self-assurance.

The AAUW study focused on academic achievement, particularly   11
in science and math, and on the different, and often unconscious, ways that teachers treat boys and girls.

The study found that many teen-age girls "learn" that they are not   12
good at math and science and see this as a personal failure. Boys who are not good at math, meanwhile, tend to dismiss the subject as unimportant.

This lower self-esteem among girls, the study found, translates   13
into fewer fulfilled ambitions and curtailed career goals, as well as insecurity about looks.

Likewise, the study found that teachers encouraged and expected   14
more from boys and tended to coddle or ignore girls. It went on to conclude that teachers and families have a greater impact on teen-agers' self-esteem than do their peers.

This is probably true. There is nothing more important than a   15
loving and supportive family and perhaps nothing more influential than a challenging and inspiring teacher. Far too many children have neither.

But I also think that we can't discount the impact children—   16
particularly girls—have upon each other.

Several of my friends have daughters, and we have talked about   17
this. Girls can be incredibly mean to each other. There aren't very many of us who don't know this first-hand.

In the sixth grade, my friends stopped speaking to me. I was hurt   18
and baffled.

I had no idea what happened until two years ago when my friend   19
Christa Beth told me that I had been shunned by official vote during a secret Saturday afternoon meeting in the restroom of the Palace Theater.

"It was your turn," she said.   20

The next year, Christa Beth said, she was shunned. By then, I had   21
moved on.

Christa Beth apologized and said she had felt guilty for years. I   22
was surprised that she remembered. I thought I had forgotten, but I hadn't and I don't suppose that anyone ever does.

Those are the kinds of things that stay with us for the rest of our   23
lives, the kinds of things that are impossible to measure in studies and surveys.

Those are the kinds of things that parents and teachers have to   24
fight. I'm not sure how. I can only share some advice that my father gave me.

"I wish I could tell you that everything will change when you   25
grow up, but the truth is, it doesn't," my father said. "The one who
changes is you.

"You can let this cripple you, or you can let it make you   26
strong."

Questions for Thinking and Discussion

1. Like Taylor, Price takes up the problem of low self-esteem among teenage women, but Price centers on different reasons for the problem. What reasons does she give for low self-esteem?

2. Price's solution to the self-esteem problem is also quite different from Taylor's. Instead of suggesting the need for legal intervention, she offers a personal solution given to her by her father: "You can let this cripple you, or you can let it make you strong." Which of the two solutions—Taylor's or Price's—do you favor? How could the two solutions be combined?

Bias Against Girls?

FORT WORTH STAR-TELEGRAM

AT THIS ADVANCED STAGE OF THE 20TH CENTURY, no American girl should continue to be subjected to what appears to be widespread, if subtle, discrimination in the classroom that blunts many girls' educational opportunity.

A recent study compiled by the Wellesley College Center for Research on Women indicates that substantial discrimination by teachers, textbooks and tests has tended to reinforce stereotyped expectations of what girls "should" study and to undermine their self-confidence and esteem.

To the extent that is true, the educational system in the United States not only is depriving young girls the opportunity to develop their own talents but also is denying them the chance to enrich the nation's intellectual and skills resources.

The report was a compilation of existing research, not original work performed by the Wellesley center, and carries a strong orientation, if not bias, toward examining the effects of the educational system only on girls. Wellesley, after all is one of the country's premier women's universities, and the study was conducted for the American Association of University Women.

On a broader level, the educational system does no favors for boys who are the "beneficiaries" of discrimination, and educators would be wise to expand their scope of reforming instruction so that *all* students receive the same encouragement and educational discipline.

Among the findings of the study are that teachers tend to pay more attention to boys than girls; textbooks still present stereotypes of women's roles and shortchange girls by failing to encourage mastery of science and math; and sexual harassment by male classmates in the schools is on the rise.

Some of the findings in the report show some internal inconsistencies, however. For instance, girls generally tend to make better grades than boys, although they score lower on standardized tests. Also, among high school graduates in 1989, 61.6 percent of girls went to college, compared with 57.6 percent of boys.

To the extent teachers and curricula compromise the educational   8
opportunities of any student, education in America is failing.

The Wellesley report, although not definitive, demonstrates that   9
policy makers and educators at all levels of U.S. education must bring
about substantial fundamental improvement in all aspects of instruction that systematically deny any young mind the opportunity to
achieve the fullest potential of her or his talents.

Questions for Thinking and Discussion

1. This article describes other problems because of biases experienced by
   women in education. What are some of these problems? Which have
   you found in actual educational experiences that you have been involved in?

2. Although this article describes a somewhat different set of problems
   than the ones discussed in Taylor's article, there may be some overlap.
   For instance, which of the problems discussed in this article are the
   result of sexism? How much of the sexism discussed in the article "Bias
   Against Girls" do you think is intentional?

"Western Wall" Syndrome Hampers Girls of Today

KATHLEEN PARKER

GIRLS HAVE IT TOUGHER. 1

So say researchers who already knew this, inasmuch as they are 2
women, but apparently felt they had to prove it statistically so that
others would believe it.

The research findings have been published in a book—*Meeting at* 3
the Crossroads: Women's Psychology and Girls' Development—by Lyn
Mikel Brown and Carol Gilligan.

The book summarizes five years of study of girls ages 6 to 18. In 4
an interview with *People* magazine, Brown summed up their findings:
"Girls learn to silence their own ideas and ignore their own instincts
when they come up against what we call the wall of Western culture."

The wall is manifested in many ways. 5

Girls often are shortchanged in schools, for instance, where the 6
authors say boys are encouraged to speak up and take risks. Girls, on
the other hand, more often are graded on the neatness of their papers.

Television and movies support the wall, the authors say, convey- 7
ing the image of superwoman as role model. Young girls today aspire
to the image of the tall, thin, perfect woman with a full-time job,
wonderful husband and adorable children.

This message of perfection begins as girls enter adolescence. 8
When they are 8, 9, and 10, girls are encouraged to be physical, and
outspokenness is tolerated, say the authors. But as girls enter the
so-called age of womanhood, they are told to be "ladylike," roughly
translated as quiet and submissive.

Boys of that same age, meanwhile, are increasing their physical 9
activities through organized sports.

It always has been tougher to be a girl, largely due to certain 10
biological factors that are inescapable. At the age of 11, 12, or 13, girls
are forced into the responsibility of tending their bodies, a burden that
brings childhood to a screeching halt.

Boys, meanwhile, are allowed to be children—some would argue 11
indefinitely.

The Western wall of culture is real, to be sure, but it is not 12
insurmountable. Through years of hard-fought battles, women have

begun scaling the wall, creating options for our daughters never before imaginable.

It is important that young girls not forget this fight, that they not   13
take for granted the opportunities they do have. Ignoring the past carries grave penalties.

For evidence, one need only look to the new Russia, where young   14
girls are being treated to a taste of Western culture. Liberated from communism, the women and girls of Russia are being herded backward toward a sexist-driven oppression.

The new Russia is a men-only club where women are judged,   15
hired and used according to their looks and their willingness to submit to sexual advances, according to a recent story in the *Los Angeles Times*.

"Businessmen come right out and say they don't take girls for   16
professional positions," says a senior economics student. "They say they do hire girls as secretaries, and then they look them up and down. If they don't like the way you look, they say, 'We don't need a girl like you,' and if they do, they let you know that your responsibilities may include those of a prostitute."

Many Russians apparently feel that sexism is supported through   17
President Boris Yeltsin's message—through word and example—that woman's place is in the home, according to the *Times* article.

Consequently, young girls in the new Russia do not aspire to   18
careers.

Repelled by a hostile workplace, young Russian girls daydream   19
about getting married, staying home and raising children. It's an interesting turn of events for a country where equality once was legally required.

Questions for Thinking and Discussion

1. In your own words, what does Parker mean by the phrase "Western Wall Syndrome"? How is this "wall" the same problem discussed by Taylor, Price, and the writer of the *Ft. Worth Star Telegram* article?
2. Parker compares the roles played by little girls and little boys. She concludes that, for several reasons, it has always been "tougher to be a girl" in our society. Do you believe this statement is true, especially based on your own experiences and experiences of friends, relatives, or children? In what ways might it be *harder* to be a little boy?

Ohio College Says Women Learn Differently, So It Teaches That Way

SUSAN CHIRA

THE PITCH IS A SIMPLE ONE: small, Roman Catholic women's college   1
in pastoral setting near lake offers the nation's only program tailored to
the different way women learn.

Selling itself as a unique experiment in women's education, Ur-   2
suline College is using a revamped curriculum and a retrained faculty
to test the theory that women learn better when they work together in
small groups and relate what they study to their lives.

In so doing, this small college near Cleveland is placing itself at   3
the center of a larger debate among educators and feminists: Do
women really learn and think differently, or does that view trap women
in the very stereotypes they have been trying to dispel?

"Our approach reflects the different ways boys and girls are   4
socialized," said Gary Polster, a professor of sociology at Ursuline.
"Boys are raised to be more independent, aggressive and competitive;
girls are raised to be a lot more group-oriented, and they work best in
cooperative ways. Ours is not the traditional classroom set up 100
years ago by men for men."

FEMINISM OR SEXISM?

But the one-year-old experiment is drawing fire from some other   5
educators of women.

"Even if men and women are socialized to be different, I would   6
still say taking that approach is a dangerous one," said Judith Shapiro,
provost of Bryn Mawr College in Pennsylvania, one of the nation's
leading women's colleges. "It is likely to perpetuate differences. I think
it can be feminism doing the work of sexism."

With its wooded campus cloaked by mist from a drizzle on one   7
recent day, Ursuline College seemed far from this ideological fray. But
after years of trying to refine their educational mission, the faculty here
seized on theories that may be controversial, but reflected their own
experience teaching women.

The college offers a core curriculum based largely on a widely   8
discussed 1986 book, "Women's Ways of Knowing," by Mary Field

Belenky, Blythe McVicker Clinchy, Nancy Rule Goldberger, and Jill Mattuck Tarule (Basic Books). The book itself is part of an intellectually respectable yet fiercely debated school of thought that includes the Harvard psychologist Carol Gilligan, who believes that women have a distinct style of moral reasoning.

"We latched onto it; we said, 'This is written about our students,' " said Sister Rosemarie Carfagna, director of Ursuline Studies, as the core curriculum required of all students is called. 9

LEARNING TO BE ASSERTIVE

Two-thirds of Ursuline's 1,600 students are women returning to college. Many are recently divorced, Sister Rosemarie said, and many are new at asserting themselves. Teachers here believe it is especially important for these students to link their experiences to their education. 10

The book's authors and other researchers have found that women of all ages tend to be more hesitant than men to voice their opinions, less comfortable with the kind of argumentative intellectual style that is a hallmark of most elite universities, and more likely to doubt their intelligence. 11

"Women's Ways of Knowing" also argues that the classic stages of intellectual development, in which students eventually move from simply parroting what teachers say to creating their own theories, are different for many women. Women tend to defer to authority more than men do and to need more personal connection with what they study along the way, the authors argue. 12

Ursuline's core curriculum, Sister Rosemarie said, is designed to combat these problems and propel its students through these developmental stages. The college offers students a series of seminars run the way the authors of "Women's Ways of Knowing" believe that many women learn better: emphasizing the links between what they study in class and their own lives, working in small, supportive groups in which students feel free to try out ideas, and featuring teachers who do not act as authority figures but as "midwives" to students' thinking. 13

SOAP OPERA AND LIFE

For example, the required first-year seminar at Ursuline is devoted almost entirely to coaxing students to write and speak their own opinions, trying to shake off their tendency to say what they think the teacher wants, Sister Rosemarie said. The seminar is the first of three that form the heart of the core curriculum. 14

In her class recently, students presented their final project: an 15
extended soap opera that tells the story of a pregnant teen-ager reel-
ing from shock to shock. The baby she is carrying is handicapped,
and she has to consider abortion, adoption or bring up the child
herself. Her boyfriend lands in jail on a drug charge and infects her
with AIDS.

The girl playing the pregnant teen-ager, Yolanda Franklin, was 16
herself a teen-age mother. Sister Rosemarie said she is careful not to
allow such classes to disintegrate into group therapy. Rather, the idea
is to help students become more confident and more sophisticated in
expressing their own beliefs.

"Coming here has enabled me to be my own person—able to say 17
what I felt instead of what everyone else wants me to say," said Lisa
Samarin, a student in the seminar. "Sister Rosemarie made us decide
what our values were. She'll pull it out of you."

EXPERIENCE AND ANALYSIS

The second-year seminar aims to combine the emphasis on per- 18
sonal experience with more traditional academic methods of analysis.
It is thus an interdisciplinary humanities course that focuses on several
cities in different historical periods but that also includes discussions
about women's lives in those eras. Students read classic works like
Machiavelli's "The Prince," but they also read feminist critiques of these
texts. They not only study the ideas of such thinkers as Simone Weil,
but they also learn about her life. In the third year of the core curriculum, students are coaxed to integrate both the personal and the academic approaches so that ethical and personal commitments drive
their academic and career choices.

These are deliberate ways to build the "empathy" that the authors 19
of "Women's Ways of Knowing" say many women need to feel involved
in their studies.

"Traditional education has denied the role of feeling in the learn- 20
ing process," said Ann Trivisanno, a professor of English who also
teaches the core curriculum. "Women have traditionally learned from
life experience. We start with that and then move them forward. We
don't stop there."

This focus on combining personal experience with traditional 21
academic methodology is what sets Ursuline College apart from other
women's colleges, which also pride themselves on their supportive
atmosphere, said Blythe Clinchy, one of the co-authors of "Women's
Ways of Knowing." She and Jadwiga Sebrechts, executive director of
the Women's College Coalition, a Washington-based umbrella group,

say Ursuline is the only college in the country to embrace these ideas so completely.

Do Men Argue More?

Students say they feel the difference. "When I used to have   22
discussions with men in high school, they tended to be more absolute,
concrete, and argued a little bit more," said Lisa Stevens, a first-year
student. "Here, you have more of a chance to consider other people's
perspectives and others' answers to their problems."

But not everyone is cheering. Some have criticized both the   23
book's authors and Ms. Gilligan for over-generalizing from interviews
and failing to conduct standard empirical studies, which would have
male control groups to test the assumptions. Others say that while the
researchers may have accurately described the way many women are
brought up to think and behave, basing an education on those differences will not help women to remedy the very powerlessness that
forced them to adapt many of these traits.

"Saying that we're more maternal and caring and cooperative and   24
contextual just reinforces that behavior," said Susan Faludi, the author
of "Backlash: The Undeclared War Against American Women" (Crown
Publishers, 1991). "It's sort of a self-fulfilling prophecy."

One-third of Bryn Mawr's students, for instance, major in science,   25
often a male preserve. Bryn Mawr is succeeding, Ms. Shapiro said, not
because the college believes women need different kinds of teaching
from men but because women know they are attending a school run
by and devoted to women.

But teachers at Ursuline say they believe their approach will help   26
women break away from stereotypes. Asked what Ursuline graduates
will have that they did not have before, Sister Rosemarie replied,
"Moxie."

Sister Rosemarie and her colleagues said they believe that their   27
approach could work for men, too. Many of the principles the college
endorses, like teachers' shunning lecturing and guiding students to
develop their own ideas, are standard ideas advocated by many education reformers.

"This is a different way, not necessarily only for women or all   28
about women," said Leslie Pina, an associate professor of interior
design.

Four percent of the college's presidents are men, most of whom   29
come for its nursing courses. But the faculty consider Ursuline primarily a women's college and their mission to help women take their place
in the world.

Donna Mattia, who returned to college after having children,   30
believes the college is helping her do just that. "I feel as if my voice is
not being heard, and I wasn't sure how to use my education to voice
my concerns," she told her classmates in the final speech of her
introductory seminar. "But I was gently forced into writing introspec-
tive essays, and the more I wrote, I learned I had the ability to write
and voice my concerns and that people would listen to me."

Questions for Thinking and Discussion

1. Ursuline College takes an extreme position on the problem of women
   fitting into an educational system: The College segregates women from
   men. What advantages does Chira cite for this arrangement? What
   disadvantages? Do you think that the advantages outweigh the disadvantages?
2. The curriculum for women at Ursuline College emphasizes "the links
   between what [students] study in class and their own lives. . . ." What
   do you think this means? What kinds of activities might these classes
   include? What areas of your own education have taken this approach?

Writing Projects

1. Several readings in this chapter emphasize that women have suffered from a loss of self-esteem in education. If you are a man, write a biographical sketch of a female student at your college. If you are a woman, write an autobiographical sketch on your own experiences in education. In either case, answer this question:

   For the female being written about in this paper, has self-esteem been a problem in education? If so, in what ways?

2. In general, what do the writers in this chapter view as the major problems facing women in education today? Write a paper that summarizes and categorizes these problems.

3. Articles by Jordan and Parker discuss how teachers often treat boys and girls differently in class. For instance, Jordan discusses how research shows that even "when boys did not answer [in class], teachers were more likely to encourage them to give an answer or an opinion than they were to encourage girls." Parker says that "boys are encouraged to speak up and take risks," whereas girls "are graded on the neatness of their papers." To test the idea that males and females are often treated differently by teachers, write a paper based on some observations you make of a class, either in college or perhaps high school, junior high, or even elementary school. As you observe the class, take notes over issues such as these following:

   How often the teacher calls on the males as opposed to the females

   How often the males and females *volunteer* responses

   What kinds of responses the teacher gives to males as opposed to females. (For instance, does the teacher praise males only? Does the teacher challenge males only? Does the teacher's tone of voice change when males are addressed?)

4. Chira's article argues that it is a good idea for women to be placed in a separate learning environment—a separate college—away from men. Write a paper that investigates the advantages and disadvantages of all-women colleges. For supporting information, you might draw on material from Chira's article, and you might also seek out some further sources on the subject in your college library. Decide whether you think that all-women colleges are what American women in the 1990s need.

8

Innovations in Education

ANY ONE WHO HAS VISITED WALT DISNEY WORLD in Florida has experienced the sections of the park that try to help us experience what the future will be like. For years, educational theorists have also dreamed about the future—the future of education. For instance, early in the twentieth century, a group of educators calling themselves "progressivists" sought to reform America's educational system for the future. Since then, each generation of educators has developed its own set of reforms in an attempt to improve schooling for learners.

The articles in this chapter offer a variety of new "wrinkles" on education: a new grading system, new places to hold classes, and new curricula. Some of these "innovations" aren't really so new, but instead are a return to older principles. As you read these articles, try to evaluate the innovations that the writers are proposing. Are they too advanced? Will they work in real life school settings? As you read, too, think about innovations you might propose to remedy some problem areas in the American system of education.

Tomorrow's Lesson: Learn or Perish

MICHAEL D. LEMONICK

THE GROUP IS TRUDGING along a pathway through the forest, looking   1
something like an extended family on vacation: small children, teenagers, middle-agers and older people. But when the walkers suddenly
emerge in a wide meadow, it is clear that something strange is happening. On one side of the clearing stands the gray-clad army of Robert E.
Lee, and on the other the dark blue-uniformed infantry serving under
George Meade. As the hikers stand and watch, bugles sound, guns
begin to fire and the battle of Gettysburg is under way.

Real as it seems, the entire scene has been staged. The year is   2
2067, and the spectators are students who are learning about the battle
in the safety of a classroom through the technology of virtual reality. By
putting on special goggles and bodysuits, the generationally mixed
students "enter" the bloody scene and experience it as if they were
really there. The sights, smells, sounds—perhaps even the sensation of
warm summer breezes against the skin—all help make an indelible
impression. In the course of their studies, the pupils will experience
many other important historical events that have been carefully re-
enacted and digitally filmed. The technology also enables them to
transport themselves to far-off places, ranging from the top of Mount
Everest to the moons of Jupiter.

This kind of total-immersion experience, already being explored   3
in places such as the Massachusetts Institute of Technology's Media Lab
and the University of Washington's Human Interface Technology Lab,
will be just one part of a great leap in learning that will take place in
the middle of the 21st century. Part of the change will be technological:
highly advanced computers will serve as both tutors and libraries,
interacting with students individually and giving them access to a
universe of information so vast that it will make today's Library of
Congress look like a small-town facility.

An even more fundamental change will be the almost complete   4
breakdown of education's formal rigidity. It will be replaced by instruction tailored to the individual student. For example, instead of forcing
most 10-year-olds to sit through 10 months of fifth grade while a few

152

gifted ones skip forward and others fall back, all the children will learn at their own pace, taking several core courses and a wide variety of electives.

The standard high school diploma will be replaced by a series of achievement goals. Advancement into college, a trade or a career will be based on the attainment of those personal goals. The venerable concept of apprenticeship, which thrived in 18th and 19th century America, will be revived: young people will divide their time between school and training with mentors in areas ranging from carpentry to wildlife biology. At the same time, adult education will boom as workers retrain for new jobs, bone up on developments in fast-moving fields and learn new skills and hobbies for their retirement years.

As with the last big revolution in education—the imposition of universal public schooling in the mid-1800s—this one will be driven by the Federal Government. The impetus will be political, social and economic. Such competitors as Japan and the European Community, which pour substantial resources into education, have already caught up with and surpassed the U.S. in the quality of their workers, and the trend will continue. In America a growing, uneducated, unemployable and mostly minority underclass will put increasing pressure on society to pay more than lip service to education.

The result will be a federal effort that will rank as, to quote Jimmy Carter's response to the energy crunch, "the moral equivalent of war." Much more money will be funneled into public schools to upgrade them physically and boost teachers' salaries dramatically. Teaching will become, as it was in the past, a hero-like profession that lures some of the brightest college graduates. A massive public relations campaign will promote teaching as a career and learning as a central theme of national life.

Competition from low-cost, entrepreneurial private schools will pressure public institutions to abandon such inefficiencies as the tenure system. They will also give up the 10-month school year, a relic of the time when students had to do farm work in summertime. Year-round schooling is a more efficient use of resources; summer breaks tend to make the first and last months of the term virtually useless anyway.

Beyond the first five grades, the standard curriculum will probably disappear. Basic mathematical, reading and writing skills will still be required of advanced students, along with, for Americans, a solid background in U.S. history and government. But there will be greater specialization for students who want it. The mass-production approach to the high school diploma will vanish in favor of competency tests in subjects as diverse as physics, metalwork, music and graphic design.

Potential employers and college admissions officers would then have a much more specific idea of a student's skills and training.

Learning will no longer stop with high school or even college.   10
Specialized knowledge will become obsolete so quickly that adults will be encouraged to take frequent breaks from work, subsidized by their employers, to catch up. "Learning vacations," even for entire families, will become a major part of the travel industry as well as a big moneymaker for colleges whose campuses and faculty would otherwise be idle.

The loosening of strictures will throw older and younger people   11
together in the same classrooms. That might pose an instructional problem: What level does the teacher aim for? But within a few decades, technology will make it possible to provide tailored instruction within a single class. Students will become adept at using interactive multimedia, a system consisting of computers, exhaustive data bases of information, moving images and sound.

The suitably epic term for such an educational odyssey is "knowl-   12
edge navigation," a term coined by James Dezell, president of EduQuest, a division of IBM. In an experimental EduQuest program, students reading a passage from Tennyson's epic poem *Ulysses* can select a distinguished actor to read it aloud, call up a panel of experts to discuss the text, or read background on the Trojan War. Most important, students will receive this information in any order that suits them. The technique is expected to help open up vital areas of study that transmit many of the ethical underpinnings of a society. "How do we pass on morals and ethical issues to our kids?" asks Dezell. "Most of those issues have been examined in the great works, but those things are very difficult for a student to read." Multimedia programs, he believes, will make literature—and thus these ideas—far more accessible.

Computer-aided instruction will be a key to solving the problem   13
of adult illiteracy, according to Kent Wall, co-creator of the Buddy System, a program now used in Indiana public schools and homes. "Suppose Mom's out shopping," Wall imagines. "Johnny, the fourth-grader, is in bed. And Dad's sitting there thinking about the fact that he can't read, or maybe he reads at the second-grade level. But if Dad can go over and find the "on" button, he can teach himself how to read. He doesn't have to raise his hand and say, 'I'm illiterate.'"

If computers take over so much of the job, what role will be left   14
for the teacher? A different yet essential one, say the experts. Rather than just presenting information and issuing instructions, like a coach directing a football team, the teacher will inspire, motivate and serve as referee for the human-to-human discussion that computerized in-

struction is designed to provoke. A teacher will thus act more like the floor captain of a basketball team, directing the overall flow of action but allowing other team members to take the lead when the situation warrants it. "Teachers will become much more like facilitators, guides," says Hugh Osborn, director of the New Media Group at public TV station WNET in New York City. "They won't be able just to have their answer book and have that be the main thing that differentiates them from the students."

The greatest mystery for the next century is whether scientists   15
will discover fundamental ways to affect how the mind learns. The human brain has evolved over millions of years to process information in a certain way—the very act of perceiving the world is an integral part of the way it is understood. Can learning speed and capacity be "souped up"? While scientists have found ways to improve the learning ability of people with damaged and dysfunctional brains, nothing has yet emerged that could radically improve a normal brain's ability. No secret pill or process is on the horizon, just a steady enhancement of abilities people already have. And the most powerful ingredient will be motivation, since the working world will become ever more knowledge driven and information intensive. In the 21st century, nothing will be more fashionable—and essential—than doing one's homework.

Questions for Thinking and Discussion

1. This article is a glowing view of the future of American education. Lemonick seems to have faith that some things in society will change radically. What are the main changes Lemonick predicts? Which of these appeal to you, for yourself or for your children? Which of the changes seem farfetched, unworkable, or not necessarily good?

2. Lemonick also foresees that teaching will become a very attractive profession. He tells us that a "massive public relations campaign will promote teaching as a career and learning as a central theme of national life." Why does the present attitude in the United States toward teachers makes Lemonick's "massive public relations campaign" necessary?

Guiding Kids With a Curriculum of Compassion

KAREN S. PETERSON

FIFTH-GRADER CHANELLE MATTHEWS wants to know more about   1
being deaf. "How did you learn to sign?" she asks Linda Kennedy, 42,
who converses with the help of an interpreter.

"Little by little, the same way you learned to talk," Kennedy says.   2

Chad Jensen, 10, wonders "Is it hard when people look at you   3
real funny when you use sign language?"

No, Kennedy says. Besides, "If they talk slowly, I can understand   4
them" by lip reading.

This is disabilities awareness day at Swansfield Elementary   5
School [Columbia, MD]. The entire school, K–5, spends the day with
the disabled, including the blind and their seeing eye dogs, the wheel-
chair-bound playing basketball, and people with AIDS.

Marissa Schwartz, 10, is just a bit anxious about meeting some-   6
one with AIDS. "I'm kind of scared. But I'm kind of eager, too," she
says.

These kids don't know it, but they're learning compassion, re-   7
spect and appreciation of diversity. The school has celebrated this day
for years. But today it is being incorporated into a new, formal "values
education" program.

Such values programs are catching fire nationwide. "This is going   8
on in every state in the union, to one degree or another," says Thomas
Lickona, author of *Educating for Character* (Bantam, $12.50). Some
schools started a decade ago, he says. But "within the last two or three
years, programs are being hammered out everywhere."

Why? With high teen pregnancy rates and kids into drugs and   9
crime, "There is a realization that society is in trouble," says Joan
Palmer, who helped design Howard County's program in Maryland.
And when society is in trouble, "it looks to schools for answers."

There is a sense, Lickona says, that many "families have dropped   10
the ball," leaving kids "in a moral vacuum."

Current programs tend to be different from those that "gave   11
values clarification a bad name in the late '60s and '70s," Palmer says.
Those programs taught kids that morality is "relative, subjective, and
situational," says William Kilpatrick, author of *Why Johnny Can't Tell
Right From Wrong* (Simon & Schuster, $23).

But isn't moral truth often hard to pin down? Whose values does   12
one teach?

The most effective new programs teach "what is ethical conduct   13
in daily life," Lickona says. "We can agree on 98% of it: how to treat
each other with respect, not to cheat on tests, not to call each other
names or duke each other out." The two "overriding" values, he says,
are respect and responsibility.

Yes, there are thorny moral issues such as abortion and the right   14
to die, experts say. But dwelling on the controversies "puts the cart
before the horse," says Kilpatrick, an education professor at Boston
College. That is "talking about all the exceptions to the rules, without
teaching kids what is moral in the first place."

There is evidence that the new programs help, says Lickona, an   15
education professor at State University of New York, Cortland. "Some
of the best data shows that if you start in kindergarten, and children
get it all through the elementary years, it makes a difference in attitudes
and behavior."

Here in Howard County, Palmer met with representatives of   16
virtually the entire community at twice-monthly meetings over 18
months. A task force came up with a list of 18 values including
honesty, integrity and responsibility. Each school decides how to implement its own program.

Phillip Audain, 9, can sum up what Swansfield's disabilities day   17
teaches him: "We all have more things in common than stuff that's
different."

The abstract concept of values comes alive here at Swansfield.   18
One of today's most effective guests is Bill Demby, who lost part of both
legs in Vietnam. In the gym, Demby supervises wheelchair basketball,
pitting some excited kids placed in wheelchairs against the permanently disabled.

In classrooms, Demby shows mesmerized kids how he puts on   19
his two prostheses. And one can see where young Audain gets his
attitude. Demby's repeated message: "I am disabled. But you and I are
more alike than different," he says.

Fifth-graders at Swansfield embrace this special day. But they do   20
have some disagreements about teaching "values" per se in school.
"The teachers can talk about it," muses Paul Sutusky, 10. "And the kids
might *look* like they're listening. But you never know. They might do it
to get good grades."

For David Early, 10, the case for values education can't be over-   21
stated. "They already teach values in school. But we should do it
more!"

Questions for Thinking and Discussion

1. Peterson's article is about "values-based education," which is a currently popular idea. What is a "value"? Which of the values Peterson speaks about do you agree ought to be taught in elementary and secondary schools? What other values do you think ought to be taught?

2. To what extent have you been taught values in your college classes? In what ways are the values that your college teachers hold in agreement with your own values? In what ways are they different?

New Grading System Earns an "F" from Houston Parents

ASSOCIATED PRESS

AHHH, THE ANXIETY, ANTICIPATION AND DOOM wrought by The Report Card. Will it be stuffed with A's, or marred by F's?   1

In 57 Houston schools, student grading has been updated for the '90s, with "connecting" and "expanding" among descriptions replacing traditional marks.   2

But the unconventional system gets a big fat F from some parents.   3

"My husband went through the roof. He was furious. He thought it was stupid, and we couldn't tell anything from it," said Donna Gilger, whose daughter is in kindergarten at Herod Elementary School.   4

Students are pegged to one of eight stages: discovery, exploration, developing, expanding, connecting, independent, application and synthesis.   5

The new report cards are intended to assess student performance more meaningfully and give parents a better idea of how their children are developing socially, emotionally, academically, aesthetically and physically in the early grades.   6

The system was developed by teachers in the Houston Independent School District. Committees of parents, teachers and administrators at each school involved voted to adopt the scale. It was used by 23 schools last year.   7

School officials said the new system is meant to eliminate the arbitrary nature of traditional grades.   8

"It's in the process of being improved," said Janice Heffer, who directs the district's early childhood program. "We're not saying this is perfect, but it is much better than what we've had."   9

Questions for Thinking and Discussion

1. This article describes an entirely new way to grade elementary school students. How effectively do you think this new system would have worked for you when you were a child?
2. If you had developed a new way of grading schoolchildren, in what ways would your system have been similar to or different from the one being used in these Houston, Texas, schools?

State Board of Education Studies Proposal For Year-Round Schools

TONY TUCCI

THIS COLUMN PROBABLY WON'T WIN US ANY FRIENDS among teachers   1
and students. But we've wondered for a long time why we don't keep
our schools open year-round. It just seems to be a logical solution to
overcrowding problems, and more economical use of our school facilities.

Now comes a report that the [TX] State Board of Education is   2
considering year-round schools as a way to resolve the financial bind
which will occur as a result of court-ordered redistribution of state
education funds. The court has said that state aid must be equalized,
which would mean either an increase in taxes or taking funds from
richer districts to give to the poor.

State School Board Member Will Davis was quoted in *The Dallas*   3
Morning News last week as saying: "Year-round schools make all the
sense in the world. We are going to pursue this idea and pursue it
hard."

One of the leading proponents of year-round schools is Charles   4
E. Ballinger, executive director of the National Association for Year-
Round Education. He testified before the board last week.

Ballinger said that studies show that a long summer break dis-   5
rupts the learning process and actually may be harmful. "Vacations are
important, but they don't have to be three months long. They can come
in shorter, less disruptive blocks of time," Ballinger said.

Vacation breaks can either be staggered, so that the schools are in   6
use all the time, or single-tracked, where all students have the same
schedule. In Los Angeles, which has year-round schools, students are
assigned to one of four calendars so that a quarter of them are always
on vacation. Parents are allowed to choose their preference.

"Year-round education is an idea whose time has come," Ballinger   7
said. "It makes no sense to keep closed half a year the school buildings
in which America has invested a quarter of a trillion dollars while we
are undereducated and overcrowded."

Ballinger pointed out that the present school calendar never was   8
an educational calendar, but was based on the needs of an agricultural
society.

Those days when children were needed to help on the farm in the   9
summertime are long past. It makes one wonder why educators didn't
propose year-round schools long ago.

Questions for Thinking and Discussion

1. The plan Tucci discusses in this article is already part of educational systems in a good many cities across the United States. If you have attended school year-round, what do you think of it? If you haven't, how do you think you would have responded if Tucci's plan had been in place when you were in elementary or secondary school?

2. One part of Tucci's article quotes Charles E. Ballinger, associate director of the National Association for Year-Round Education. Ballinger makes the following statements in the article:

   A long summer break "disrupts the learning process and actually may be harmful."

   The "days when children were needed to help on the farm in the summertime are long past."

   Based on your experiences, how accurate are these two statements?

Schools at the Workplace Bringing Families Together

MARY JORDAN

PATRICK DUNN PULLS OVER NEAR AMERICAN AIRLINES in his gray Ford   1
van and drops his 7-year-old son, Corey, near a busy runway.

As 75,000 daily passengers come and go, the father and son stick   2
to their quiet routine. The older Dunn settles into work at the Miami
International Airport post office; the younger one studies nearby in one
of the nation's most unusual elementary schools.

The single parent and first-grader are part of an experiment born   3
of practicality, one bringing families together by moving schools to the
workplace.

"I can punch out for lunch with my video camera and run right   4
across the field to the school," said Dunn, who works near the main
terminal. "I got him [on tape] singing songs for Christmas and playing
Louie the orangutan in a *Jungle Book* play."

The nation's first workplace school opened in Miami six years   5
ago. It consisted of classrooms constructed by a private employer on a
job site and run by the public school system. Since then, three more
have followed, including Corey Dunn's school at one of the world's
busiest airports.

The convenience is catching on. Minneapolis and New York city   6
recently opened similar schools. Dozens of other cities, including Los
Angeles, are negotiating with businesses interested in making an on-
site elementary school the hottest perk since the health club.

"It's quite an ingenious situation," said Gordon M. Ambach, ex-   7
ecutive director of the Council of Chief State School Officers. "It's not
that different from the good old days of small towns, when the school
was a block from the mill or factory."

In a country where more than 2 million children between the   8
ages of 5 and 13 come home alone from school, many officials say,
these schools fit the times. Along with enabling children to sit behind
desks yards from their parents, the schools match their hours to the
workday.

"The trend is an accommodation by business to the needs of the   9
nontraditional work force," said Foster C. Smith, senior vice president
of the National Alliance of Business. Along with the intangible benefits,

162

like peace of mind for the working parents, Smith said there are "turnover and productivity aspects that make this a financially smart thing to do."

Esterlene Lewis, chief of the airport's community affairs, said that the $400,000 the airport authority spent to build the school has been well worth it. The airport also pays for maintenance, utilities and security, with the school system providing the teachers, desks and books.

For one thing, Lewis said, attendance has improved. Some parents are apparently reconsidering taking a day off if they have to haul their child into school anyway. Others aren't staying home because they have to go to a school play or teachers' meeting.

"There is a lot of interest in this," said Sidney Thompson, superintendent of Los Angeles public schools. "It's good sense."

It is also practical. In cities like Los Angeles, New York and Washington, real estate for new school buildings is increasingly scarce and expensive. An answer is to allow businesses and industries to donate their land or buildings, often in return for tax credits.

Likewise, millions of suburban residents now work as far as an hour or more from their children's neighborhood school. For people like Donna Sands, who works at Miami airport's credit union but lives in Hialeah, the arrangement is a life-saver.

"I love it," said Sands, the mother of Jason, 5, and Jennifer, 7. "Sometimes I fight traffic 40 minutes in the morning, but at least I'm spending that time with my kids."

While many parents struggle to stitch together care and transportation for their children before and after school, the Miami airport school stays open from 6 a.m. to 6 p.m.

The regular Dade County school day runs from 8:30 a.m. to 3 p.m., so that time is free for parents. Parents pay a small fee—$1.20 an hour—for any extra time their child spends in the school.

Christopher T. Cross, who runs education reform efforts for the Business Roundtable, said that zoning codes and regulations hinder more headway. For instance, the Miami schools—also located in a hospital and bankers' insurance group—include only kindergarten, first and second grades. At the third grade, expensive state requirements kick in, such as a mandated number of library books and playground space. In New York City, regulations prohibit schools in high-rises if they are above the bottom floors.

New York City school Chancellor Joseph A. Fernandez was leading Miami schools when the effort began there in the late 1980s, and he is now pushing it in New York.

Questions for Thinking and Discussion

1. The plan that Jordan outlines in this article is very much like the plan for daycare already in place in many corporations in the United States. The difference, of course, is that these facilities are for school-aged, rather than preschool-aged, children. What are the pros and cons of having children attend school where a parent or caretaker works? How might this arrangement affect children, both positively and negatively?

2. In the view of Gordon M. Ambach, quoted in Jordan's article, this arrangement is "not that different from the good old days of small towns, when the school was a block from the mill or factory." In what ways is this arrangement *really* like being in a small town and in what ways is it not?

Commuter Students Up to Speed on Learning

Elizabeth Mehren

THE JOKES AND THE PUNS were probably inevitable. "Choo-Choo U," this rapid-transit approach to education was immediately dubbed. Students, lurching while the 7:45 a.m. train pulls out of this suburban station an hour south of Boston, were said to be "on the fast track." The Massachusetts Bay Transportation Authority just couldn't resist touting its new "commuter classroom" as "an alternate route" to learning.

But if you ask the 12 adults who have signed up for the three-credit undergraduate course offered jointly by Dean College and the MBTA, the proof is in the principles—in this case, "Principles of Management," the subject they are studying three mornings each week.

"I'd wanted to go back to college for a long time," said Kathy Harber, a 44-year-old legal assistant at a large Boston law firm. "I'd used every excuse in the world to avoid doing anything about it." When it turned out Harber could use her commute time as college time, "that was what finally got me off my duff."

At the Boston leasing company where she is a senior secretary, Avia Johnston 43, said executives had urged her for some time to sign up for college courses. But the prospect of navigating a university bureaucracy was too intimidating for Johnston, a grandmother of two whose formal education stopped with high school.

"This was the incentive I needed," she said. "It's social, you get to meet people, it's small and it's stimulating."

The idea of turning the commuter rails into college classrooms was the brainchild of Joy Evans, director of continuing education at Dean College, a small two-year institution in this community southeast of Boston. Evans learned that a similar effort had been conducted between 1971 and 1986 by Adelphi University on New York's Long Island.

In the '90s, Evans reasoned, a commuter classroom made more sense than ever. Colleges have satellite campuses in shopping malls, after all. Trains offer a captive audience. And time is a precious premium that no working American can afford to overlook.

"Obviously, this program appeals to people who are trying to get   8
that little edge by using their time more wisely," said John Haley Jr.,
general manager of the MBTA.

To Robert Anzenberger, a Northeastern University professor and   9
longtime train commuter who is teaching this first course for Choo-
Choo U, the appeal of a commuter classroom is as clear as the old
equation that dictates that time is money.

"You've seen all those bumper stickers—'It's the economy, stu-   10
pid.' " Anzenberger said. "Well, we're so deep into a recession that it's
very difficult for people working in corporations to get to traditional
classes."

While market research and a survey of train commuters showed   11
substantial interest, only 12 pioneers actually ponied up the $330-
tuition fee and agreed to devote their morning commutes to the pursuit
of higher learning. Still, MBTA and Dean College officials says the
students make up in enthusiasm what they lack in numbers, and two
more courses are under discussion for the next school term.

Anzenberger said the eagerness and discipline of his commuter-   12
students has come as a surprise.

"I've been pleased to find out how motivated and how extremely   13
bright they are," Anzenberger said. "I didn't expect people in an undergraduate course to exceed the people in my MBA program."

Another unexpected aspect of teaching on a train turns out to be   14
learning to accept the state of constant motion, Anzenberger said. His
65-ton classroom travels at 60 m.p.h., snaking through the suburbs as
he uses his collar microphone to shout out something about "the Wall
Street solution."

"You really have to keep your two feet planted," he said. "You   15
literally have to start thinking in terms of art and choreography."

Students say another hidden benefit is that the class provides a   16
new kind of camaraderie. Their out-of-classroom work for "Principles
of Management" means they are often in contact during the day. And
when they board the train at night, they tend to sit together and talk
about their schoolwork.

"That really is one of the big rewards," Anzenberger said. "You're   17
not staring at the back of someone's head for decades at a time."

Of course, taking on a college business course three mornings   18
each week also means giving up the time that is usually reserved for
newspapers, magazines and pulp fiction.

Anzenberger's only male student, 35-year-old electrical engineer   19
Michael Sullivan, held up his "Contemporary Management" textbook
and quipped that "instead of reading the papers, now I'm reading
something useful."

Jean Cataldo, a receptionist in a Boston law firm, said she was   20
thrilled to find a reason to use her brain on her morning commute. As
for her paperback novels, Cataldo, 55, said with a smile: "There's still
the trip home."

Questions for Thinking and Discussion

1. Mehren cites several advantages of this "Choo-Choo U." educational
   innovation. What are some advantages that Mehren doesn't discuss?
   What are some disadvantages?
2. Mehren discusses how college courses have been offered in places such
   as shopping malls. If you were working with college administrators to
   find new places to offer courses, where might you suggest? Why do
   you think these places would be especially effective spots for conduct-
   ing classes?

Writing Projects

1. Prepare a paper about a school district with which you have direct experience. Then, outline what you see as the three areas in the school district most seriously in need of reform. Using specific examples to support your case, focus the paper on explaining *the severity of the problems* and *why they are so serious.*

2. Since most of us have grown up under a traditional grading system, the Associated Press article about the grading system in Houston is perhaps a bit startling, just as it was to some parents in that city. Write a paper on the traditional ABCDF college grading system (or whatever grading system is used at your college), and argue for or against the system. Ask yourself questions such as these: Does it work? Why or why not? Should it be replaced? What would be a better system? Why?

3. Write a paper about the three innovations you find most appealing in this chapter. Try to connect these three innovations by explaining some of their shared goals. For instance, you might discuss how they all share the goal of helping students get along better in their complicated world. Or, perhaps you could describe how the innovators seem to want students to feel more comfortable about themselves and their relationship to others.

4. In her article about values-based education, Peterson implies that there are just a few values we can as a society agree on to teach young people. These values are *honesty, integrity, compassion, respect, appreciation for diversity,* and *responsibility.* Working with other members of your class, interview five teachers or administrators and five parents about the values they believe should be taught in public schools. Then, write a paper outlining the values that came up most often in your interviews. How does this values list compare to the one in Peterson's article?

9

The Value of College

IN 1975, WRITER CAROLINE BIRD PUBLISHED *The Case Against College,* a book that outlined her belief that college is an unnecessary luxury for many people. For instance, Bird said that college often serves no other purpose than to be a place where young people can hang out until they are old enough (and responsible enough) to hold jobs.

No doubt many of you have gone through a process of trying to decide whether you really wanted to go to college. You might even have asked yourself this question:

Is college really worth the time and money?

All of the readings in this chapter in one way or another address this question—what is the value of going to college? As you read them, notice how they explore financial benefits of college, as well as other less obvious benefits. Notice, too, how some of the readings are about the process people go through when they try to decide if college is right for them. Finally, notice how the writers discuss the plight of people who don't go to college. How limited are their opportunities?

Mother, Son at Odds on Education

Abigail van Buren

DEAR ABBY: Our middle son, Andy, is a very intelligent young   1
man of 19. He went to college for one year just to please us, then he
quit, saying, "I don't want to waste any more of my time and your
money."

His grades were fine, but he says he prefers working with his   2
hands. He's now enrolled in a trade school and we're so disappointed
in him!

I'm not putting down people who work with their hands, Abby,   3
but it seems to me that people who work with their hands do so
because they aren't smart enough to work with their minds.

Andy's father is a professional man, and both of Andy's brothers   4
plan to enter professions.

Please say in your column that a college degree is absolutely   5
necessary these days. After Andy graduates from college he can do
anything he chooses, but we desperately want him to have a college
degree first.

ANDY'S MOTHER

DEAR MOTHER: I disagree. College is *not* for everybody. If Andy   1
prefers to work with his hands, that's what he should do.

It's not true that people work with their hands because they aren't   2
smart enough to work with their minds. Some handwork requires
more skill, talent and know-how than many professions. You do your
son a tremendous disservice by telling him he's "disappointed you" and
urging him to go to college. Change your tune.

Questions for Thinking and Discussion

1. Place yourself in the position of Andy, the college-aged freshman in this
   letter written by his mother to Dear Abby. If you were Andy, what
   would you do: go to trade school or go to college? Why?
2. Abby starts her response letter to Andy's mother by saying that "College
   is not for everybody." Explain why you agree or disagree with this
   statement.

Letter by Linda Kaufman

Ann Landers

Dear Ann Landers: I've been reading you for years, but I never   1
dreamed that one column in particular would change my life completely.

Four years ago, a 41-year-old man wrote and told you how he   2
wanted to start college but was afraid of what the 18- and 19-year-old
college students would say and how he would fit in. He also was
concerned about not graduating until he was 45.

Your reply, which I will never forget, was this: "When you are 45   3
years old, you will be a 45-year-old WITH or WITHOUT a college
degree."

A light bulb went off in my head, and I applied to Harper College   4
in Palatine, Ill. In May, at the age of 41, I will be graduating with an
associate of arts degree. My concern about the young college students
was nonsense. They are terrific and helped me fit right in.

My advice to anyone who is thinking about going to college at   5
any age is this: GO. You'll enjoy it, and you'll feel great about yourself.
Thanks, Ann, for that advice. I owe you a lot.

—Linda Kaufman, Schaumburg, Ill.

Questions for Thinking and Discussion

1. This letter to Ann Landers by Linda Kaufman is a follow-up to one
written by a 41-year-old man some years earlier. This man had wanted
to "start college but was afraid of what the 18- and 19-year-old college
students would say and how he would fit in." If you are a "non-
traditional student" (age 25 or older), to what extent was this "fitting
in" a concern of yours before you enrolled in college? If so, has it
turned out to be hard to "fit in"? In what ways? If you are a traditional
student, how do you view the non-traditional students in your classes?

2. Kaufman gives the following advice to "anyone who is thinking about
going to college," no matter what his/her age: "GO. You'll enjoy it, and
you'll feel great about yourself."

This view contrasts the position taken in the letter to Abby by Andy's
Mother (above). Explain who you think has the better case: Linda
Kaufman or Andy's mother?

What's a Diploma Worth?
A Thousand Bucks a Month

ASSOCIATED PRESS

THAT COLLEGE DIPLOMA HANGING ON THE WALL is worth $1,309 a   1
month in extra pay.

At that rate, it takes the typical four-year graduate just a little   2
under two years to make up the cost—not counting the pay and
experience he would have earned working rather than studying.

On average, people with bachelor's degrees earn $2,116 a month,   3
a Census Bureau study said Wednesday. High-school graduates earn
$1,077 a month.

Tuition, books, room and board for four years at a public univer-   4
sity averaged $19,880 in 1990, a survey by the College Board found.
The cost of education has since risen to more than $23,000 for the four
years.

Prestigious private universities cost far more.   5

Is it worth it?   6

"As my job search threatens—I've gotten four rejections al-   7
ready—it's kind of depressing, especially considering how much education costs today," said Don Modica, 21, a senior who pays more than
$18,000 a year to attend Notre Dame.

Despite the cost, Americans increasingly prize a college degree.   8

In 1990, one American in four had a bachelor's degree or higher,   9
the Census Bureau said. That's up from one in five in 1984.

But a diploma doesn't always open the doors to high pay and   10
security.

"It isn't like it used to be," said Susan Miller, president of   11
the Annandale, Va., job-placement firm Susan Miller and Associ-
ates Inc. "You have an edge to start, but it's not the guarantee it used
to be."

People with degrees in engineering, computer science and other   12
technical fields can get well-paying jobs when they graduate, Miller
said. Everyone else is "out there in the job market competing with the
high-school grads."

"If someone comes through college and they have no work expe-   13
rience, they're clueless," Miller said. We see college grads starting as
receptionists."

Questions for Thinking and Discussion

1. This newspaper report about the amount of money a college diploma is worth in the work force says that a "college diploma hanging on the wall is worth $1,038 a month in extra pay." Is this salary the primary reason why you are in college right now? If not, what other reasons have you had?

2. This report indicates that on the average high school graduates earn $1,077 per month. How suitable is this salary at covering the "basic necessities" of a single eighteen year old? How suitable for covering the necessities of a *married* eighteen year old? How suitable for covering the necessities of a married thirty year old with a family? Do some calculating on paper about how people in each of these situations might spend a monthly salary of $1,077.

Useless U?

JACOB WEISBERG

THE FIRST JOB ROGER LABRADOR, a 1992 graduate of the University 1
of California at Santa Cruz, landed after graduation was working as a
short-order cook for $4.25 an hour. Things have improved slightly
since then. He's now making $5 an hour at a health-food store.

Pragmatists might be inclined to say that's what Labrador de- 2
serves for majoring in studio art. But consider the case of his classmate
and girlfriend, 22-year-old Kimberly Brewer. She majored in biology,
thinking she'd be able to get an entry-level job with a bio-tech firm or
a veterinarian. But the bio-tech firms told her she needed a graduate
degree, and the veterinarians told her they wanted someone with
"hands-on experience." She is now working at a rubber-stamp factory
for $6.25 an hour.

"Out of all the people I went to school with," says Labrador, "I 3
only know one person who got a real, high-paying job. Nowadays,
people don't care if you have a degree."

Statistics bear out the pair's experience. A recent survey of Cali- 4
fornians who returned to community college for job training after
getting a bachelor's degree showed that almost 10 percent have incomes of less than $8,000, a figure slightly below the poverty line.
But it's not just California graduates who are wondering about the
real value of their diplomas. According to a 1991 study by the National Center for Education Statistics, 40 percent of all 1990 graduates
felt the work they did in their jobs did not require a college degree.
In the U.S., a great many of us go to college with the naive assumption that a diploma will bring us economic success. While it's true
that college graduates make more money in the long run, it's also true
that four years at a university is no longer the best path to making a
lot of money, nor is it even a guarantee of a secure middle-class
existence.

For those who are so intensely focused at age 18 that they know 5
how they plan to make money, four or more years doing something other than making it is likely to be a waste of time. With four
years of college now costing as much as $100,000, a $139 yearly
subscription to the *Wall Street Journal* is probably a better investment.
As Robert Wallach, president and CEO of Robert Plan, an urban
auto-insurance agency, proudly told that newspaper, "We have the
lowest proportionate number of college graduates on staff in the indus-

try. I don't want the valedictorian. I want the kid who sold cigarettes in the bathroom."

Indeed, a look at the *Forbes* 400 shows little correlation between the accumulation of degrees and the accumulation of wealth. First on the list is software whiz-kid Bill Gates, who dropped out of Harvard in 1975 to start Microsoft, from which he has earned a cool $6.3 billion. Another example is Michael Dell, one of whose computers I'm writing this on. Dell dropped out of the University of Texas after starting his own company, which later became Dell Computers. He is now 28 years old and worth $310 million.

It's not just cyberpunks who can make it without a sheepskin. Being booted from Brown didn't do much harm to Ted Turner's career. Nor did dropping out of the University of California at Los Angeles hurt show-business tycoon David Geffen, who was a multi-millionaire at 25 and is now, at 49, worth a billion dollars. After a few semesters of college, Geffen left to get some real training in the mailroom of the William Morris talent agency. Of course, the Morris agency, like most employers, did not hire people without college degrees. When Geffen's transcript arrived in the mail, he intercepted it and substituted a forged letter. Even the talent agency was more interested in the credentials than the talent.

The ranks of college dropouts include a lot of highly literate people as well, even a few intellectuals: poet Maya Angelou, *Vanity Fair* editor E. Graydon Carter and National Public Radio legal-affairs correspondent Nina Totenberg. The highly motivated usually manage to educate themselves. It is an American tradition as old as Ben Franklin.

Even if college isn't a reliable passport to an upper-middle-class existence, you could still argue it's a good place to get an education, to broaden your mind and learn about the world. But intellectually and academically, college is in a bad way. Consider the titles of some recent books about the American university: *Killing the Spirit, Illiberal Education, The Closing of the American Mind, ProfScam, The Hollow Men* . . . the list goes on.

Things are looking grim even at the highly selective Ivy League schools. It was big news last spring when a survey of 3,119 Ivy League undergraduates reported by the magazine *U.S. News and World Report* found that only half the respondents could name the two senators from their home state, and only 41 percent could name at least four members of the U.S. Supreme Court.

The Ivy League, though, represents only seven schools; there are now thousands of colleges in America, partly as a result of the GI Bill. Passed by Congress in 1944, the bill made it possible for millions of World War II veterans to go to college. As a result, colleges swelled into universities, and a lot of new colleges sprang into being. But in looking for ways to finance their existence, many of these institutions have become little more than corporate subsidiaries, centers for "research" that have little to do with opening the minds of the young.

The professors at these schools are often more focused on secur- 12 ing tenure by publishing their own work—a crucible known in academia as "publish or perish"—than on teaching, and leave the actual work to T.A.s (teaching assistants), graduate students with little more training than the undergraduates. At the University of California at Berkeley, there are 1,742 of these teaching assistants, and at Harvard University—the school ranked number one academically in the survey published by *U.S. News and World Report*—there are about 850 of them.

The wars over political correctness have also turned many cam- 13 puses into battlefields, where there's more debate about what students should be studying than there is actual studying of anything. As critic Robert Hughes points out in his new book, *The Culture of Complaint,* the current controversy over multicultural versus traditional curricula assumes that what people read in school is so important because everyone knows few graduates will read anything other than the occasional bestseller once they graduate. This is proof, if any were needed, of the failure of the system. What are colleges doing if not fostering the curiosity that will make their graduates into lifelong readers?

If college is so dismal, why are we more intent than ever on the 14 idea that everyone must go? This year, more than a million people will graduate from college; in 1960, fewer than 400,000 received degrees. Part of the reason is the social function that the university has come to play in American life. For most of us, college is our first chance to live away from home, to learn about drinking, drugs and sex. And it affords us the chance to do it in a sheltered, protective setting. It introduces us to kinds of people we've never met, and creates avenues of social mobility. The belief in college also stems from a kind of misplaced egalitarianism that says if everyone has the same credential, credentials will somehow cease to matter.

The result, however, is almost precisely the opposite. Today, 15 paradoxically, a college diploma is considered both essential and nearly meaningless. Since employers can no longer rely on a college diploma, per se, to have much value, they rely more and more on specialized graduate-school programs to train prospective employees. Hence, the recent boom in M.B.A.s. Roger Labrador and Kim Brewer, the two UC Santa Cruz graduates who couldn't find good jobs, are both planning to continue their studies—he's thinking abut graduate school; she's taking animal-health technology courses at a community college. The problem with this is that four years to get your ticket punched before moving on to real training isn't a very efficient use of time.

Some efforts are under way to reconsider what the experience of college is all about. S. Frederick Starr, the president of Oberlin College in Ohio, and Gerhard Casper, the new president of California's Stanford University, have both suggested making college three years instead of four. This has drawn a hostile reaction from other university presidents, who consider the four-year plan eternally fixed. In fact, it's a historical accident. Harvard took the four-year scheme from Cambridge in 1636. Soon afterward, Cambridge switched to three years. Casper argues that dropping the fourth year would force colleges to think harder about what it is they want to teach students. 　16

In many ways, the problem lies not with colleges themselves, but with what our society expects from them. We need to get away from the idea that a B.A. or B.S. is the single necessary credential for any sort of advancement—or even an automatic hallmark of academic achievement. People graduating from high school should be encouraged to take the time to consider their options, and to try different things before they go off to spend four years at a college. Had Labrador and Brewer worked in the real world before going to college, they might have spent those four years differently and been better prepared for the realities of the job market. 　17

We need to recognize that a great many people don't want, can't afford and won't benefit much from such a diversion. The cure is not to cut off opportunities for going to college; it's to think more seriously about who goes and why they go. Instead of moving toward a system where everybody goes to college, we should think about creating a situation where everybody who wants to can, but no one feels her life will be ruined if she doesn't. College should be a choice—but not an automatic one. 　18

Questions for Thinking and Discussion

1. In contrast to the news report on salary expectations in the "What's a Diploma Worth" article, Weisberg indicates that college does not really prepare people for high paying jobs. If it is true, as Weisberg says, that "four years at a university is no longer the best path to making a lot of money," would there still be enough good reasons to attend college? Explain.

2. Weisberg believes that college helps people mature. He writes:

   "For most of us, college is our first chance to live away from home, to learn about drinking, drugs and sex. And, it affords us the chance to do it in a sheltered, protective setting."

   How legitimate is this reason for attending college? If you were going to use this reason to sell the existence of a state university or a community college to a group of taxpayers, what would you say to them?

New Elitism: The College Class

Bettijane Levine

It's the salesman's best pitch: "Invest now, and you'll have enough   1
for your kids to go to college." Who could say no? What parents don't
want diplomas for their children? With all the noise about the need for
higher education, who dares dream that a child can succeed without
benefit of a degree?

And what are the alternatives, anyway?   2

Sure, some have climbed to the top without that degree. Lack of   3
college did not stop Peter Jennings from becoming a top newscaster,
or David Geffen from becoming Hollywood's richest man, or Steve Jobs
from pioneering personal computers, or Jackie Collins from becoming
a bestselling novelist.

But aren't Jobs and Jennings—and dozens of other high-profile   4
types—exceptions to the rule? Perhaps they are genetically gifted with
a talent, drive and/or intellect that is not standard issue.

Not so, say analysts studying education in the United States. They   5
are simply the obvious success stories in a nation of potential successes
whose talents are not being tapped.

Mark Tucker, president of the nonprofit National Center on Edu-   6
cation and the Economy in Rochester, N.Y., and other experts say
talents of non-college-bound youngsters are not valued. They get no
respect, are educationally abandoned or ignored—and leave high
school with no preparation and no credentials to help them dive into
the economy's mainstream.

They say that U.S. schools do not assess the average high school   7
students' talents or skills and there is no way to know what potential
may lie beneath an undistinguished academic record.

"In the U.S., if you don't go to college, you're nothing. That's   8
absurd," says Tucker. "This is abominable elitism."

At the William Morris agency in Los Angeles, for example, the   9
company won't even hire you for the mail room if you haven't finished
college.

Says Larry Blaustein, vice-president of the agency: "The mail   10
room is part of our trainee program. We require a four-year degree,

although many of our kids have also been to law school or have their master's."

Because so many corporations now use the "diploma test" to   11
gauge whether applicants even get through the door to interview, the prognosis for much of the country's youth seems cloudy: The U.S. Department of Labor estimates that less than 50 percent of young people start college, and only 50 percent of those ever graduate. This leaves approximately 75 percent of those seeking jobs without the one asset—a diploma—employers increasingly require.

Critics of the system say education need not be synonymous with   12
college: You can be an educated person without a degree, or be a dunce with one.

Says Robert Reich, U.S. secretary of labor: "America may have the   13
worst school-to-work transition system of any advanced industrial country. Short of a college degree, there is no way someone can signal to an employer that he or she possesses world-class skills."

If today's attitudes continue, those who admit to not holding   14
degrees will have little chance to make their mark. They will earn about 40 percent less in their lifetimes than those who have that piece of paper, according to the U.S. Department of Education. Meanwhile, the income gap between haves and the have-nots continues to widen.

"In the 1950s it was perfectly possible for a middle-class Cana-   15
dian teen-ager like me to leave school and find a job in banking," says Jennings, ABC-TV's top-ranked anchor. "I started doing the cash book, then became a teller. I truly loved the work. There were a number of children of respectable families who started there with me and have since risen to the top in the Canadian banking system. But the field has become so complicated now that it requires specialists. This is true about life in general, and it is certainly true about journalism."

Jennings says it's naive for even the most gutsy or self-motivated   16
people to assume they will be able to flourish without college nowa-days.

"In the agricultural era, you could earn a decent living and lead   17
a good life without college," he says. "After that, in the industrial era, you could leave school early and still prosper as an industrial worker. Now those jobs are all done by machines."

Since the 1970s, Jennings says, possibilities have dwindled for   18
those with no college. "In the new world order, the imperative is for higher education."

Mark Tucker, of the National Center on Education and the Econ-   19
omy and an adviser on education to the Clinton administration, fo-cuses on the impact the educational system has on society. He is not pleased with what he sees.

"Ours is one of the most elitist educational systems of all the   20
advanced industrial world. We concentrate all resources on college-
bound kids," while the others "leave high school having achieved only
a seventh- or eighth-grade level of literacy. The result is that we are
forced to compete not with Japan and Germany on quality, but with
Thailand and Mexico on wages and hours."

Tucker says "other nations educate almost everybody to the   21
standard which we in the U.S. think appropriate only for those who
are going to college." That is why real wages in those nations go up,
while here they go down. "It is also why our income distribution
pattern in the past 20 years has changed in shape from the diamond
[equitable] to the pyramid—which is what you would find in a banana
republic."

Tucker concludes: "Any sensible soul would realize we must find   22
a way to educate the 70 percent of youngsters who are not likely to get
a college degree almost as well as we educate those who are going to
get one.

"It's essential," he adds, "or our country will be torn apart."   23

Herbert Kohl, author of 32 books on education, says the United   24
States developed "a nation of disposable kids, whom we see as a
problem rather than a possibility." It is not possible to believe that all
these kids are uneducable, he says. "We have this whole group who are
very poor, who grew up in a hard world, and who find more immediate
financial reward on the streets. But you could never call them dumb."

Questions for Thinking and Discussion

1. Levine's article is about American society's attitudes toward people who
   don't have a college degree. She points out that some experts see such
   people as "a nation of potential successes whose talents are not being
   tapped." How many people do you know who are not college bound
   but have "talent"? What talents do they have that might contribute to
   the welfare of the rest of society?

2. Mark Tucker, an expert on noncollege educated people, sees the elitist
   attitude toward people without college degrees as having the potential
   to cause our country to "be torn apart." What is Tucker talking about?
   How valid do you think Tucker's idea is?

Graduation Address: Spring 1993

CHRISTOPHER GUTHRIE

I'D LIKE TO TELL YOU A LITTLE STORY about my father. He died two
years ago, but I don't think he would mind at all if I immortalized him
a little bit today. He was born in 1918 in Mount Carmel, Illinois, a little
town in the southern part of the state on the Wabash River. His father,
who worked on the railroad, died of tuberculosis three months before
my dad was born. His mother, however, remarried a couple of years
later and would, over the years, have eight more children—making my
father the oldest boy in a family of eleven kids (he also had two older
sisters). My father's step-dad never had a real job. In fact, my father
never did know precisely how his step-father made a living outside of
telling me once that he "traded things."

Supporting a wife and eleven kids by "trading things" is not
exactly a career path designed to promote prosperity. And it didn't. My
dad's family was poor, dirt poor—so poor, in fact, that my dad had to
leave school in the fifth grade to get a full-time job working as a hired
hand for a local farmer in order to help support his family. And he
never returned to school. He eventually would enlist in the army, serve
in Europe during World War II, marry my mother, and move to
Chicago after the war. And, he had a pretty good life himself: he and
my mother raised four children, he made a living operating heavy
roadbuilding machinery, and he eventually became the owner of a
service station.

But my father still had some regrets. One summer in the late
1960s, he got me on as a laborer for the construction company he
worked for at the time. I always look back on that summer with a great
deal of fondness. You see, my father was not the easiest man in the
world to get close to. But that summer, working together and sharing
lunch together every day, I was probably closer to him than I had ever
been before or since. Anyway, one day that summer, while we were
having lunch, my father told me something that he had never mentioned before. We were talking about the civil engineer who always
accompanied our crew—he was the man who designed the roads we
worked on. My father didn't like him, although I can't repeat the exact
words he used to describe him. And then my dad said, "You know, if
I could have gone to college, that's what I'd be today, a civil engineer.
I think I'd be pretty good at designing roads and bridges." And that
was it. I never heard him mention it again during his life.

But what he had said stuck with me. And, I think it did because 4
I realized that, despite the many positive things he'd achieved, my dad
regretted the opportunity he had missed when he was forced to leave
school in Mount Carmel. It wasn't his fault, of course. Times were hard,
and he did what he had to do to help his family. Nonetheless, it was a
missed opportunity, and he still regretted it forty years later.

My father's story is not unique, of course. Everyone accumulates 5
at least a few regrets in life. It's part of the human existence, I guess. In
fact, if a person had to count all the regrets most humans collect during
the course of their lives, I think it would be clear that my father's regret
over his missed educational opportunity was a fairly common one.
There are probably many people in this audience today who, like my
father, were forced by circumstances beyond their control to miss an
educational opportunity that might have led them down a different
path in life. I would also guess that most of these people, once again
like my father, have not brooded too much on this regret and have
gone on to make rich and rewarding lives for themselves and their
families. But, I also suspect that every once in awhile, just as was the
case with my dad during that lunch break in 1969, a nagging question
will occasionally pop to the forefront of their consciousness—a question of what might have been if they somehow had been able to take
advantage of that educational opportunity they have been forced to
pass on earlier in their lives.

This brings me to you, soon-to-be graduates of Tarleton State 6
University. Maybe you're the first person in your family ever to graduate from college; maybe you were forced to postpone your college
plans when you were younger due to family or financial concerns and
have only come back to complete your education later in life; maybe
you come from a long line of college graduates in your family. But,
regardless of your own individual story, all of you—due to your own
hard work, plus the sacrifice and encouragement of your family and
friends, plus a little luck—have been able to take advantage of an
incredibly important educational opportunity. While you are still going
to have some regrets in your lives, at least you won't ever have to
wonder, like my father did, about what you could have done if only
you had finished school. For even though some of you plan to go on
to graduate or professional school, most of you will complete your
formal education today when you walk across the stage and receive
your diploma from Dr. McCabe.

But, the next move is yours, ladies and gentlemen. You have been 7
given a chance that many others never had. You have a college education. The choice before you now is whether you're going to make the
most of it, or whether you're going to squander it. Few people go

through the trouble of graduating from college with the intention of wasting their education, of course. But it happens.

   As you go through your lives, you will encounter a variety of frustrations and temptations that will encourage you to put yourself ahead of the rest of society, that will tempt you to put what you feel is good for you ahead of what *is* good for everybody else, yourself ahead of the rest of society, that will lead you to think that the entire universe revolves around your needs and that everyone else is here to serve and further those needs. These temptations are powerful, and they are especially powerful in today's volatile economic climate where everything is so unsettled and uncertain. The urge to "get what's yours" and say to heck with everyone else thrives in a climate such as this. But, ladies and gentlemen, you have to resist following this path. We all want you to be successful. But you also have to live with yourself. At least when my father wistfully wondered what his life would have been like if he had been able to stay in school and become a civil engineer, he could find comfort in the fact that he had done his best with those chances he did receive in life and that he had also done his best, however small, to make this world a better place. But what comfort can a person find when he or she looks back on a life filled with callous disregard for the feelings and hardships of others, filled with disdain for the society which provided him or her with the chance for a college education in the first place? No one here today wants any of you to look back on a life such as this. My father's regret over his missed educational opportunity was tragic in its way, but it was one he could live with. However, to regret wasting one's abilities and education is another story altogether.

   So, graduates of Tarleton State University, we all congratulate you on your achievements. We all celebrate the fact that you have made the most of your educational opportunities. And, we are all very proud of you. All I ask is that you continue to make us proud of you in the future and, even more importantly, that you will be able to be proud of yourselves.

   Thank you.

8

9

10

Questions for Thinking and Discussion

1. In this graduation speech, Guthrie says that "missed educational opportunities are tragic in a way." How is he using the term "tragic" here? What are some examples of your own missed educational opportuni-

ties or those of people you have known? Do you consider these missed chances to be tragic? Why or why not?

2. Guthrie discusses two different kinds of regrets. On the one hand, there are regrets involving missed educational opportunities. However, Guthrie seems more concerned about other kinds of regrets. What are some of these regrets? In what sense is Guthrie talking about morality?

Writing Projects

1. Since you have committed yourself to attending college this term, you probably have done some serious thinking about *why* you are here. Drawing on your own ideas, observations, and experiences, write a paper entitled "My Philosophy of the Value of College." This paper should explain what value college serves for you and others.

2. It has been said that the value of higher education sometimes takes years to appreciate. In other words, things people learn at one phase of their education come to mean more when they are in later stages of life or career. In a paper, explore how an older person regards the value of his/her college education.

   Select an older person over the age of sixty who attended college earlier in life. Interview the person and ask about ways that he/she now sees the value of that college education. Try to get your interviewee to speak on specific ways about his/her life and its relationship to the college education.

3. Several of the writers in this chapter paint rather bleak pictures of the job market, even for college graduates; however, these people are speaking in generalities—not necessarily about specific career fields.

   Assume that you are writing to fellow students in your major field. Prepare a report outlining the prospects in your major field for getting the kind of job you would like. As your sources of information, interview three professors in your major field and three practitioners in the field.

4. One of the "Questions for Thinking and Discussion" at the end of the Dear Abby piece raises the issue of whether college is for everybody. What do you think?

   Write a paper in which you attack or defend this premise: *Every American should attempt to attend college.*

10

The College Party Scene

IN THE FAMOUS MOVIE *Animal House,* the mythical Delta fraternity is depicted as the worst Greek organization at Faber College. The Deltas are best known for their low grade point averages, their being on "double secret probation," their toga parties, and their distinctively rowdy members such as "Bluto" Blutarsky. Despite the humorous portrayal of early 1960s college life in this movie, there is a serious side that the film doesn't show. For instance, to what extent did the Deltas disturb the peace and property of other people during their parties? Did the actions of the Deltas harm the reputation and future recruitment of students by Faber College? If a sequel were made to *Animal House,* how many of the Deltas today would be paying the price for the lifestyle of their college years?

The readings in this chapter look at the 1990s college party scene from a variety of views. One article is about a fraternity that gets out of control; another is about the aftermath of spring break parties in Ft. Lauderdale, Florida. As you read these pieces, try to think about party life as you have seen it so far in college. Does it resemble what the writers of these articles are describing? What are the real purposes of party life, and what is the point at which "letting off steam" goes too far?

Hey, Give Us a Break . . .

WILLIAM BOOTH

IF THE FUTURE OF AMERICA is to be measured by the promise of its 1
youth, then let us crack open the door of Room 721 during the height
of Spring Break and enter the lair of the Betas, shall we?

To say that what we have here is the nightmare of every motel 2
maid who has ever lived is the kind of pure exaggeration that stories
about Spring Break are inevitably full of.

True, there is the matter of the cans. 3

Actually, many, many beer cans, enough aluminum to give the im- 4
pression that one has entered some kind of municipal recycling facility.

And true, here and in the motel rooms all up and down the 5
beach, there are soiled pieces of what was once laundry, and towels
with unusual patterns not placed there by their manufacturers, and
collateral pizza products in the vicinity of the various bathrooms, and
sticky substrata created in the wake of early-morning consumption of
flavored alcohols, and ashtrays so rich with organic matter that one can
almost hear new life forms evolving.

But so what? 6

The Tau Phi Betas of Southern Connecticut State University in 7
New Haven have been busy boys. They have been relaxing almost
without pause for five days. Certain niceties, such as sprucing up, have
had to wait.

For it is Spring Break, a few sunny weeks when hundreds of 8
thousands of America's college students descend on Panama City Beach
and its fading rival, Daytona Beach, to unwind, to relax, to learn what
metabolically dangerous quantities of a disturbingly brown cocktail
called the "Mudslide" can do to the human body.

Hey! The Betas have been studying hard all semester. Or at least 9
those Betas still in school. Several are now out in the real world,
perhaps making decisions about your loan applications or operating
heavy machinery in the vicinity of gas mains. So back off.

See it their way: When they left New Haven, the snow was waist 10
high. Imagine it: Cold. Dark. Awful. A gray, industrial, medieval horror
show. New Haven . . . in the winter.

Then, after 22 hours of interstate driving, after circling Washing- 11
ton twice on the loop, after the Burrito Supremes, after the Big Gulps,
after surviving the dangers of scurvy while packed into a 15-passenger
van, they arrive here, a virtual paradise, the "Redneck Riviera" of
Florida: warm, bright, summery, beautiful. Heaven, if heaven were a
tacky strip of goofy golfs and T-shirt shops.

The Betas needed this. Dammit, they earned it. And God bless 12
them for it! America need not fret. It's all going to be okay.

For these beefy American frat boys, with their Greek tattoos on 13
their butts, with their silver loop earrings, their backward baseball
caps, their crystals on leather necklaces, their boxer shorts hanging
down from the nascent beer bellies—these kids are all right.

"Spring Break! Who the hell invented it?" says Dominic Alfieri, 14
president of the Betas, as he lounges, shirtless, brown-skinned and
warm, on the beach-side deck of the Holiday Inn, quaffing a plastic
mug of beer, rubbing his gut, feeling good, looking cool and well
toned, watching his female counterparts stroll by wearing bikinis with
bluejean shorts unbuttoned and pulled halfway down their backsides,
as the deejays play UB40 covering the Sonny and Cher anthem "I Got
You Babe."

"Sleep as late as possible and drink as early as possible," explains 15
Beta brother Patrick Morrissey, in answer to the question: Why?

And indeed, the Betas are partying fairly seriously now, and to 16
understand the concept "fairly seriously," one should understand that
one Beta, after a long day of relaxing, claims he flipped his rented jet
ski, cracked his tibia, then went bungee jumping, then went to the
bars, then went to the hospital.

"A total animal," Alfieri says. 17

On the balconies, their fellow Spring Break revelers are now 18
howling. Howling and whooping are important. A few days ago, a pair
of occupants were evicted after performing sexual acts upon their
balcony to the applause of the crowds below.

A lizard scrambles across the beach-side deck. "Eat him!" Beta 19
brother Steve Soboliski says. And a visitor has absolutely no doubt that
someone might eat a living lizard if it hadn't barely escaped into the
sea oats.

This inn, which is aswarm with its own security people and 20
reputed to be tame compared with other locales, is filled to capacity
with college students. So too is almost every motel along a 10-mile
strip of bars, fast-food pits, buffet spreads and liquor emporiums called
Panama City Beach.

For years, Fort Lauderdale reigned as the supreme gathering spot 21
for Spring Break. But Lauderdale elders, pushed by year-round resi-

dents, eventually tired of the annual invasion, and so their police began to enforce laws against public drinking eight years ago. Imagine!

So the party moved to Daytona Beach, which has the advantage   22
of permitting Spring Break revelers to drive on the beach. But even Daytona Beach has its limits, and so the word is now out among the students that Daytona police aren't quite as . . . *relaxed* as the long-suffering authorities in Panama City Beach, who prefer not to arrest underage guzzlers, but instead make them pour out their beers onto the sand.

"In 1990, Daytona was totally out of control," says deejay Jon   23
Barry, who has been working Spring Break for the past few seasons. "It couldn't last. You had all these people with $200,000 condos within a beer's throw of Spring Break and they just got sick of it."

And so, even Daytona started cracking down.   24

"When a couple of people dive off the balconies here, they'll close   25
it down here too," Barry says. "No place can stand this for long."

Yes, well, right, okay, fine. The Betas' present hotel is not the first   26
the boys have occupied this week. So what? There was a little problem at the first one. A problem that involved a law enforcement official and repeated use of the word eviction and the retention of certain deposits in excess of a thousand dollars.

The Betas admit they were noisy. They admit they were messy.   27
"The owner considered a messy room a hazard," Beta brother Walter Dolan says. "If you can believe it."

They concede that they might have even been obnoxious. A piece   28
of furniture was used for purposes not intended. An air conditioner was mistakenly dislodged.

"Of course, one of the guys put his head through a door," Alfieri   29
says.

God bless the Betas!   30

True. All true. There is wretched excess, there is war-whooping   31
and public lewdness and Technicolor yawning from balconies. There is much roadside stumbling. There is scamming (using extremely lame pick-up lines), mashing (making out) and raking (sleeping with or upon others).

But it is all so controlled, so socially appropriate, so well super-   32
vised and ultimately harmless, with its designated drivers and con-doms with Nonoxynol-9 given away free at the bars (wishful thinking!), that the entire Spring Break phenomenon can be seen as something almost sweet. Decadent for sure, a trifle dangerous perhaps, but sweet.

Consider this. It is late at night, and a crowd of hundreds of   33
rowdy college students are drinking, smoking and dancing on the

beach. A pair of Panama City Beach officers, without guns, without threats, simply wade into the throng to check a couple of IDs. A few beers are quickly poured out onto the sand. A few students scatter. But it is not a bust. It is mom and dad telling the kids to turn down their stereos.

Let France have Paris. We've got the Velcro Pygmies playing really 34 loud though not distractingly good rock-and-roll at one of Panama City Beach's super-clubs with 21 bars, while nearly professional topless dancers from Tallahassee masquerading as "visual communications" majors from FSU compete in the hot bikini contest, and nearly professional collegiate athletes with decades of work on Nautilus machines enter best buns contests, while down on the beach, Sherry Campbell and her gang from Penn State are doing beer bongs.

"Yummy!" Campbell yells as her friends suck the bong dry. 35

A word about beer bongs. These are funnels with plastic tubes 36 attached that sell for $3.95 at almost every commercial establishment on Panama City Beach. Operating them is fairly simple. You fill up the funnel with beer and·then hold it over your head and then the beer floods into the mouth. Gulp. All gone.

"They've been selling like hot-cakes," says one beer-house pro- 37 prietor. "That and anything to do with condoms. Condom key chains. Condom earrings. Just a lot of condoms."

The males here maintain that the females have sexual relations 38 with them during Spring Break. Where they do this alleged activity is somewhat mysterious, given the fact that it is not unusual as in the case of Theta Phis from Indiana's DePauw University next door to this visitor, to have 25 guys in two motel rooms.

Where the intimate moments take place, according to sources, 39 include bathrooms, the beach, elevators and yes . . . in the rooms late at night while others sleep, or more accurately, lie quietly in beer-bonged coma-sleep states.

Many of the female Spring Breakers are asked if the whole holiday 40 is not more of "a guy thing" than "a girl thing," given the atmosphere of drunken frat rats chanting at hot dog-eating contests, behavior that wouldn't exactly be celebrated in, say, the corridors of the feminist studies department of the University of California at Berkeley?

"I'm appalled," says one woman from DePauw, who asked not to 41 be quoted by name. "They'd never get away with this at school. Never."

Yes. But others are less appalled. 42

"Look, a lot of guys are jerks. But a lot of them aren't," says Beth 43 Griffin of Ohio State. "It's a party. It's Spring Break. I've seen some girls screaming at good-looking guys. It's a time when everybody can go totally crazy in a controlled environment."

And indeed, for a week or two in a honky-tonk beach town filled   44
with college students and various predatory types and the luckless
Brown family from Washington, Ind., that is exactly what is happening.

Imagine some normal family showing up here at Panama City   45
Beach in March and not knowing it's Spring Break.

Meet Ken Brown, a 47-year-old firefighter, who did just that with   46
his wife and two young daughters.

"It was the war whoops that we noticed at first," says Brown.   47
Then there were the repeated, late-night, hungry calls for "Melissa."
But it's not so bad. Brown even says he finds the whole circus . . .
interesting.

"I always wondered what it was like," says Brown, who never had   48
a Spring Break, what with the need to work and the Vietnam War.
"Now I know. Sorta hedonistic, isn't it? Sorta like ancient Rome must
have been."

Questions for Thinking and Discussion

1. This article is comic, but much of the comedy is actually satire. Who
    or what do you think Booth is satirizing? Why?
2. Beth Griffin, one of the students quoted in this article, says that spring
    break is a time when students can "go totally crazy in a controlled
    environment." What do you think she means by this comment? How
    accurate is her comment? Do you think her comment justifies the
    existence of spring break?

Cities Eager to Follow Lead of Lauderdale

TAO WOOLFE

NOW THAT THE CITY HAS BROKEN THE BACK OF SPRING BREAK, other cities   1
want to learn how to get rid of their annual collegiate bacchanalia.

Mayor Jim Naugle has been invited to talk to a group of business   2
owners in Galveston. The topic: "Is There Life After Spring Break?"

Galveston is deluged with as many as 500,000 college students   3
during Mardi Gras and spring break, Mayor Barbara Crews said.

Last year, police shot a spring-breaker wielding a gun on the   4
beach, said John Caskey, president of the University Area Association,
the civic organization that invited Naugle to speak.

"We don't want this place to be perceived as a wild, violent place,"   5
Caskey said.

Larry Kelly, mayor of Daytona Beach, Fla., said he would also like   6
Naugle to come talk about taking the spring out of spring break, which
runs from mid-March to mid-April.

Daytona Beach, a city of about 65,000 inherited many of Fort   7
Lauderdale's 350,000 annual partiers in the late 1980s.

"I don't think we have as big a problem as Fort Lauderdale   8
because we have so much space," Kelley said. "On the other hand,
there is a feeling in our community that the spring breakers have taken
away our image as a family-oriented city."

Kelly and Fort Lauderdale Police Capt. Paul Urschalitz said crime   9
increases during spring break not so much because of the college
students, but because of people who come to prey on the students.

"If you look at the arrests here during spring break, you'd find   10
that 68 to 69 percent of those arrested are [drifters] from Central
Florida," Kelly said.

Daytona Beach reported eight rapes in the first part of March,   11
compared with seven during all of last March.

But Kelly said there were mixed feelings about getting rid of   12
spring break because so many businesses thrive on it. That was, and
still is, a concern in Fort Lauderdale.

Earlier this year, a group of business owners in Fort Lauderdale   13
began a campaign to lure spring breakers back. Welcome-back book-
lets were mailed to thousands of sororities, fraternities and travel
agencies.

But tourism officials and police estimate that no more than   14
20,000 spring breakers came to the city this year—the same number
as last year.

"We're going to start our campaign earlier this year and fax   15
invitations directly to the offices of college newspapers," said Don
Meyer, owner of Concierge Consultants, one of the businesses seeking
breakers.

But Naugle, tourism officials and police say spring break will   16
never return.

"Spring break was a wonderful period in our history, and now   17
we're entering another great time," said Naugle, referring to the European, Canadian and South American tourists who now come to the city
year-round.

Fort Lauderdale's former Mayor Bob Cox told students in the late   18
1980s on national TV that they were no longer welcome in the city. But
most spring-break historians credit its demise to tougher law enforcement. The city passed a law in 1986 that prohibits walking or driving
with open containers of alcohol. It was, and is, strictly enforced.
Capacity limits on clubs along the beach were also strictly enforced.

"It just wasn't any fun for them anymore," Urschalitz said.   19

The city then began to actively seek international tourists. That   20
continuing campaign was successful, according to hoteliers.

The international tourists tend to spend more money on clothes   21
and buy more expensive meals, said Francine Mason, spokeswoman
for the Greater Fort Lauderdale Convention and Visitors Bureau.

In 1992, she said, visitors spent $1 billion more than in 1985, the 22
peak year for spring break. It is estimated that students dumped about
$125 million into the local economy during the peak years. There also
have been 1 million more visitors than in 1985, she said.

Alan Chane is the owner of the Bahia Cabana Beach Resort, a   23
popular spring-break hangout.

"One night in 1983 or '84, some spring breakers threw the Coke   24
machine into the swimming pool," Chane said. "They destroyed rooms
and had no respect. I never want to go back to spring break. It would
be a giant step backwards."

Questions for Thinking and Discussion

1. This article is about the "adult" and business community's responses to
   the party scene surrounding spring break. If you or anyone you know
   has ever traveled to Florida for spring break, how justified are the

criticisms in the article? How justified do you think Ft. Lauderdale was in trying to eliminate spring break?

2. Ft. Lauderdale's steps were obviously extreme. What other actions might these cities have taken that could better have controlled the destructive aspects of partying during spring break while still permitting young people to enjoy themselves? What advice or plan would you give the mayors of these cities if you were asked to address their group?

"Party Schools" Find the Image Is Difficult to Shed as Efforts to Curb Alcohol Abuse Have Limited Success

CHRISTOPHER SHEA

THE CALIFORNIA STATE UNIVERSITY AT CHICO has been trying for years to shed its image as a "party school." For most of the 80's, Chico State was the site of Pioneer Days, a beer-soaked spring festival that turned Chico into a mecca for college-aged students from across the state.

The university banned Pioneer Days in 1987, but the partying went on. "There used to be a keg on every single porch in town every single Friday," says Chico State senior Todd McKendrick, remembering what the university was like when he arrived as a freshman. "It was a matter of just grabbing a cup and walking around."

Chico State cracked down further on out-of-control students by banning alcohol in dormitory rooms. Mr. McKendrick, who is president of the campus interfraternity council, says he finally notices a change in student behavior. Sort of.

"You don't see the festival atmosphere. People get as drunk as they ever have, but they're more responsible about it," he says.

A LONG, UPHILL BATTLE

Ambiguous gains and a long, uphill battle are the norm for colleges trying to lose reputations as havens for partying. Their administrators, like many others, have unleashed a barrage of programs to curb alcohol abuse and to narrow the gulf between students' academic work and their social lives.

Many students say some progress has been made, although some of the change has more to do with appearance than behavior. Alcohol consumption continues at stunningly high levels, students say, but there is also a growing awareness that a reputation for non-stop raging can be counterproductive.

196

Such an image, many note, is always shaped by a minority of 7
students, anyway.

"The vast majority of students are drinking in moderation, but 8
you've got a significant minority drinking at extraordinary levels,"
says Philip W. Meilman, director of the counseling center at the College of William and Mary. In a survey that Mr. Meilman helped conduct, one in five college students reported having gone on at least
three drinking binges in the past two weeks. On the other hand, the
same survey found that 53 percent of students had one drink a week
or less.

A number of forces have combined to make outrageous excess a 9
little less chic. Students say they are worried about the possibility that
their degrees may lose value in a tight job market if their college has a
reputation as a party school. Students at Central Michigan University
cited that reason whey they protested against *Playboy* magazine last fall
for scoping out their campus in preparation for a new list of the
nation's biggest party schools. *Playboy* had placed Central Michigan on
the infamous 1987 list of the "Top 40" such schools. (Chico State was
the champ in 1987.)

Central Michigan in the 1980's was home to The End of the 10
World, a bacchanalian spring celebration that often led to confrontations between drunk students and police. As recently as two years ago,
the university's annual football game with Western Michigan ended in
beery riots.

'STUDENTS HAVE TO DO MORE'

A few students spoke out after *Playboy's* list appeared, but the 11
outcry this time was far louder. Among the protesters were leaders of
several student organizations. "Students were afraid the reputation
would tarnish their degrees," says Julie Ann McMahon, president of the
Residence Hall Assembly. "I've had friends graduate and go on to job
interviews as far away as Idaho, and the interviewer will say, 'Hey, you
go to that party school.' "

Sarah Barrett, president of the Panhellenic Council at Central 12
Michigan, says: "Especially with the job markets the way they are,
students have to do more than just party."

She adds that much else has changed since the days of The End 13
of the World celebration. Under a tough new alcohol policy, for example, students not only must bring their own alcohol to fraternity and
sorority parties, but they also must check their supply with a bar-
tender, who keeps track of how much each student has drunk.

Playboy ultimately decided to scrap its new list, citing a lack of student interest.   14

Fraternities and sororities on many campuses, concerned about   15
their potential liability for alcohol-related accidents and hazing injuries, have embraced many of the reforms that colleges have been urging them to adopt for years.

A Greek system at the University of Texas that flouted university   16
rules helped land the institution on *Playboy's* list. "We used to have the reputation of being sort of a renegade system, an animal-house reputation," concedes Bryan Barksdale, president of the inter-fraternity council at Texas.

RETREAT FOR LEADERS

Today, no Texas fraternity or any of its members can even buy   17
kegs. Houses can throw only BYOB parties. New members learn about safe-sex, liability, and alcohol issues at a mandatory day-long conference. There's also a retreat for leaders of each pledge class, who deal with the issues in more depth on a two-day camping trip.

Tough university enforcement of its new rules, combined with   18
pressure from national chapters, makes reform a matter of life and death for fraternities and sororities, Mr. Barksdale says, and pledges are told to listen hard to what they learn in the university-sponsored sessions. "If people go in there with a negative attitude, about half-way through they realize the gravity of the situation that faces us as Greeks," he said.

But old habits die hard. Last month, seven members of Texas's   19
Delta Sigma Phi fraternity were suspended or expelled by the campus chapter after pledges complained that they had been "paddled," forced to eat cat food, and ordered to rub Ben-Gay ointment on their testicles.

Shedding the party-school label, say those who have attempted   20
it, often means tackling head-on a myth with a life of its own.

"Images are terribly important, as are standards," says Paul L.   21
Moore, vice-president of student affairs at Chico State.

Tired of seeming permissive, the Chico State faculty voted two   22
years ago to limit to two the number of courses students could repeat without a penalty. "A large majority of the faculty are very pained by that sort of reputation," says James M. Postma, a chemistry professor and chairman of the faculty senate.

ADVISERS IN APARTMENTS

Over a period of several years Chico State copyrighted its insignia   23
to keep entrepreneurs from capitalizing on the university's decadent

image. The Chico State Wildcats rarely used to be seen on T-shirts without mugs of beer in their hands. "Now the 'party animals' are just hanging around with nothing in their hands, looking stupid," says Robin S. Wilson, president of the university. Chico State struck a deal with owners of some local apartment buildings to place upperclass advisers in apartments to serve as liaisons to hard-to-reach off-campus students.

At Central Michigan, officials have been pressing professors to hold Friday classes as scheduled—and not to bow to students' wishes for a three-day weekend. "We were getting to the point where we had only Monday, Tuesday, and Wednesday classes," says James L. Hill, vice-president for student affairs. "To be frank, that was a better deal for the faculty than for the students." 24

Central Michigan officials have also revised admissions brochures, moving up and highlighting academic messages and dropping some pictures of students hanging out and having a good time. 25

Many observers single out the University of Miami as a case study in how to reform a party-school image. 26

A decade ago, Miami was known mainly for its football team and its sunny clime (which gave it the nickname "Suntan U"). "My best friend's sister went through here seven years ago, and that's basically what it was—basket weaving and all that," says Lisa Kagan, a peer-adviser on the Miami campus. 27

'PEER-TO-PEER COUNSELING'

Now, she says, "I think there's a much more positive atmosphere. You see signs warning about alcohol abuse when you walk around campus. Guys in fraternities are showing up to do peer-to-peer counseling." 28

Residential colleges, built between 1984 and 1989, set a new tone for the campus. Each of five residential colleges houses between 400 and 600 students. A number of faculty members and their families live in the colleges, each of which has a budget for cultural events in the range of $70,000. 29

Alletta Bowers, editor in chief of the undergraduate newspaper, the *Miami Hurricane,* says they have helped the university make important strides toward academic serious-mindedness. "You tend to see fewer parties in residential colleges because there are RA's on every floor, and that breaks it up a little bit," she says, referring to resident advisers. 30

But she adds that the campus has not left fun worshipping entirely behind. "It seems like the campus is split between people who want to go to the pool all the time, and those who take their studies seriously," she says. "It's a transitional phase." 31

The colleges serve about 40 per cent of the student body. Administrators are working on ways to let the students who commute share in some of the advantages of such a system.   32

Even elite institutions are working to change their undergraduate culture. When James O. Freedman assumed the presidency of Dartmouth College in 1987, he said he wanted to make Dartmouth a more attractive place to "creative loners and daring dreamers" who prefer solitary tasks like translating poetry and playing the cello to buddying around with their classmates.   33

Surveys have found that Dartmouth students drink more than any of their Ivy League counterparts, and Mr. Freedman and other administrators were afraid the reputation was scaring off quiet scholars.   34

A few campus wags who think translating poetry is for geeks have sneeringly dubbed the "creative loner" the "creative loser." To be sure, students have resisted some administration proposals—notably a plan to place graduate students in undergraduate dormitories to increase the intellectual level of informal discussion. Fraternities, which have been on a tight rein in recent years, are among those crying foul.   35

MORE HONORS THESES

But the proportion of seniors who do honors theses at Dartmouth has jumped from 11 per cent to 17 per cent under Mr. Freedman's tenure. Undergraduates have more opportunities to work directly with faculty members, and the college has gone to great lengths to highlight the achievements of its academic superstars, who are many.   36

Andrew Beebe, president of the Dartmouth Student Assembly, underscores why change is hard at Dartmouth, and at so many other places: "The fraternities definitely don't cultivate an intellectual atmosphere. But what kind of bar social scene does, anywhere?"   37

Questions for Thinking and Discussion

1. Do you consider your college to be a "party school"? If so, why? What specific features help place the school in that category? If not, why not?

2. In contrast to the students interviewed in Booth's article about partying in Panama Beach, the college students in this article seem extremely concerned about the reputation of their college. How important is the reputation of your college to you? How important do you think it is to your peers?

Letters from College Students

ANN LANDERS

Dear Ann Landers: You asked college students to respond to the 1
letter by Magdalene and Thomas Naylor. They cited a recent study by
the U.S. surgeon general. The study reported that the nation's 23
million college students drink nearly 4 billion cans of beer and enough
wine and liquor to bring their annual consumption of alcoholic beverages up to 34 gallons apiece.

I'm a senior at Penn State. While I'm sure there are many boozers 2
on this campus, the majority of the students are too busy with their
workload and part-time jobs to get bombed and fool around with
drugs. This school is expensive and hard to get into, and the standards
are high. You either produce or you are out of here.

—R.D.

Dear R.D.: The mail resulting from the column has been heavy 3
and fascinating. Although I received a variety of responses, the next
letter reflects the viewpoint of the majority who wrote:

From Ann Arbor, Mich.: The Naylors are right on. Please, dear 4
Ann, don't add to the problem by playing it down or denying its
existence. I have had to change dorms twice in order to get away from
the nightly partying and incessant noise.

Los Angeles, the University of Southern California: The Nay- 5
lors know what they are talking about. But in all fairness, Ann, the
freshmen are the worst. For many, it's the first time they have been
away from home, able to do as they please. They can't handle the
freedom and they go a little nuts. I know this is true because I was one
of them.

Dallas: Please don't name my school but it is religion-based and 6
supposed to be pretty strict. The rules are: no alcohol on the premises
and no sex in the dorms. If my parents knew what went on here they
would yank me back home in no time flat.

San Diego State: The Naylors are right, but I don't think it's 7
different outside of school. College is for learning about life as well as
what's in the books. It is also a last crack at hell-raising.

Boise, Idaho: This comes right out of the *Seattle Post-Intelligencer,* 8
and it didn't shock me in the least: "In Moscow, Idaho, more than 80
percent of the students treated at Gritman Medical Center's emergency

room at night are alcohol-related cases. On weekends there are at least 10 a night. Alcohol has been involved in five student deaths this fall, four of which involved drunken driving."

New Haven: I realize any letter with a New Haven postmark is ⁹ immediately suspect but this one is for real. At Yale, like anyplace else, you find your own crowd. There's something for everybody. There may be heavy drugs here, but I haven't seen any. What I do see is a lot of wine and vodka but not among serious students and campus leaders.

Atlanta: I'm a sophomore at Georgia Tech. My first night in the ¹⁰ dorm during freshman orientation, I got a blistering headache from the aroma of marijuana. Many a night we had a friend sleeping on our couch because his roommate was having noisy sex and he couldn't sleep.

Chicago: Get real. There's booze, pot, sex and anything you want ¹¹ on any campus in the country. Like everything else in life, people are free to choose what they want. After a month of acting like an animal, I decided it was no fun at all, just foolishness, but I had to go through it to get to where I am now. It was part of growing up.

Dear Readers: If you want a real picture of what's happening, ask ¹² the people in the middle of the action. I did and they told me.

Questions for Thinking and Discussion

1. These letters written by college students from across the country are intended to show a broad spectrum of attitudes about party habits at their schools. Which of the attitudes best reflects your own personal set of beliefs?

2. The San Diego State student seems to justify alcohol and drug use by arguing that college "is a last crack at hell-raising." Furthermore, this writer argues that college is "for learning about life as well as what's in the books"; therefore, because drug and alcohol abuse exist outside college, they should be part of a student's education. How logical do you find this argument?

College Students and Alcohol

ANN LANDERS

Dear Ann Landers: Thank you for encouraging readers to recognize that alcohol consumption by college students is a serious threat to the nation's health and safety. These are the young people who will be running our country in a few years, and we can't afford to lose them.

Your reply to "A Former Party Animal" cited some alarming facts about college drinking. You pointed out that the total amount college students in the United States spend on booze is $5.5 billion a year. What does that huge amount of money buy? Well, here are some startling figures:

One study found that alcohol consumption is one of the major reasons for absenteeism among college students. That same study showed that 25 percent of student deaths are associated with alcohol. Also, alcohol is involved in 90 percent of campus rapes. According to the 1991 College Alcohol Survey, 70 percent of administrators said alcohol is a major contributor to campus violence and is a factor in 40 percent of academic problems.

Regarding our hopes for tomorrow: More than 7 percent of this year's freshman class—more than 120,000 students—will drop out because of drinking. Between 240,000 and 360,000 of our current 12 million college students will eventually die of alcohol-related causes.

With the help of the Surgeon General Antonia R. Novello, the U.S. Center for Substance Abuse Prevention has developed "Put on the Brakes," an educational and informational campaign designed to help administrators, faculty and students create safer, healthier and more challenging environments at our institutions of higher learning and in their communities.

—Vivian L. Smith, M.S.W., acting director,
Center for Substance Abuse Prevention

Dear Vivian Smith: While many readers will be shocked by these statistics, they are not surprising to me.

My mail is an unerring indicator of what is happening in our society. I have been aware for several years that alcoholism among 16- to 28-year-olds is a serious public health problem.

While some preach moderation, I'm for total abstinence. Those
who don't touch the stuff won't have to worry about how much is too
much or when to call it quits.

Questions for Thinking and Discussion

1. Landers suggests that, as far as she is concerned, the only reasonable
   answer for college students is "total abstinence" from drinking. She
   goes on to say that those "who don't touch the stuff won't have to worry
   about how much is too much or when to call it quits." How reasonable
   do you find her solution for people in your generation at college? What
   other solutions might you pose?
2. Assume that you were going to give a speech to fellow college students
   urging them to control their alcohol use. If you were going to select *two
   of the statistics* given in Smith's letter to use in this speech, which two
   would be most convincing? Why?

Writing Projects

1. In the final letter to Ann Landers in this chapter, a student writes:

   After a month of acting like an animal, I decided it was no fun at all, just foolishness, but I had to go through it to get where I am now. It was part of growing up.

   In what ways do this student's experiences resemble your own at college? Write a paper comparing or contrasting this student's party scene experiences with your own.

2. In his article in this chapter, Christopher Shea cites a survey by Philip Meilman, director of the counseling center at the College of William and Mary, that seems to show that there is a small core of heavy drinkers and a large group of very moderate drinkers. For instance, Meilman found that one out of every five students "reported having gone on at least three drinking binges in the past two weeks." However, 53 percent of students in the study reported that they "had one drink a week or less."

   Working with a research team of five classmates, randomly survey fifty students at your campus to see how similar Meilman's survey information represents the situation at your college. Prepare a paper in which you show your findings and then try to explain why your study would result in findings similar to or different from those in Meilman's research.

3. Booth's article is a largely negative portrayal of Greek life on campus. In truth, a good many fraternities and sororities have tried very hard to be positive organizations working for the good of their campuses. Write a paper arguing the thesis that a certain fraternity or sorority of your choice is a positive force on your campus.

4. Though none of the writers in this chapter have said so, parties are by no means a new idea. In fact, parties have been part of the fabric of college life for centuries. What is their real purpose? If an administrator at your school were about to ban all parties connected in any way with the college, how would you respond? Write a paper to be delivered to such a college administrator that defends the need of parties to be permitted on campus. At the same time, provide this administrator with ways to carry out parties without serious destruction of humans or property.

11

College Athletics

IT IS NO SECRET that many controversies have plagued college athletics in the 1990s, but these controversies are really nothing new. According to Frederick Rudolph in his book *The American College and University: A History,* during its early development in the nineteenth century, college athletics was often criticized because it conflicted with the functions that colleges saw themselves serving.

The readings in this section deal with some major problems facing intercollegiate athletics in the United States in the 1990s. As you read these sections, try to look at the broad picture and ask yourself some of these questions: What purposes do intercollegiate athletics serve on a college or university campus? How are problems related to those purposes? Who (if anyone) is at fault? Is the entire student body (men and women) being treated fairly by the current system of intercollegiate athletics? Are there any reasonable ways to reform problem areas in the system?

College Sports, Inc.: The Athletic Department Vs. the University

Murray Sperber

A GENERATION AGO, when I was an undergraduate at Purdue, college sports were on the margin of university life. Today, at Purdue and many other schools, athletic departments are much larger in size and scope, and they make greater demands on their institutions than ever before. Although I am a fan of college sports, I have long wondered whether and to what extent their increasing importance complements or corrupts the academic mission of their host universities.

After intensively researching these questions for a number of years, I came to one absolute conclusion: intercollegiate athletics, especially the big-time version, has become College Sports Inc., a huge commercial entertainment conglomerate, with operating methods and objectives totally separate from, and often opposed to, the educational aims of the schools that house its franchises. Moreover, because of its massive hypocrisy and fiscal irresponsibility, College Sports Inc. places many colleges and universities under the constant threat of scandal and other sports-induced maladies.

A great number of myths shield college sports from careful scrutiny and burden any discussion of the subject. The following refutations of the most common of these myths should introduce readers to the realities of College Sports Inc.

MYTH: *College sports are part of the educational mission of American colleges and universities.*

REALITY: The main purpose of college sports is commercial entertainment. Within most universities with big-time sports programs, the athletic department operates as a separate business and has almost no connection to the academic departments and functions of the school—even the research into and teaching of sports is done by the physical education department.

The reason why elite athletes are in universities has nothing to do with the educational missions of their schools. Athletes are the only group of students recruited for commercial entertainment purposes—not for academic reasons—and they are the only students who go through school on grants based not on educational aptitude but on their talent and potential as commercial entertainers.

> When you go to college, you're not a student-athlete but an athlete-student. Your main purpose is not to be an Einstein but a ballplayer, to generate some money, put people in the stands. Eight or 10 hours of your day are filled with basketball, football. The rest of your time, you're got to motivate yourself to make sure you get something back.
>
> —Isiah Thomas, former
> Indiana University basketball
> player, now a Detroit Pistons star

The system does not make sense. If colleges searched for and awarded scholarships to upcoming rock stars so that they could entertain the university community and earn money for their schools through concerts and tours, educational authorities and the public would call this "a perversion of academic values" and would not stand for it. Yet every year American institutions of higher education hand out more than 100,000 full or partial athletic scholarships, worth at least $500 million, for reasons similar to those that would justify grants to rock performers.

MYTH: *College athletes are amateurs, and their athletic scholarships do not constitute professional payment for playing sports.*

REALITY: A school gives an athlete a "full ride" grant worth up to $20,000 a year in exchange for the athlete's services in a commercial entertainment venture, that is, playing on one of the school's sports teams. If the athlete fails to keep his or her part of the agreement and quits the team, the institution withdraws the financial package—even if the athlete stays in school as a regular student. Moreover, once the athlete uses up his or her playing eligibility, the school is under no obligation to continue to pay for the athlete's education—even though the athlete may be many semesters from graduation. Most schools stop the grants.

In its *NCAA Manual,* the National Collegiate Athletic Association lists the "benefits" of an athletic scholarship: free tuition and fees, room and board, and textbooks, as well as free tutoring, athletic medical insurance, rehabilitation expenses, on-campus career counseling, and advice from nonuniversity professionals. The athlete's freebies cost regular students thousands of dollars a year. Indeed, given escalating tuition and other school costs in the 1990s, the cost to a regular student for what an athlete receives in exchange for playing on a school's athletic team will soon reach $25,000 a year.

At one time in NCAA history, athletic scholarships were given for four years and, once awarded, could not be revoked. In 1973, under pressure from coaches who wanted greater control over their players and the ability to "fire" them for poor athletic performances, the NCAA instituted one-year scholarships, renewable annually at the athletic department's discretion. [11]

Under their current terms, athletic scholarships appear indistinguishable from what the Internal Revenue Service (IRS) calls "barter payment for services rendered." According to IRS rules, "If you [the athlete] exchange your property and/or services of another [a school's athletic scholarship], you have taxable income," and you are a professional. [12]

Ironically, the NCAA itself endorses the concept of athletic scholarships as noncash payments when it forbids various "practices [that] constitute 'pay' for participation in intercollegiate athletics," among them, "complimentary admissions [to sports events] in excess of four per student-athlete per contest." Why does the fifth "admission" become "pay," whereas the first four are proof of a student-athlete's amateur standing? The IRS should consider athletic scholarship holders professionals and tax them accordingly. [13]

MYTH: *For college athletes, the opportunity of a university education is as important as playing intercollegiate sports.* [14]

REALITY: Formal and informal studies of why athletes choose colleges indicate that they make their selections primarily for athletic—not academic—reasons and that they consider universities as the pathway to professional sports. Specifically, top high school athletes want to play for a college coach with a winning record, on a team with a winning tradition, in the hope of receiving the best preparation for professional or Olympic careers. In addition, they want to "start" as freshmen and to receive maximum media exposure during the college careers. They believe that, if these ambitions are satisfied, they will be pro draft choices of Olympic team selections and acquire lucrative professional contracts. How coaches make use of these ambitions was explained by basketball's Larry Brown: "Every kid I recruited for college felt that he had an opportunity to play in the NBA, and I liked them to have those expectations. So they give themselves—their trust—to you from day one, hoping to reach that goal." [15]

That very few college athletes ever fulfill their dream of professional sports is irrelevant to the dream's power over them and to its role in shaping their college careers, especially their willingness to devote as many as 60 hours a week to their sports and their frequent inability to sustain a serious course of studies. Jim Walden, head football coach at Iowa State University, says that in his sport "not more than 20% of [16] the football players go to college for an education. And that may be a high figure."

MYTH: *What about those athletes like Bill Bradley and Tom McMillan who were outstanding in sports and in the classroom? Don't they prove that the system works?* 17

REALITY: In any large sample of people in any endeavor, there are always a few at the high end of the bell-shaped curve. The renown of Bradley and McMillan successes in sports *and* in academics suggests that intercollegiate athletics is a system that works for only a few. No one bothers to name all the outstanding Americans who were once top college students but not athletes; they are not unusual, and higher education is supposed to produce them. 18

Harry Edwards, a sociologist at the University of California, Berkeley, has done extensive research on the time constraints on college athletes and concludes that NCAA Division I-A football players spend up to 60 hours a week during the season on their sport; basketball players spend 50 hours a week. Edwards succinctly explains the time dilemma that confronts most college athletes: "Education is activist. You have to be actively involved in sports 50 hours a week, maybe living in pain, you can't be actively involved [in your education]." 19

Edwards' comment also hints at the unrecorded hours that athletes spend on their sports: the time in recovery, the hours passed getting over headaches and other pains acquired in scrimmages, games, and so on. One former college basketball player described life under a coach who ran hard practices: "It was all you could do to drag yourself back to the dorm each day. By the time you ate and got back to your room, it was 8:30, and all you could think about was getting your weary bones in bed and getting some sleep. Who had time to study?" This player had placed second in his high school graduating class and had intended to prepare for medical school, but he had been channeled instead into physical education. He did not graduate from college. 20

If the coach demands that player spend 50 or more hours a week on a sport, an athlete cannot refuse—unless he or she wants to drop the sport and lose the athletic scholarship. And most athletes, because of their dream of making it to the pros or the Olympics, willingly participate in full-time sports regimens. Football and men's basketball programs are notorious for the time they require and the physical demands that they make on players, but many nonrevenue sports also require constant sacrifices from athletes. A recent NCAA survey noted that "women basketball players at major colleges spend as much time at their sport as their male counterparts." However, university authorities believe that a full-time student who is pursuing a meaningful 21 degree should devote at least 40 to 50 hours a week to attending classes and studying—and that students who are ill-prepared for college, including large numbers of athletes, should spend significantly more time than that on their studies.

Even in an athlete's off-season, the time required for sports does not drop appreciably. A former athletic director at Southern Illinois University explained that, for off-seasons, many coaches have "the mentality of 'more is better' . . . the longer the out-of-season practice and the longer the weightlifting session, the better." In addition, the new high-tech machines, rather than cutting time from an athlete's training, have added to it. Coaches now demand longer hours on the Nautilus to increase strength and conditioning, and athletes are required to spend more time viewing videotapes of their own and their opponents' performance.

To put in perspective the amount of time that a college athlete spends on a sport, consider that the federal government allows a regular student receiving a work/study grant to spend *a maximum of 20 hours a week on his or her university job* (e.g., shelving books in the library). The government's rationale is that more than 20 hours a week cuts into the amount of time needed for a normal course of study by a full-time student. Nevertheless, according to Harry Edwards' figures, intercollegiate athletes regularly exceed this federal guideline by as much as 200%.

MYTH: *College sports provide an excellent opportunity for black youngsters to get out of the ghetto and to contribute to American society.*

REALITY: Harry Edwards claims that many athletic programs treat black athletes as "gladiators," bringing them to campus only to play sports, not to obtain an education. And the low graduation rates of black college athletes support Edwards' thesis. From 1972–73 through 1985, Memphis State University, with men's basketball teams that were predominantly black, *did not graduate a single black player;* from the early to the mid-1980s, 4% of the black players on the men's basketball team at the University of Georgia graduated.

Most schools with major athletic programs, and many schools with smaller ones, recruit black athletes much more intensively and systematically than they do regular black students. In addition, some schools fund their "black gladiators" by diverting money from such scholarship sources as the Basic Educational Opportunity Grants, earmarked for academically motivated minority students.

The final irony of the "black gladiator" situation is that many schools, instead of trying harder to locate and educate future black teachers, doctors, business leaders, and so on, spend large sums of

We've got the deal spotted. If they [athletic programs] don't get enough money, they steal it out of the education budget.

—Don Tyson, chairman of Tyson Foods and a member of the Arkansas Higher Education Committee, commenting on the multimillion-dollar athletic department deficits in his state

money recruiting and then maintaining in college a group of black youths who are often the least prepared and the least interested in acquiring college educations.

MYTH: *College sports are incredibly profitable, earning huge sums of money for American colleges and universities.*   28

REALITY: One of the best-kept secrets about intercollegiate   29
athletics—well-guarded because athletic departments are extremely reluctant to open their financial books—is that most college sports programs lose money. If profit is defined according to ordinary business practices, of the 802 members of the NCAA, the 493 members of the National Association for Intercollegiate Athletics (NAIA), and the more than 1,050 junior colleges, only 10 to 20 athletic programs make a consistent (albeit small) profit. In any given year, another 20 to 30 break even or do a little better. All the rest—more than 2,300 institutions—lose anywhere from a few dollars to millions of dollars annually on college sports.

Questions for Thinking and Discussion

1. How many of Sperber's "myths" about college athletics are you familiar with? Though Sperber doesn't provide reasons, why do you suppose Americans believe those myths? Have these myths intentionally been invented and spread by people? What do you think would happen if large numbers of people connected with universities began to challenge these myths, just as Sperber has?

2. Sperber is highly critical of the role of athletics in colleges today, but he also ignores the positives. What *positive* contributions can athletics make to the entire college or university setting? Do you think the positives outweigh the negatives?

UNLV Basketball Star Suspended After Review of His English Paper

Douglas Lederman

The University of Nevada at Las Vegas suspended its top basket- 1
ball player last week after determining that a tutor had written part of
an English paper for him.

University officials insisted that they had broken no National 2
Collegiate Athletic Association rules in certifying the senior player, J. R.
Rider, as eligible to compete last fall.

But they acknowledged that the revelation about Mr. Rider was 3
another black eye for a sports program desperate to shed its image as
a renegade.

Nevada-Las Vegas suspended Mr. Rider after an internal re- 4
view found sufficient evidence that he may not have deserved a
passing grade in a summer-school correspondence course he took
at a community college last summer. Mr. Rider's grade in the English course was based at least partially on a paper that a tutor had
helped him write, and passing the course allowed him to continue
playing.

That revelation was one of several reported by the *Las Vegas* 5
Review-Journal this month. The newspaper first reported that an instructor at the community college had felt pressured by UNLV coaches
and sports officials to give Mr. Rider a passing grade. After that story,
Nevada-Las Vegas released a statement saying its own review had
found no improper behavior.

A few days later, however, the *Review-Journal* published a report 6
questioning whether Mr. Rider had done his own work for the course.
Accompanying the story were two pages from an assignment, which
appeared to have been done in different handwriting. Three assignments also misspelled Mr. Rider's given name, Isaiah.

The *Review-Journal* also disclosed that Mr. Rider had received 7
credit for a course on premenstrual syndrome.

After the second story, Nevada-Las Vegas again looked into Mr. 8
Rider's status, said David Chambers, the university's athletics compli-
ance officer. The university's inquiry was hampered, its officials said,
because Mr. Rider's file at the community college had been emptied—
by whom, they did not know.

COMPELLED TO ACT

Based on the *Review-Journal's* findings and the university's own   9
evidence, Mr. Chambers said, Nevada-Las Vegas officials felt obliged to
suspend Mr. Rider before last week's games in the National Invitation
Tournament. Mr. Rider is expected to enter the National Basketball
Association draft in April.

Mr. Chambers said the university believed it had not violated   10
NCAA rules. Last fall, when it certified Mr. Rider to play, Mr. Chambers
said, it had no evidence suggesting that the player should not have
been eligible. As soon as that evidence emerged this month, Mr.
Chambers said, the university suspended Mr. Rider.

Robert C. Maxson, the president of Nevada-Las Vegas, said the   11
university had asked Joseph A. Malik, executive director of the Commission on Colleges of the Northwest Association of Schools and
Colleges, to look into the broader issues surrounding the Rider case.

"We may not have broken the rules, but the question is, Was it   12
sound educational practice?" said Mr. Maxson. "I think that's what we
have to look at in this situation. I want to know if this was an isolated
incident or a pattern. And if we've got problems, let's fix them."

For the Runnin' Rebel basketball program, the suspension of Mr.   13
Rider was the latest in a long line of public embarrassments.

President Maxson was locked for years in a power struggle with   14
Jerry Tarkanian, the basketball coach, who was forced to resign last
March. Mr. Tarkanian, long watched by NCAA investigators, was finally done in by his 1987 recruitment of Lloyd Daniels, a high-school
star who read at the sixth-grade level. The NCAA is weighing about 30
charges of improper recruiting and other violations.

Ironically, Nevada-Las Vegas plans to release in the coming weeks   15
a set of proposals for revamping the oversight of its sports program.
They include standards for monitoring the academic progress of its
athletes, designed to prevent problems like Mr. Rider's.

Questions for Thinking and Discussion

1. In this news report, Lederman describes a situation that is probably all
   too common. What forces do you think might cause an athlete to try
   to cheat his or her way through college? Which of the issues discussed
   in Sperber's article can help explain the pressures on athletes to practice
   unethical behavior?

2. Based on your experiences and observations, how typical is this alleged situation? In other words, are athletes often given exceptional chances to pass in order to stay eligible? What actual situations can you think of as further examples?

Two Dreams Cross Paths in College

HARRY BLAUVELT

OHIO STATE TAILBACK ROBERT SMITH, a gifted student-athlete who   1
wants to become a doctor, will make his moves under a media microscope beginning Saturday when the Buckeyes open practice.

Last August, with a superb freshman season behind him, the   2
outspoken runner hit a nerve when he quit the team, accusing his
coaches of emphasizing athletics over academics. He returned to football in March but hasn't softened his stance on the system.

"College athletes are like indentured servants," says Smith, paus-   3
ing during a recent dinner at a restaurant near campus. "Amateurism
is a myth. If colleges are going to treat sports like big business, let's take
it all the way and pay the players."

Smith's story attracted national attention, triggering charges that   4
college athletics are running amok.

"When you leave the field, coaches don't care how you're do-   5
ing in class unless it becomes important to them because there is a
problem—then they'll act," says Smith, 20, a pre-med major with a 3.1
grade-point average (scale of 4.0). "But I don't think that's just an Ohio
State thing."

Dr. John Frank, former standout tight end for Ohio State and the   6
San Francisco 49ers, agrees.

"Go anywhere in the country and you'll see athletics empha-   7
sized, whether it's Ohio State or Stanford or a Division III school," says
Frank, friend and mentor to Smith. "That's not any big surprise—it's
not a perfect world. But you can't blame colleges for emphasizing
athletics.

"Athletes have to seize the opportunity to get an education, and   8
that's what Robert has done. He's a good kid, he stands up for his
principles and he's a tremendous asset to Ohio State."

Smith, 6-2, 202, is one of the hardest workers on the team, and   9
arguably the best-conditioned. Although not all his teammates agree
with what he did, most respect his courage. He is strong-willed,
idealistic, confident—qualities that sometimes rub people the wrong
way.

"I don't think I'm bigger than Ohio State football, but Ohio State   10
is not going to dictate my life, either," says Smith, whose first game will
be Sept. 5 against Louisville. "I know there is lingering animosity. But

if I know something is wrong, I won't back down and that bothers a lot of people."

"There is a stereotype that premier athletes . . . don't care about their intellectual development," says Richard Lapchick, director of the Center of the Study of Sport in Society at Northeastern University. "But here is a young man who says academics are his priority. That sends a strong message." 11

For Smith, the term student-athlete is not an oxymoron. Pounding would-be tacklers is not as important to him as hitting the books. 12

Questions for Thinking and Discussion

1. This news report about Robert Smith when he was still in college illustrates the frustrations some athletes feel who want more from their time on scholarships than just athletics. Based on your experiences, is Robert Smith the exception or the rule at your college or university? How?

2. Smith offers a solution to the "indentured servant" status he sees college athletes serving: "If colleges are going to treat sports like big business, let's take it all the way and pay the players." How do you regard this solution to the problem?

Leveling the Playing Field in Athletics

KATHY SWINDLE

A LITTLE MORE THAN A YEAR AGO, Donna Lopiano walked away from   1
her 17-year job as women's athletic director at the University of Texas
at Austin and became executive director of the Women's Sports Foundation in New York, an organization formed in 1975 to promote and
encourage women in sports.

During her stint at UT, Ms. Lopiano was credited with estab-   2
lishing the women's athletic department as one of the best in the
country.

While some miss her aggressive presence at UT, Ms. Lopiano says   3
she took the foundation job because she feels she can accomplish a
greater good: promoting sports for women and raising funds for female
athletes nationwide. She regularly speaks on behalf of the foundation
across the country. Last week, Ms. Lopiano, 46, spoke in Dallas at the
Association for Women Journalists' annual banquet. We asked her to
discuss the changes taking place in women's sports, as well as what she
perceives as continued inequities:

Q: **You once said that athletics is a right for boys and a privi-**   4
lege for girls. Has this outdated mode of thinking begun to change,
in your opinion?

A: I think it has already. I think the people who are balking   5
under TITLE IX (the federal statute that outlaws educational discrimination based on sex) are the dinosaurs, the old guys. The people
who are bringing the (discrimination) lawsuits now are the dads
on behalf of their daughters. This is the first generation of fathers
to grow up thinking that their daughters had the same opportunities. All of a sudden the daughter wants to play sports and somebody tells her she can't play and dad's mad. Everybody knows that
sports is where you gain confidence and learn to set goals. The world
has changed and the athletic dinosaurs aren't willing to acknowledge
it.

Q: **What are the advantages, both physically and otherwise,**   6
of encouraging our daughters to participate in sports?

A: In high school, girls who participate in sports are 80 percent   7
less likely to get pregnant and 90 percent less likely to use drugs.

They're three times as likely to graduate from high school. The teen-age girl who participates in sports reduces her lifelong risk of breast cancer. Research shows that they (female athletes) have higher levels of self-confidence, higher levels of self-esteem and are less prone to depression.

Women realize that what's at stake is their health. Men play sports, but women are much more eclectic. They grew up without a sports focus. Women lift weights, they exercise, they'll fit sports and fitness around their lives in a much more eclectic way than men will. As people become more and more educated (about fitness benefits) it becomes more and more ludicrous for coaches to say that football is more important than gender equity.

Q: **Why do girls drop out of sports more often than do boys? How can we change this?**

A: One reason is opportunity. Look at girls playing Little League baseball—girls don't play after Little League. They're not as likely to receive support—both financial and parental support. Parents are typically neutral on sports (for girls) but they're positive on sports for boys. They're encouraging their boys to go out and throw a ball, and the girls are receiving Barbie dolls. Unless the girls take the initiative, these things don't happen. They don't see their pictures in the newspapers, they don't hear about their sports exploits on the TV or radio. The people who control the media are 97 percent men. They still devalue women's sports.

We're caught in the middle of a massive change where all of the changes haven't caught up yet. The athletic directors are backward, the media is backward. We're witnessing a significant transformation period. Any change of this magnitude is accompanied by resistance. That's part of the change process. I don't think there's going to be a turning back this time.

Q: **How did you become involved in sports? Was there someone in your life who encouraged you?**

A: I had a family that was not tied to stereotypical views as to what girls could do. It was an expectation that I would go to college and be as successful as my brother. I wanted to be a pitcher for the New York Yankees. It didn't occur to me that being a girl would prevent me. I was drafted No. 1 in the Little League but they wouldn't let me play because I was a girl. I rationalized that maybe I wasn't big enough to play ball.

No matter where I speak around the country, women are always coming up to me and saying, "You know, I wanted to play second for the Cubs." And that's the first time they've said it. We've completely erased the aspirations of women in sports.

Q: **You're known as someone who speaks her mind, is suc-**   15
cessful, and champions the causes of women. Any one of these
qualities would cause some people to dislike you. What are your
thoughts about this?

A: If you don't say what's right, then you condone what's wrong.   16
It's that simple. Behind everything you do, there has to be some notion
that this is the right thing to do.

Questions for Thinking and Discussion

1. This article, an interview with one of the most influential college
   women's sports figures in America, raises the question of whether
   women receive fair treatment in college athletics. Lopiano believes very
   much that participating in college sports is advantageous to women.
   What advantages do you find beyond those that Lopiano speaks of?

2. Lopiano also indicates that the attitudes of college women and men
   toward athletics differ:

   Women realize that what's at stake is their health. Men play sports, but
   women are much more eclectic. They grew up without a sports focus.
   Women lift weights, they exercise, they'll fit sports and fitness around their
   lives in a much more eclectic way than men will.

   What does she mean by these claims? How accurate do you think they
   are for most men and women at your college?

"The System" Feeds on Sports Mania

TOMMY DENTON

> Games played with the ball, and others of that nature, are too violent for the body and stamp no character on the mind.
>
> Thomas Jefferson, Aug. 19, 1785

CONSIDERABLE IRONY SURROUNDS THAT QUOTATION from a letter written by Jefferson, founder of the prestigious University of Virginia, to Peter Carr more than two centuries ago. [1]

If the gentleman from Monticello could return and see how the nation he helped to conceive has fallen under the maniacal sway of games played with the ball, he would most likely begin drafting a new version of the Declaration of Independence. [2]

Jefferson's beloved university at Charlottesville is still prestigious academically, but like many other good schools, it has sullied its sterling reputation by compromising a part of its scholastic soul for the allure of collegiate/professional sport. [3]

Dick Schultz, former athletic director at Virginia, resigned last week as executive director of the National Collegiate Athletic Association. An NCAA investigation accused him of condoning illicit loans to student athletes during his tenure at Virginia in the mid-1980s. [4]

He denied the charges, but felt that all his work to elevate the NCAA would be lost if his remaining would leave any hint of doubt about the integrity of the organization. [5]

By most accounts, Schultz was the respected, squeaky-clean director who would lead the NCAA out of the muck of big-bucks scandals in recent years. Even he was not immune, though, and that raised a question in the minds of athletic directors, coaches, university presidents and sports columnists across the land: Can "The System" be cleaned up? [6]

Of course it can't be "cleaned up." There's too much invested in keeping the system accelerating toward ever-higher thresholds of athletic "excellence"—however subtle and sophisticated the graft and corruption may have to become to get there. [7]

College sport—primarily football and basketball because they are the big money-generators—is to "amateur student-athlete" as Serbian ethnic cleansing is to territorial dispute resolution. The object is to win, and hang the disagreeable side effects. [8]

222

Systems are created by people, who structure their systems ac-   9
cording to the values that give them meaning as people. The people
who create the college athletics system value winning above everything
else, and they are willing to pay for it.

They will pay huge salaries for athletic directors who will raise   10
enormous amounts of money for stadiums, domed arenas and state-of-
the-art training facilities. They will also pay huge salaries for coaches
who will be expected to win.

They will open "opportunities" to the athletes themselves and   11
create in their young minds an attitude of entitlement to all the material splendor that life has to offer.

Never mind that too many of them will never meet the intellec-   12
tual and ethical standards of the academy, much less actually graduate
with a degree that will have far more meaning in 20 years than the
yellowed clippings of "big games" that the rest of the world long ago
will have forgotten.

In the process of supporting this system, the university has be-   13
come a harlot, shamelessly tendering its academic integrity in exchange for currying favor with contributing alumni and for a place in
the entertainment sun.

Most everyone recognizes the hypocrisy within the present ar-   14
rangement. Those who favor "The System" wish to eliminate its hypocrisy by shedding the pretense and paying the players outright, as the
formerly amateur Olympic Games is now doing.

That response seems to strike at the core of the values of "The   15
System": Money talks and amateurs walk. Calculate the price of "success" and cut the deal. That's the American way, isn't it?

The rest of us, alas, simply watch the spectacle, knowing that the   16
corruption cannot and will not stop until "The System" is completely
dismantled. We also know that will not happen because of the American mania to pay any price to be entertained and stimulated to the
primal core.

Robert F. Kennedy, in a speech during his brief, ill-fated 1968   17
presidential campaign, called on his compatriots to re-examine some
collective assumptions. His comments struck a familiar chord about
misplaced values in a nation caught up in self-indulgent calculation
and distracted from what is truly important.

Kennedy's words of 25 years ago are equally relevant today: 18

"The gross national product counts the destruction of redwoods   19
. . . napalm and nuclear weapons . . . television programs which glo-
rify violence to sell toys to our children. Yet the gross national product
does not allow for the health of our children, the quality of their
education, or the joy of their play. It does not include the beauty of our

poetry . . . the integrity of our public officials . . . neither our wit nor our courage, neither our wisdom nor our learning, neither our compassion nor our devotion to country. It measures everything, in short, except that which makes life worthwhile; and it can tell us everything about America—except why we are proud to be Americans."

Questions for Thinking and Discussion

1. Like Sperber, Denton is obviously very pessimistic about college athletics. Unlike Sperber, though, he offers a solution: The "system" can't merely be "cleaned up" but instead it must be "dismantled." What do you think about this solution? Is it viable? How might it be carried out? What effects would such a solution produce?

2. Denton shows nonparticipants (the general student body, other fans, parents) as mere spectators who can only "watch the spectacle, knowing that the corruption will not stop until 'the system' is completely dismantled." In contrast to what Denton says, offer a course of action that might be followed by nonparticipants to challenge corruption in college athletics.

Sack Athletic Scholarships

ALLEN BARRA

"OF THE MAKING OF REFORMS," Confucius is said to have said, "there is no end." With regard to college sports, he might have added: Especially when the reforms are half-hearted.

If the N.C.A.A. is serious about making reforms in college sports, there's one sweeping measure that is simple, fair and economically advantageous: Do away with athletic scholarships.

Scarcely a week goes by without news of some fresh scandal involving the football programs at our major schools. Steroids at Notre Dame. Chaos at Oklahoma. The off-campus activities of the Miami Hurricanes alone could have kept Don Johnson and the crew on "Miami Vice" busy for another season. And how serious is the N.C.A.A. about solving these problems?

The N.C.A.A.'s usual response, when it gets around to taking action, is to punish thousands of students and student athletes by barring their school's teams from TV and post-season competition. Of course students and student athletes are easier to punish than coaches and administrators; they have no rights.

In a recent issue of *Sports Illustrated* the writer Douglas Looney suggested that a return to one-platoon football would cut the average school's athletic budget by nearly 25 percent, largely because the N.C.A.A.'s current limit of 95 scholarships per year could be reduced to 69.

Why not go a step further? Since most of the schools that compete in big-time football would lose money if not for TV, why not save everyone a lot more money by eliminating athletic scholarships entirely?

Today's college athletes are professionals in every significant way except one: they don't get paid. They are there not to learn but to make money for the colleges. The money is a fact of life and can't be done away with so long as millions of alumni and fans are willing to pay for tickets and turn on their TV's. What's to be done short of turning 18-year-olds into legitimate professionals?

For starters, colleges can get out of the business of being a cost-free minor league for the National Basketball Association and National Football League. The elimination of athletic scholarships would mean that football and basketball players would be ill prepared for pro sports. But why should that concern colleges?

Colleges would be forced to try something new: to field teams 9
comprising college students, not future pro draft picks. There would
be no more preferential treatment for "scholar-athletes." Nevertheless,
more athletes would graduate because they would be entering college
as students, not athletes.

Without athletic scholarships, we'd really find out if students 10
from Miami play football better than students from Notre Dame. More
to the point, we'd find out if Miami and Notre Dame, once their
recruiting machines are gone, are really better than, say, Northwestern
and Georgia Tech.

The primary objections to this come, as you'd expect, from the 11
coaches and N.C.A.A. administrators. It would cut down on revenues,
they say. But why? Even if the networks paid less for a game played by
nonscholarship athletes, the schools would still earn big bucks; certainly more than it would have cost them to field the teams.

The second objection is stickier; the elimination of athletic schol- 12
arships would mean fewer minority—mostly black—athletes. Though
this would be true, at least for a while, it wouldn't necessarily mean
fewer minority college students. There may be nothing that can be
done about the vast sums of money N.C.A.A. sports are bringing in,
but something can be done about how it's spent.

Most colleges put most of their basketball and football money 13
back into their sports programs. Eliminate athletic scholarships and
the money saved could go toward putting minority students in school.
In this case, though, the minority students given aid would be ones
with aptitudes for math instead of 20-foot jump shots.

Then, the millions brought in by college students would at least 14
benefit college students. Instead of sending thousands of uneducated
ex-jocks out to face a hostile society every year, colleges would have
the chance to send thousands of professionals into a society that needs
them badly.

Questions for Thinking and Discussion

1. In contrast to Tommy Denton's solution of "dismantling" the college
   athletics system, Barra believes the solution is to eliminate athletic
   scholarships. If scholarships are given for athletics at your school, what
   do you think would happen if they were eliminated? Would the positive effects outweigh the negative ones?
2. Barra and Murray Sperber both discuss the problem of commercializ-
   ing college athletics. In what ways are these two writers' views about
   the reasons athletes are in college similar?

Writing Projects

1. These articles present conflicting views on what the so-called "scholar athlete" is and what he or she can be. In their discussions, both Sperber and Barra doubt whether real scholar athletes even exist; however, Blauvelt provides one example: Ohio State's Robert Smith.

   Write a paper on the general topic of the *scholar athlete on your campus*. Base your paper on an interview with an actual scholar-athlete on your campus. You might explore one of these questions:

   What do scholar-athletes see as their greatest problems in trying to balance two roles?

   How do scholar-athletes balance their time as students and athletes?

   What recommendations do scholar-athletes make to younger athletes that might help them become successful both in their studies and on the playing field?

2. What are the central problems in college athletics—the ones most in need of reform? Write a paper that summarizes in detail the three or four primary problems discussed by the authors in this chapter.

3. Since so much concern is voiced about whether athletes graduate from college (Sperber, Denton, Barra), prepare a project that investigates the whereabouts of five athletes who have (within the last three years) completed their athletic eligibility at your school. Did they complete degrees? Even though they were pressed to be both a student and a athlete, were they able to compete well enough in the classroom?

   You might interview friends of athletes, athletic directors, coaches, and journalists to find out where the athlete you have chosen has gone.

4. One of the controversies in the readings in this chapter is athletic scholarships. Although such scholarships are very prevalent in U.S. colleges and universities, Barra argues that they should be eliminated. Write a paper arguing for or against athletic scholarships at your college.

12

The Changing American Family

THIS CHAPTER DESCRIBES CHANGES that have been taking place in the American family. Most of us have heard statistics from sociologists, politicians, and talk show hosts about how the family has declined in this century. Whether it has actually "declined" or just "changed" is a matter of debate. Whatever the case, what constitutes a typical American family is certainly *different* from what it was 100 years ago: More women are working away from the home, more children live in single parent families, and more men have responsibility for child care.

The articles in this section provide a picture of the causes of changes in the family, the results of these changes, and the future of the family in the next century. As you read these articles, think about your own family or other families you have known. What is the "shape" of your family or one you are familiar with: Is it a "traditional American family," or is it a variation from that norm? Is this family experiencing the difficulties that these writers speak about? What is the family doing to cope with problems?

Finally, as you read these articles, think about the future. What do you think a family will be like in the next century? Will changes taking place in the family be advantageous to all members of the family? Or, will the family unit disappear entirely? If so, what might replace it that can serve the same function?

Rethinking the American Family

Lauren Tarshis

How would you define the typical American family? Is it two parents and their children living together? A divorced mother living alone with her kids? An extended family of many generations? A foster family of kids from different families and backgrounds?

The answer, of course, is none of the above. And all of the above. The American family has changed radically over the past 30 years. And today, as any sociologist would tell you, there is simply no such thing as one typical family.

But then, you probably know this, since your generation is on the front lines of these changes. Look at your own family and at those of your friends. Chances are, some—even many—of your parents are divorced. Fifty percent of all of today's marriages end in divorce and 26 percent of today's kids live with a single parent.

It's likely that your mother works outside the home, as 60 percent of all mothers do, and that she shoulders some of the burden for supporting your family. Depending on what part of the country you live in, you might know some kids who live in foster homes or in extended families where many generations of relatives share responsibilities for raising the kids and paying the bills.

You know what these changes have meant for you and your friends. What you'll see in this issue of *UPDATE,* our first of the year, is that the changes in American families have had profound effects on American society as well.

Storm of Change

These changes didn't just happen. They've been evolving slowly for 30 years, since the early 1960s. While popular television shows of that period—*Leave It to Beaver, Father Knows Best, The Donna Reed Show*—were glorifying suburban family life, America was heading into a storm of social change. By the mid-'70s, the attitudes of many young Americans would have little in common with those of their own parents, let alone TV's mythic Cleaver family.

Paving the way for these changes were leaders of the women's movement, who urged women to rethink their roles as wives and mothers.

231

Galvanized by these feminist leaders, thousands of young women   8
postponed marriage to pursue college and careers. As the women's
movement gained momentum in the late 1960s, universities and corporations were forced to reevaluate policies that were "sexist," or
discriminatory toward women. Women of all ages poured into the
work force, including fields like medicine and law that had been
dominated by men.

RELAXED DIVORCE LAWS

Meanwhile, many states began to relax their divorce laws, making   9
it quicker and easier for men and women to end unhappy marriages.
Between 1950 and 1975, the number of Americans seeking divorces
tripled each year.

Other social forces, too, would reverberate through American   10
family life. As attitudes about premarital sex changed, more and more
young couples decided to postpone marriage to try living together.
Birth control became widely available, which allowed couples to carefully plan the timing and size of their families. Finally, the 1973
Supreme Court case *Roe* v. *Wade* legalized abortion throughout the
country, which limited the number of marriages spurred by accidental
pregnancies.

What have all these changes in family life meant for American   11
society? It depends on whom you ask.

Many politicians, religious leaders, and social critics believe that   12
the American family is in a state of crisis. They believe that today's high
divorce rates and number of women in the work force have caused
serious problems for kids, including high rates of teen suicide, drug
abuse, and crime.

These experts are particularly alarmed by what they see as the   13
disintegration of family life in low-income areas, where as many as
85 percent of all families are on welfare and headed by single women.
Without strong family structures, these experts say, kids have little
chance of avoiding the cycle of poverty and the lure of drugs and
crime that pervade so many of America's poor communities. A growing chorus of politicians from both the left and right insist that
government should do more for America's poor families and their
children.

Others, however, including many sociologists, argue that the   14
American family isn't crumbling. It's simply changing to accommodate
changing American life-styles, as it has numerous times over the past
300 years.

In the 1700s, when most Americans were rural farmers, families   15
were primarily economic units, to which even young children were

valued contributors. Marriages tended to be arranged, and extended families stuck together.

By the late 1800s, most Americans had flocked into cities seeking   16
new job opportunities, often leaving extended families behind. Young couples began to marry for love. Women demanded—and got—more say in family decisions.

SOUNDING THE ALARM

Sociologist Edward Kain notes that throughout history, social   17
critics have sounded the alarm over changes in family life. At the turn of the century, for example, social critic John Watson warned, "In 50 years, there will be no such thing as marriage."

Marriage and family life survived, of course. And Kain and other   18
sociologists believe it will survive the current round of changes. They say that while the traditional family is on the wane, other "alternative" family structures are emerging. Many single men and women are having or adopting children to raise on their own. Single mothers are moving in with their parents, seeking emotional and financial help.

Experts like Kain admit that America's changing dynamics have   19
not been easy, particularly on kids. Current studies suggest that divorce can have long-lasting emotional effects on children. And today's harsh economic climate is making it tough to get by even for two-parent families. Indeed, the majority of today's mothers work because they have to, not because they want to.

We hope this issue of *UPDATE* gives you the perspective you   20
need to understand how one of life's most personal matters—our families—have reshaped American society. It will take decades to know with any certainty how these changes will pan out. Because ultimately, the real answers lie not in statistics or the prophesies of sociologists. They lie in the futures of young people like you.

Questions for Thinking and Discussion

1. This article summarizes changes that have occurred in the last thirty years in the American family and offers reasons why these changes have taken place. Which of these reasons seem more important?

2. Since Tarshis argues that there is no such thing as a "typical American family" today, do we still really have the family as a central unit in our society, or is it being stretched so much that we may actually be moving away from it entirely? Is there still a reason for the family, even if it has an entirely different shape than it did thirty years ago?

America's Family Time Famine

WILLIAM R. MATTOX, JR.

MANY PARENTS IN AMERICA TODAY are out of time. Out of gas. Running on empty. "On the fast track of two-career families in the go-go society of modern life, the most rationed commodity in the home is time," observes syndicated columnist Suzanne Fields. And the children of today's overextended parents are starving—starving from a lack of parental time, attention and affection.

Parents today spend 40 percent less time with their children than did parents in 1965, according to data collected from personal time diaries by sociologist John Robinson of the University of Maryland. In 1965, parents spent approximately 30 hours a week with their kids. By 1985, parent-child interaction had dropped to just 17 hours a week.

These changes are presenting significant challenges to American family life. Parents today employ a variety of time-management strategies to meet their work and family responsibilities. In roughly one-third of all two-income families today (one-half of those with preschoolers) spouses work complementary shifts to maximize the amount of time children are cared for by at least one parent. The most common "tag-team" arrangement is one in which the father works a standard 9-to-5 job and the mother works part-time in the evenings or on weekends.

Other two-income households work concurrent shifts. Families in which the youngest child is of school age often choose this strategy to minimize the amount of time parents are unavailable to children during non-school hours. Same-shift arrangements are also common among families in which both parents have a high attachment to their careers and in those in which limited employment opportunities leave few alternatives.

Whether couples adopt a tag-team arrangement or a same-shift strategy, two-income households spend considerably less time with their children than do breadwinner-homemaker households. (Although there are certainly some traditional families that suffer from father absence due to the time-demanding nature of the sole breadwinner's work.) This discrepancy is most pronounced in maternal time with children. In fact, research by University of Virginia sociologists Steven Nock and Paul William Kingston shows that employed mothers of preschool children on average spend less than half as much time with their children as full-time mothers at home. Moreover, Nock and Kingston show that employed mothers do not compensate for this shortage in quantity of time by devoting a higher proportion of the time they do spend with children to "high quality" child-centered activities such as playing with dolls, going to the park, or reading.

Time pressures can be especially daunting for single parents— 6 and especially harmful to their children. Children in single-parent homes usually receive less parental attention and supervision than other children. Not only is one parent absent from the home (and research by sociologist Frank Furstenberg shows that three-fourths of all children of divorce have contact with their fathers less than two days a month), but the other parent is overloaded with money-making and household tasks. Indeed, Robinson's data show that, on average, single mothers spend 33 percent less time each week than married mothers in primary child-care activities such as dressing, feeding, chauffeuring, talking, playing, or helping with homework.

Moreover, children in single-parent families often have very ir- 7 regular schedules. One study found that preschool children of single mothers sleep two fewer hours a night on average than their counterparts in two-parent homes, in part because harried mothers find it difficult to maintain a consistent bedtime routine.

SIBLING REVELRY

Kids aren't just missing out on time with their parents. Thanks to 8 the "birth dearth," they are also missing out on interaction with siblings.

In 1975, 62 percent of all women aged 40–44 had given birth to 9 three or more children over the course of their lifetimes. In 1988, only 38 percent had done so. The percentage of those giving birth to just one child rose from 9 to 15 percent during this same time period.

Some regard the decline in family size as a positive development 10 because it means children today receive more individualized attention from their parents than did children a generation ago.

Even if this were true—and sociologist Harriet Presser reports 11 "not only are Americans having fewer children than ever before, they are spending less time with the children they have"—it can hardly be argued that a one-child family generally has as rich a family experience as a larger family. Even if an only child receives more individualized parental attention, he still misses out on the intimate joys of having brothers and sisters—playing wiffle ball in the backyard, exchanging gifts at Christmas time, double-teaming Dad in a wrestling match on the family room floor, attending a sibling's ballet recital, and (later in life) reminiscing about old times at family reunions.

Today's fast-paced family life is also eroding the development of other aspects of what sociologist David Popenoe of Rutgers University says "is arguably the ideal child-rearing environment": 12

> a relatively large family that does a lot of thing together, has many 13
> routines and traditions, and provides a great deal of quality con-
> tact time between adults and children; regular contact with rela-
> tives, active neighboring in a supportive neighborhood, and
> contact with the world of work; little concern on the part of
> children that their parents will break up; and the coming together
> of all these ingredients in the development of a rich family sub-
> culture that has lasting meaning and strongly promulgates such
> family values as cooperation and sharing.

Eating dinner together is one time-honored family tradition some 14 believe is on its way out. "The family meal is dead," columnist Jonathan Yardley has written. "Except on the rarest occasions—Christmas, Thanksgiving, certain religious holidays—when we reach down to the innermost depths of the tribal memory and summon up turkeys and pies, roasts and casseroles, we have given up on what was once a central element in American domestic life."

Research on the prevalence of regular family mealtimes is mixed. 15 Some reports claim as many as 75 percent of all families regularly dine together, while others suggest less than 35 percent do so. Whatever the case, polls taken by the Roper organization show that the proportion of families that dine together regularly declined 10 percent between 1976 and 1986. This helps explain why heat-and-eat microwavable dinners for children to prepare alone are "the hottest new category in food products," according to a food industry spokesperson.

Whatever the virtues of microwavable meals and other conven- 16 ience foods, there is reason to be concerned about children routinely feeding themselves. As Suzanne Fields observes, "The child who grazes, standing in front of a microwave eating his fried chicken, biscuits, or refried beans, won't starve, but he may suffer from an emotional hunger that would be better satisfied if only Mom and Dad were there to yell at him for every pea he slips onto the knife."

So MANY BILLS, So LITTLE TIME

So how did American families run out of time? Growing eco- 17 nomic pressures have a lot to do with the American family time crisis.

One of the supreme ironies of recent economic developments is 18 that while America has experienced steady growth in its gross national product, the economic pressures on families with children have risen significantly. How can it be that at the same time we hear so much about the longest peacetime economic expansion in our nation's history, we also hear talk that economic pressures have grown so much that many families today must have two incomes?

Wage stagnation is one big reason. During the 1970s and '80s, 19 constant dollar earnings of American husbands grew at less than 1 percent per year compared to a real growth rate of 3 percent per year in the 1950s and '60s. Moreover, for some occupational and demographic groups—particularly non-supervisory workers and males under age 25—real wages have actually fallen since 1973.

While wages have stagnated, taxes have risen dramatically. In 20 1950, a median-income family of four paid 2 percent of its annual gross earnings to the federal government in income and payroll taxes. Today, it pays 24 percent. In addition, state and local taxes, on average, take another 8 percent from the family's gross income.

Moreover, the erosion in the value of the personal exemption (the 21 tax code's chief mechanism for adjusting tax liability to reflect differences in family size) has shifted more of the federal income tax burden onto the backs of families with dependents. Had the exemption kept pace with inflation since 1950, it would now be worth close to $7,000. Instead, it stands at $2,050.

On top of this, families are finding their take-home pay does not 22 go as far as it once did. As economist Sylvia Ann Hewlett puts it, families today are "like hamsters on a wheel," running hard just to keep up.

Over the past 25 years, increases in the cost of several major 23 family expenses—housing, health care, transportation, and higher education—have significantly outpaced the general inflation rate. For example, Joseph Minarik of the Congressional Joint Economic Committee has calculated that the typical 30-year-old man could get a mortgage on a median-priced home in 1973 with 21 percent of his income. By 1987, a median-priced home mortgage would take 40 percent of a typical 30-year-old's gross income.

The cost of housing, which is typically a family's single greatest 24 expense, is tied directly to crime rates and school districts. As crime rates have risen and school performance has declined, an under-supply of housing in good school districts with low crime rates has driven the price of housing in such neighborhoods way up. Thus, parents who value safety, education, and time with children must either live in areas with poorer schools and higher crime or divert time from children to market their labor in order to purchase a home in a safe neighborhood with good schools. That is a quintessential Hobson's choice.

PERRIER AND TEDDY BEARS

Growing economic pressures aren't the only reason families have [25] less time together. A number of cultural factors have also played a major role.

"Unbridled careerism" is partly responsible for the decline in [26] family time, says Karl Zinsmeister of the American Enterprise Institute. "For years, one of the most cogent criticisms of American sex roles and economic arrangements has been the argument that many fathers get so wrapped up in earning and doing at the workplace that they become dehumanized, losing interest in the intimate joys of family life and failing to participate fairly in domestic responsibilities," he writes. "Now it appears workaholism and family dereliction have become equal opportunity diseases, striking mothers as much as fathers."

The devaluation of motherhood stands behind such trends. As [27] Zinsmeister notes, "Today, women are more likely to be admired and appreciated for launching a catchy new ad campaign for toothpaste than they are for nurturing and shaping an original personality." Ironically, this has a detrimental impact on fatherhood as well. So long as child-rearing is viewed as a low calling for women, it is unlikely that it will take on increased significance for men.

Apart from unbridled careerism, some of the reduction in family [28] time has been driven by a rampant materialism that places a higher premium on obtaining or retaining a "Perrier and Rolex life-style" than on investing time in a larger kin group.

"Increasingly, Americans are pursuing a selfish individualism that [29] is inconsistent with strong families and strong communities," writes University of North Carolina sociologist Peter Uhlenberg. "This movement is fueled by the media, most especially television (both in its programming and advertising), which suggests that personal happiness is the highest good and that it can be achieved by pursuing pleasure and material goods."

Indeed, it has become all too common for parents to buy material [30] goods for their children in an attempt to compensate for their frequent absence from the home. Harvard University child psychiatrist Robert Coles calls this the "teddy bear syndrome":

> Some of the frenzied need of children to have possessions [31] isn't only a function of the ads they see on TV. It's a function of their hunger for what they aren't getting—their parents' time. The biggest change I have seen in 30 years of interviewing families is

that children are no longer being cared for by their parents the way they once were. Parents are too busy spending their most precious capital—their time and their energy—struggling to keep up with MasterCard payments. They're depleted. They work long hours to barely keep up, and when they get home at the end of the day they're tired. And their kids are left with a Nintendo or a pair of Nikes or some other piece of crap. Big deal.

SWIMMING UPSTREAM

Of course, not all parents are trying to "buy off" their children 32 with Teenage Mutant Ninja Turtles gear or overpriced sneakers. Many are struggling to raise responsible children and to transmit family values such as sharing, responsibility, commitment, and self-control. But these families are finding themselves swimming upstream against an increasingly unfriendly culture that instead promotes casual sex, instant gratification and selfish individualism.

Whereas once institutions outside the family, such as schools, 33 churches, the mass media, and businesses, formerly reinforced the inculcation of traditional values, today they are often indifferent or downright hostile to family values and the rights of parents to pass on such values to their children. Many parents sense that they are being undercut by larger institutional forces. And they recognize that children who lack the self-esteem that comes from parental attention and affection are especially vulnerable to negative peer and cultural influences.

"DOING THINGS TOGETHER"

Some opinion leaders in government, academia, and the mass 34 media view initiatives designed to increase family time—especially those that recognize the legitimacy and strengths of the breadwinner-homemaker family model—as an attempt to "turn back the clock" rather than "facing the realities" of modern family life. These leaders overlook the fact that concerns about family time are not limited to those who believe the traditional family model is ideal.

A 1989 Cornell University study found that two-thirds of all 35 mothers employed full-time would like to work fewer hours so that they could devote more time to their families. And when respondents to a 1989 survey commissioned by the Mass Mutual Insurance Company were asked to identify "extremely effective" ways to strengthen the family, nearly twice as many opted for "spending more time together" than listed "full-time parent raising kids."

Moreover, most Americans do not sneer at the past the way 36 elitists do. As Whitehead observes:

In the official debate (on family issues), the remembered past   37
is almost always considered a suspect, even unhealthy, guide for
the present or future. . . . But for the parents I met, the remembered past is not a dusty artifact of the good old days; it is
an important and vital social resource. Parents take instruction
from their own family's past, rummaging through it for usable
truths and adopting—or modifying or occasionally rejecting—its
values. . . . In the official language, the family isn't getting weaker,
it's just "changing." Most parents I met believe otherwise.

Americans believe "parents having less time to spend with their   38
families" is the most important reason for the family's decline in our
society, according to a recent survey. And most parents would like to
see the work-family pendulum swing back in the direction of home.

To be sure, most children would not object to spending more   39
unhurried time with their parents. Indeed, when 1,500 schoolchildren
were asked, "What do you think makes a happy family?" social scientists Nick Stinnett and John DeFrain report that children "did not list
money, cars, fine homes, or televisions." Instead the answer most
frequently offered was "doing things together."

Questions for Thinking and Discussion

1. Mattox lists several culprits responsible for the problems experienced,
   especially by traditional families. What are some of these culprits? How
   accurate do you find his statement (in his quotation from sociologist
   Peter Uhlenberg) that Americans have become too taken with personal
   happiness to make families run successfully?

2. Mattox, quoting sociology David Popenoe of Rutgers University, indicates that the "ideal child-rearing environment" includes a relatively
   large family that does a lot of things together, has many routines and
   traditions and provides a great deal of quality contact time between
   adults and children; regular contact with relatives . . . and contact with
   the world of work. . . . "Similarly, Mattox distrusts families with only
   one child: "It can hardly be argued that a one-child family generally has
   as rich a family experience as a larger family."

   What do you make of the position Mattox takes on this matter? How
   does it square with your own family experiences? Are children who
   do not have the family experience that Mattox promotes somewhat
   deprived?

How America Is Choosing Between Family and Self

Christine Wicker

The American tug of war between self and family draws few spectators. It's waged around kitchen tables, amid car pools, with whispers over the phone. Every day, in a million little ways, it pulls people who love each other together or apart.

To find out just how Americans balance family life and freedom, I traveled across the country, stopping in cities most likely to reflect the voices of mainstream America.

I rode Seattle's ferries and Phoenix's city buses. I walked the malls in Lexington, Ky., and flagged down joggers at the edge of Minnesota's Lake Harriet. In Nashua, N.H., recently named the best place to live in America by *Money* magazine, I talked to mothers, to fathers and to people who hope they will never be either.

On the whole, I found Americans' love of family to be strong and deeply felt. Stories of sacrifice, compromise and generosity were commonplace. Over and over, however, people of all ages said in one way or another: "If I'm not happy, my children won't be either," "I owe myself some things, too," and "I need this job for myself."

Almost everyone felt some conflict between individual freedom and commitment to family. Many nodded agreement as the interviews began. Some laughed and said, "You've found the right person to talk to about that."

Dorothy Davis from Chicago is one of those.

When the Dream Dims

"It was about two years ago. I was riding along in the car with my husband," she says. "And I realized that I had it all—2.1 children, two nice cars, a house in the suburbs. I had the American Dream, and I wasn't happy. All this sacrifice, and nobody was happy."

Her daughter, in her mid-20s, was living with her, threatening never to marry. Her teen-age son was charming his way through school, learning very little. "I'd done so much for my kids that they'd gotten passive," she says.

241

So Dorothy invited her daughter to find her own place to live. She   9
told her teen-age son to shape up, and when he didn't, they decided
he would be better off living with his grandmother in Phoenix.

The 61-year-old grandmother, Laveta Colbert, understands   10
Dorothy's feelings completely. Five years ago, she had come to the same
realization. She told her Chicago children: "You've heard of kids running away from home? Well, this is grandmother running away. I've
done my bit for my kids."

With that, Laveta moved to Phoenix, where she has started a   11
taxicab business.

Dorothy spent part of her vacation visiting her mother-in-law,   12
making sure her son was doing well. But she isn't letting his life run
hers anymore.

"From now on, I don't care what makes them happy," Dorothy   13
says. "I care what makes me happy."

When Family Doesn't Last

Dorothy lived the American Dream long enough to find it want-   14
ing; others reached it and then watched the dream slip away.

"I waited on my husband hand and foot," say 49-year-old Kay   15
Hess, now district manager for Kentucky congressman Larry J. Hopkins. "Right down to, if there were two pieces of meat, and one was
better, I'd give him the best one."

In March of 1986, he died unexpectedly. The day after his death,   16
she learned that their business was bankrupt, they had no insurance
and the house had to be sold. "Even the bank accounts were cleaned
out," she says.

Kay had not brought home a paycheck in 13 years. When the   17
utility company asked for a $75 deposit at her new apartment, she
didn't have the money.

A year and a half after her husband's death, Kay has a job she likes   18
and a man she plans to marry. But nothing will ever be the same.
Widowhood taught her lessons about the need to take care of herself.
And she won't forget.

"They can take away monetary things and the frills of life, but   19
they can't take away my pride," she says. "And pride is independence."

When Equals Marry

As people's needs change, some couples are successfully putting   20
together the new kind of family they want: one in which both freedom
and commitment are important ingredients.

For most of his nine-year marriage, Bill Bradley, 43, has lived apart from his wife. He has been in Lexington since last October. Although he and his wife haven't lived near their families for almost two decades, Bill, who is from Lexington, wanted to try going home again. So far, his wife remains in Germany. 21

The Bradleys have no children, and both value independence highly. 22

"It's the perfect situation," Bill says of their flexible union. "We tried living together for a few years once. I'm not cut out for that." 23

The couple visits each other on holidays and during the summer. 24

The Bradleys are just one couple to whom marriage is important but having children is not. 25

Forty-three-year-old Seattle lawyer Fred Staatz and his wife married six years ago, after a long period of living together. Their lives are taken up with jobs, hobbies, travel, and each other. Children aren't in their plan either. 26

The specter of growing old without children isn't a vision that haunts Staatz. "We'll keep up our interests, so it won't be necessary to live vicariously through grandchildren," he says. "I don't see the future as a license plate that says, 'Happiness is having grandchildren.' " 27

Staatz doesn't consider himself any more selfish than anyone else, and his life is full. So, why plan for children? 28

WHEN ALTERNATIVES PREVAIL

Helen Neuharth, 36, has the same attitude about marriage that Staatz has about children. This afternoon, eating a lunch of fruit salad, listening to jazz under the canopies of Phoenix's Solar Oasis exhibit a block from her office, she's perfectly content. As usual. 29

Although she's never been married, the Mesa, Ariz., resident considers herself very family-oriented. She lives in a family neighborhood and she decided to move to Phoenix and take a job with the county because her sister lives nearby. She arranges most of the family reunions for her South Dakota clan. 30

Some sociologists would say that marriage has been edged out of Helen's life. She has so many other options—work, travel, friends, extended family—that her life has filled up without a husband and children. 31

"I'm happy," she says. "I have to work at it sometimes. You have to work at being single just like you have to work at being married." 32

WHEN MARRIAGE IS LACKING

Americans are looking for marital experiences radically different 33
from their grandparents'. Sometimes independence, even companionship, isn't enough. Spouses also want respect, and some don't believe
they are getting it.

Nancy Willis has taken a rare day off to come into Nashua for an 34
outing with a longtime friend. They've stopped for lunch at Ming
Gardens, and the dark haired 33-year-old is having what she calls "a
good old bitch session."

She caters weddings, works as a chef, takes on most of the 35
responsibility for the three children, and still she gets "nitpicked."

"All those years before I married him, I did everything fine, and 36
now I can't do anything," she says. "I can't pay the rent. I can't buy
groceries. I can't drive. I can't do anything right. I can't even cook right.
Sure, I'm a chef. But he's an *executive* chef."

Her mother put up with the same kind of treatment from her 37
father, she says. "But she didn't have any choice. In those days, you
didn't get divorces."

For six years, Josephine Cope, 46, has listened to customers talk 38
about their marriages as she styles hair at Lexington's McAlpin's beauty
shop.

"I hear a lot of women coming in here and they're not happy, but 39
they're staying with it," says Josephine, a divorced mother of two who
doesn't plan to remarry.

"I hear a lot of complaints about not wanting to do the same 40
things and ending up doing things separately or not at all. Mostly not
at all," she says. "They say they don't have freedom to do what they
want to do."

"Staying together used to be just a matter of survival," she says. 41
"Now people expect to have a relationship—in terms of doing things
together."

WHEN COMMITMENT WINS

Lots of Americans are willing to give up career advancement for 42
the sake of their spouses and children. Plenty wouldn't have it any
other way. But sometimes they feel stranded in a world no one else is
sharing.

Bill and Mary Beth Sousa of Nashua agree that she should stay 43
home during the day with their 3-year-old son. When Bill comes
home, he takes over the evening bath and bedtime stories.

They are living life exactly as they want to. But finding friends 44
who live the same way is hard. In fact, the Sousas, both in their
early 20s, don't know any other couples in their mid-20s who have
children.

"A lot of people our age feel having a child has locked us in, and 45
he's going to be a burden all our lives," Bill says. "It's like they say, 'Oh
my God, isn't he ruining your lifestyle?' "

Since Nashua's Lisa Kammler quit her job as an audiologist 46
to care for her two children full time, talking to an adult has become
a treat.

"You don't have coffee klatches anymore," she says. "Everybody 47
works. It's lonely during the day." Lisa, 33, finds herself stopping
people in the grocery store just to talk. "Sometimes it seems like I just
need an 'adult fix' " she says.

Lisa's working on her resume now. 48

One night a week, Lexington homemaker Betty Sampson, 34, 49
would go out while her husband watched their two children. She
needed the time off.

But on her night out, it sometimes seemed that all the other 50
adults were busy. She took ballet lessons, she tried quilting classes, she
visited the library. Finally, she just wandered around malls.

Soon she began postponing the outings. 51

"I had to get out and do something that would make me feel good 52
about myself."

Now, Betty works two nights a week and every other Saturday in 53
a bookstore at Lexington's Civic Center shops. "I love my job. If
something happened that I lost it, I'd find another one."

When Marriage Ends

Some people who sacrificed for their families now look back and 54
realize nothing turned out as they planned. Sometimes they wish they
had lived differently.

In a small city park overlooking Puget Sound, a 52-year-old 55
blond woman in a white uniform is reading a paperback novel. It takes
two bus rides to get home from her job as a health care aide, and on
this sunny Seattle day, she's loath to rush indoors. She will tell her story,
but she won't give her name. Her 19-year-old son still lives with her.
The husband she divorced 10 years ago recently married the woman
who caused their breakup.

Considering the way her life has gone, she wouldn't choose to 56
have children again.

"Having a child was wonderful during the marriage but after- 57
ward, it was just too hard," she says.

Lyman Palmer, 45, is a retired Navy man, the father of four sons 58
from a first marriage, now a pipe fitter. He says his marriage foundered
because he spent too much time at sea.

"If I had it to do over again, I wouldn't get married," he says. "I 59
loved the Navy. I'd stay in until they kicked me out."

Then he amends, "I might get married, but I wouldn't have 60
children."

When Role Models Fail

Some single people are opting out of marriage because the family 61
they saw as children isn't a pattern they're remotely interested in
repeating.

Diane is 21 and works two jobs: full time, she's a grocery store 62
meat packer and, part-time, she's a checker at a Nashua fast-food
burger restaurant. On her only day off, she's in a Nashua laundromat
washing clothes for herself and her older brother, who is unemployed
and lives with her.

Married? "No, thank goodness," she says, flipping the mane of 63
blond hair down her back, "I've never married, and I'm never going to
be."

Diane has been taking care of her brother as long as she can 64
remember. Even before her parents divorced, they were gone most of
the time, usually working. She has a boyfriend, she plans kids of her
own, but she won't marry.

"Why would I want to do that?" she asks. "I take care of myself 65
just fine."

Surrounded by the jewelry, stained glass and marble busts of his 66
mother's antique jewelry shop at Minneapolis' Riverplace, Thomas
Townsend is the thoroughly modern man, right down to the fashionable stubble on his chin. His parents divorced early. He's taken care of
himself virtually since childhood.

That's not to say he doesn't want a family. Thomas, 23, has just 67
called his girlfriend in California to propose. But already he knows he
and his fiancee have different ideas about how much freedom a marriage should allow.

"I have a lot of female friends," Thomas says. "My girlfriend 68
knows it's platonic with them, but she always suspects there's something lurking in the background.

"She was raised in this small-town way—to believe you finished   69
high school, got married and started having kids. And then there's me,"
he says grinning wryly, "from the big city."

When Children Leave

The young aren't the only ones asking for more freedom. Parents   70
of grown children are selling the homestead and taking to the road; if
their children want to visit them, they'll have to find them.

More than 30 years ago, when Robert and Theresa Loso began   71
their family of five children, they knew perfectly well that they would
have to wait their turn. For 20 years, Robert has put together a file of
places in 48 states that he and Theresa wanted to visit. Now their
children are grown, and, unlike any generation before them, they have
lots of life left. It's their turn now, they say.

Two years ago, they sold their New Hampshire home and bought   72
two mobile homes: one for a winter home in Florida and one to take
on the road.

Their five children are welcome to visit anywhere they stop, but   73
"when I live in any one place longer than a month," says Robert, 65,
"I get homesick for the road."

"My daughter says we threw her out," says Theresa, 62. "But we   74
made her grow up, and it was about time.

"The children are all living lives of their own. Why should we sit   75
at home and hope they're going to come visit?"

When God Leads

About the only people who say they have entirely escaped the   76
internal debate about how to live are those with strong, religious faith.
For them, the pursuit of happiness begins and ends in God's will—that
hasn't changed, they remind unbelievers, in 2,000 years.

Thirty-eight-year-old Diana Araki is jiggling a pink-bonneted   77
infant on her hip as she stands behind the card table that holds the
containers of roses she is selling.

She sells the roses every Friday outside the Seattle ferry termi-   78
nal "to supplement my husband's income, not because I need some
feeling of self-worth." On Thursdays, she works at the Unification
Church.

Diane has no doubts about how to live her life. Her husband   79
is the head of the family. She sacrifices for her family gladly. "An
individual finds his value in the sense of giving to a greater Self," she
says.

But even those people with a strong sense of their own religious   80
direction often find that society isn't willing to go along with the plan.

Twenty-year-old Michelle Farnsworth, whose home is near Seattle   81
in Bremerton, wants marriage in the Mormon temple and eight children. But so far, the junior elementary education major at Brigham
Young University hasn't found many men her age who agree with her
life plan.

"Some people are put off," she says. "A lot of people are."   82

In this modern age, even God's guidance doesn't always lead to   83
traditional marriage.

Claudia Rist, 33, and Martina Rist, 27, are both unmarried phy-   84
sicians who attend Faith Baptist Church in St. Paul. Both believe God
led them to become doctors. Both hope to marry.

But giving up their careers for a traditional marriage would be   85
difficult. Claudia can imagine herself staying single more easily than
she can imagine curtailing her work as a surgeon.

"I've put so much into this. My parents have. Everyone has. I feel   86
like God wants me to be doing this."

Martina tried training for everything from nurse to zookeeper   87
before giving in to her urge to be an internist. She knew it might be
hard to find a man who would marry a doctor.

"I go through phases where I really think about being married,"   88
she says. "But it doesn't seem as big a stumbling block as it used to. I'm
contented."

WHEN FREEDOM CHAFES

On a warm Sunday afternoon at Minneapolis' Lake Harriet, it   89
would be impossible to believe the family is anything less than it ever
was. It would seem unlikely that anyone could find a better way to live
or even that anyone is trying.

The broad, smooth faces of toddlers peer solemnly from helmets   90
as they whiz silently by, perched behind daddies on 10-speeds. Wobbly
mothers in shoe skates proceed stiff-armed, while shaky-legged children clutch their hands, careening on either side. Shirtless fathers
meditate the state of the universe from behind navy blue baby car-
riages.

Peter MacDonald is sitting alone on a park bench. Dark shades   91
shield his eyes. His 10-speed, its saddle bags filled with books, is near.

He's reading an article from the alternative press called "In Pursuit of Leisure."

Peter has lived lots of places in his 29 years. He's been through   92
counseling and read Jungian psychology. He's never been married.
Until three months ago, he was a full-time architect working as hard
as he could to become a partner in the firm. Like most of his friends,
he was buying a lifestyle.

But now he's changed his mind. He's working part time. He wants   93
to combine his work and leisure so that he will have enough time for
his own interests and the children he hopes to have someday.

He is living with a woman for the first time, and he thinks they   94
will probably marry.

"I'm beginning to realize that I don't necessarily need other peo-   95
ple," he says, "but maybe my life would be enhanced if they were
around."

Questions for Thinking and Discussion

1. Wicker provides us with profiles of a wide variety of Americans, each
   one dealing in his/her own way with the American family model. Some
   reject it, others accept it, and still others change it. Which of the people
   in Wicker's article would Mattox consider to be "selfish individualists"?
   What sort of dialogue do you suppose these people would have with
   Mattox? What would each person say?
2. Do the variations in lifestyle depicted in Wicker's article resemble the
   variations you have seen in people you have known? Do you think that
   these people can all live happily even though they do not follow the
   traditional model, or will they suffer from the prejudices of tradition-
   alists?

Care For the Elderly a Physical, Emotional Burden for Children

Lawrence M. Kutner

THE INCREASED LIFE SPAN OF AMERICANS over the last century has 1 brought joy to many families. But while many older people are healthy and productive to the end, those who fall ill tend either to recover quickly or to stay sick for longer periods than they would have a generation ago.

In 1900, only one in 10 couples between the ages of 40 and 60 2 had one or more of their parents still alive. Ninety years later, 56 percent of couples that age had at least two parents alive.

"I estimate that half the 35-year-olds today will have a dependent 3 parent alive for at least 20 years before that parent dies," said Dr. Vern L. Bengtson, a professor of sociology and director of research at the Andrus Gerontology Center at the University of Southern California in Los Angeles.

"Having aging and dependent parents at the same time as caring 4 for your own children and grandchildren will be the major domestic crisis for the 21st century," said Bengtson, who speaks from both professional and personal experience. His mother is dying in a nursing home. He is her only child.

"My children, who are in their late teens and early 20s, are in 5 various stages of dependency on us," he added. "I'm trying to promote autonomy in my children while coping with dependency from my mother."

The illness of an elderly parent affects the entire family, often in 6 ways that are not anticipated.

The financial costs of long-term care and the division of respon- 7 sibility for physical care of a frail parent are not the only changes family members must handle. Old aspects of the parent-child relationship are rekindled. Dormant sibling rivalries may resurface or be resolved.

"Emotionally, it's very difficult to face, because it means you can 8 no longer rely on your parent for support," said Dr. Lissy Jarvik, a professor of psychiatry at the University of California in Los Angeles who specializes in aging and is the author of *Parent Care: A Compassionate, Common Sense Guide for Children and Their Aging Parents* (Bantam, 1990, $10.95). "There's great anxiety. Who's going to help me now?"

Jarvik recalled how her own mother's terminal illness helped   9
them resolve old issues and feel closer to each other. "It also improved
my relationship with my sister," she said. "Even five years after my
mother's death, I feel closer to my sister."

The two best predictors of how a parent will be cared for are the   10
sex of the child and the nature of the early parent-child relationship.

Women undertake a disproportionate amount of physical care for   11
aging and ill parents. According to a 1987 survey by the American
Association of Retired Persons, 75 percent of the people who took care
of elderly relatives were wives, daughters and daughters-in-law.

Most worked full or part time as well, often giving up time at   12
work to care for a parent. Nearly 40 percent also had children at home.

"If you can choose, have daughters, because they're on average   13
more supportive in your old age than sons," Bengtson said.

The uneven distribution of responsibility for care of an aging   14
parent is a sore point, both within couples and between siblings.

Counselors routinely describe situations in which the primary   15
caretaker, who takes time off from work or other responsibilities to
cook meals or to bring a parent to a doctor's appointment, feels
unappreciated. Yet that parent openly gushes over the weekly phone
call from another of the children.

"I've talked to many people who are the primary caretakers and   16
who are angry that their siblings, who live far away, are getting a lot of
credit from the parents even though they're not carrying their share of
the burden," said Dr. Nancy K. Schlossberg, a professor of counselor
education at the University of Maryland in College Park.

Involvement in an ill parent's care also often reflects what the   17
parent-child relationship was like years before.

"An earlier nurturing relationship makes children more open to   18
caring for a sick parent," said Dr. Bonnie J. Kin, an adjunct associate
professor of psychology at California State University in Dominguez
Hills, a suburb of Los Angeles. "But when the early relationship was
cold and distant, the children are more likely to seek the least expensive institutional care."

Questions for Thinking and Discussion

1. This article describes a dimension of change in family life not explored
   in the first four articles. What are the effects of aging parents on
   modern families? Who takes care of them? Who is financially respon-

sible? What effects do caretaking responsibilities have on families? How do you think these problems might be dealt with by individuals, by the government, by religious organizations, or even by private industry?

2. Think in particular about experiences you have had in this area or observations you have made about aging relatives. What problems cited in Kutner's article have you witnessed? What are some problems that Kutner does not mention?

All Work and No Playtime

STAN LUXENBERG

UNTIL LAST YEAR, ELLEN SAHL SPENT NEARLY AS MUCH TIME THINKING about day care for her 3-year-old daughter, Victoria, as she did thinking about her own job as a secretary. She had a full-time baby-sitter for Victoria. But she was so unreliable that Sahl often had to miss work. And some days, when she did make it to the office, she spent most of her time on the phone frantically looking for substitute baby-sitters.

But today, Sahl's day-care problems are solved. And the solution came from what some people might consider to be an unlikely place: her employer, Stride Rite Corporation, a shoe manufacturer in Cambridge, Massachusetts. Last year, Stride Rite opened a state-of-the-art day-care center in the company's headquarters. Each day, Sahl brings Victoria to work and drops her off just three floors below her own seventh-floor office.

"It has really made my life less stressful," Sahl says. "I know Victoria is well taken care of, and I can see her during lunch."

Stride Rite workers are fortunate. Just 200 American companies have on-site day-care centers. Others try to help their employees by establishing "flextime," or flexible working hours. But the vast majority of families must fend for themselves. Those who can afford it hire private baby-sitters at a cost of $200 to $400 a week; many more families rely on public or private day-care centers, at an average weekly rate of $140. And countless numbers of families look for help from relatives.

Emily Sandler, a computer programmer in Philadelphia, adds one hour to her 45-minute commute by driving to her mother's home, where she leaves her 1-year-old son, Casey. Every night, she drives an extra hour to pick him up. "I have no choice," she says.

Certainly, many of these day-care arrangements work out well for both children and parents. But there are always snags and stresses.

As a result, working parents have higher rates of absenteeism than other employees and tend to be late for work more often. Many quit their jobs entirely.

LESS PRODUCTIVE WORKERS

Companies like Stride Rite have come to believe that in order to operate efficiently, they must help families cope. Distracted employees, after all, make for less productive workers. Some experts say it is cheaper to help current workers with day care than to constantly hire and train replacements.

A study by the Conference Board, a business-research organization, showed that family-care programs have helped to cut costs at many firms, including Du Pont, a chemical company, and General Mills, a food-products company. Still, most employers have not been willing to get involved. For small businesses, helping with day care may simply be too expensive. Stride Rite spent $700,000 to build its care center, and the company contributes heavily to pay for the ongoing operations of the program.

But some experts say the pressure on companies is only going to build. "More and more women are going to work outside the home," says Diane Piktialis, vice president of Work/Family Directions, a corporate consulting firm. "There is going to be an increasing demand for different kinds of assistance."

Questions for Thinking and Discussion

1. Luxenberg's article suggests a corporate solution to the time pressure problems outlined in Mattox's article earlier in this chapter. If you were an employer, would you be willing to make an investment such as the one made by Stride Rite in Luxenberg's article? What do you see as its advantages? What problems can you envision for such a system?

2. If corporate daycare becomes common for American children, how do you think it will affect their upbringing? How will they be different from those who have largely been reared in a home? What positive effects does this system offer? What negative effects? If you are a parent or caretaker of children, would you want your child to spend his/her days in a corporate daycare center?

A Capitol Issue: Saving the Family

ELLIOT NEGIN

MARIAN WRIGHT EDELMAN wants to redefine "national security."   1

Most people think national security means protecting the country   2
from external enemies. But to Edelman, one of America's leading
children's rights advocates, the gravest threat to the nation comes from
within—from poverty and the other social ills afflicting the American
family. True national security, she says, is "our ability as a nation to
protect children and promote families."

Many people are alarmed by current statistics on the family.   3
More than 15 percent of all American families with children live below
the poverty line, according to the U.S. Census Bureau. That figure
includes 12.6 million children in this country—nearly one out of every
five.

And every year, more than half a million children drop out of   4
school, more than 450,000 teenage girls have a baby, more than
75,000 children are arrested for a drug offense, and 10,000 children
die because of poverty.

"The federal government hasn't dealt with the problem at all,"   5
says U.S. Representative Pat Schroeder, a Democrat from Colorado.

"LAST ORDER OF BUSINESS"

Like a growing number of politicians—both liberal and conser-   6
vative—Schroeder believes the government must act to address the
problems of American families, and act fast.

"For 16 years I've been in Congress trying to move on issues   7
concerning the family," Schroeder says. "But families have always been
the last order of business in Washington. Families don't have powerful political-action committees. And toddlers don't give [legislators]
money for coming by their day-care centers."

But thanks to the efforts of Edelman, Schroeder, and other activ-   8
ists, "saving the family" is finally becoming a hot political issue on
Capitol Hill.

The last Congress, for example, passed the first federally funded   9
day-care program for poor children. Family advocates had been pushing for such a program for more than 20 years. And this summer, a

group of legislators from across the political spectrum announced plans to press the government for even more action. "Liberals and conservatives disagree on everything, including the time of day, but not on this issue," says Gary Bauer, head of the conservative Family Research Council.

A FLURRY OF BILLS

Family advocates in Congress hope to pass a number of impor-   10
tant pieces of "family-support" legislation this year. These bills include:

- **Parental Leave:** Most working parents find it hard to get time   11
off to care for their newborns. A recent survey found that less
than 4 percent of workers in small companies and less than 14
percent of workers in large companies have maternity- or
parental-leave benefits.

    To alleviate this problem, Congress last year passed the   12
Family Medical Leave Act. The act would require companies to grant employees up to three months of unpaid leave for
the birth or adoption of children, or to care for ill family
members.

    One hundred twenty-five countries, including every in-   13
dustrialized nation (except the U.S. and South Africa), have a
similar law. Nevertheless, President Bush vetoed it. Why? The
Bush administration believes such benefits should be provided
voluntarily or through negotiations between employers and
employees. The business community feared the law would
open the door for other federally mandated—and costly—employee benefits.

    The Family Medical Leave Act is up for consideration again   14
this year. Experts predict Congress will pass it for a second
time, but that President Bush will once again veto it.

- **Tax Breaks:** Financial stress is a prime factor in divorce, and   15
one of the biggest problems for low- and middle-income families is a lack of money.

    A bill introduced in Congress last spring by 48 lawmakers   16
aims to put more money in parents' pockets. It would allow all
parents with dependent children to deduct $3,500 from their
income on their tax returns, and to increase the amount to
$7,500 by the year 2000. Currently, families can deduct only
$2,050.

In addition to simply giving families more money, tax   17
breaks could result in a host of other benefits for families,
supporters of the bill say. They could, for example, allow more
mothers to spend time at home with their children, rather than
having to work full-time.

But the bill's advocates admit they don't know how Con-   18
gress will pay for the cost of the tax breaks—the main reason
observers say it stands little chance of passing.

- **Early-Childhood Education:** One of the most successful na-   19
  tional family-support programs is Head Start, a federally
  funded preschool program for poor children. But as a result of
  recent budget cuts, only a third of all eligible children are
  enrolled in Head Start.

  Last April, Senator Edward Kennedy (D-Mass.) introduced   20
  legislation that would significantly increase the program's
  funding. The bill would also force Congress to adequately fund
  Head Start every year. Up to now, Congress has set aside
  widely varying amounts of money for Head Start. Kennedy
  contends the amount has never been enough.

- **Childhood Hunger:** A recent survey by the Center for Dis-   21
  ease Control found that one in four poor children suffers
  from anemia, a sign of malnutrition. Both houses of Congress
  are considering bills that would enable more families to qualify
  for food stamps—free vouchers that can be exchanged for
  food.

Worries Abound

Despite this recent focus on family issues, family advocates worry   22
that many of these bills will never by enacted—or will be so watered
down that they will be inadequate.

Edelman, who has been lobbying for children's rights for the last   23
18 years, isn't optimistic. "I am convinced that a new direction will not
come from inside the political process," she says. "Politicians love to
make speeches about families and children, but when they get back to
Washington and budget battles, kids are the last things to cross their
minds.

"If change is going to come," she contends, "it will happen be-   24
cause people respond in an aggressive, sustained, and even outraged
way."

ment as essential. What might happen if no legislative
action is taken?

2. Negin seems to regard legislative actions on the family as being agreed
   upon by both conservative and liberal members of Congress. Do you
   think that American taxpayers would be willing to support the legislation that Negin speaks about regarding parental leave, tax breaks, early
   childhood education, and childhood hunger? Should they support
   legislation? Why or why not?

Writing Projects

1. Although they don't all agree about whether the changes are good or bad, the writers of these articles all recognize that changes have occurred in the American family. They all seem to be aware that further changes are coming as well.

   Write a paper that analyzes a family—your own or one you know. Base your paper on interviews with family members. The paper should examine this family by comparing it to or contrasting it with discussions about family in the articles in this section. You might focus your paper on one of these questions:

   Does the family I am examining share some of the same problems discussed in these articles?

   Would the solutions proposed by some of the writers in this chapter help the family I am examining?

2. Write a summary paper in which you pull together several of the articles in this chapter. Select one of the following topics and build your paper around it:

   Problems in the American family

   Causes of problems in the American family

   Effects of problems in the American family

   Solutions to problems in the American family

   As part of this assignment, you might quote and paraphrase from the articles in this chapter to provide evidence for your arguments.

3. Using these articles as well as your own ideas, offer solutions for reviving the American family. Or, if you think American families can't really be revived, discuss what is needed to replace them.

4. As you will recall, the article by Wicker outlines a number of different variations of modern lifestyles. Each of these is a kind of response to the idea of a family: some represent an acceptance, some a rejection, and some a modification.

   Present a paper to your class about what students at your college predict will be their version of Wicker's lifestyle variations. With a team of four other students, survey thirty students. Which lifestyle variations seem to predominate? Based on your findings, predict what you think the American family will be like thirty years from now.

13

Parenting

THE RATING "PG" THAT ACCOMPANIES SOME AMERICAN MOVIES means "parental guidance suggested." Aside from guiding children in the movies they watch, parents have to guide children in nearly every area of their lives. However, just as the structure of the American family has changed in the last three decades, so too has the role of "parental guidance." Decisions that parents have to make about guidance are often difficult and complicated.

Readings in this chapter are addressed directly to parents: past, present, and future. The readings touch on some unique problems facing modern parents: How do they guide children away from dangerous vices that they themselves may not have avoided as young people? What is the line between being too permissive and too restrictive? How should they discipline their children? This chapter describes these and several other problems. As you read the articles—whether you are a parent or may someday be one—evaluate the opinions of the writers and the experts quoted in the articles.

Risky Business

LAWRENCE M. KUTNER

THE PHRASE "DO AS I SAY, NOT AS I DO" may ring especially hollow for   1
many of today's parents, who came of age during times of sexual and
drug experimentation in the 1960s and '70s.

The concerns and risks are very different now from what they   2
were a generation ago. Convincing today's young people of that, however, can be a difficult problem, particularly for parents who don't wish
their children to follow in the footsteps they made during their own
teen-age years.

"My son asked me directly about whether I'd used drugs," said   3
Dr. Alan Marlatt, the director of the Addictive Behaviors Research
Center at the University of Washington in Seattle. He and other child
development experts advise parents to tell their children the truth
about their youthful experimentations, but to temper that truth with
discretion and perspective.

"If you talk to your children about what you've done in the past   4
but no longer do," Marlatt continued, "you're not giving them permission to do the same things."

Sexual experimentation can be another difficult topic for many   5
parents to discuss if they don't want their children to do what they did
as adolescents. Researchers who study sexuality generally agree that
sharing accurate information with teenagers about the biology and
emotions of sex is one of the best ways of preventing unwanted
pregnancy and sexually transmitted diseases.

"Television has become the leading sex educator of teen-agers   6
today," said Dr. Victor Strasburger, the chief of the division of adolescent medicine at the University of New Mexico in Albuquerque and
author of *Getting Your Kids to Say 'No' in the '90s When You Said 'Yes' in
the '60s* (Fireside Books).

"That's a scary proposition," Strasburger said, "because it's not   7
teaching them about abstinence, contraception or responsibility. It's
teaching that everyone's having sex but them."

Discussions of sexuality may include some information from   8
parents or other adults about how they reacted to the emotional and
physical changes of puberty when they were adolescents. This sort of
disclosure can be very reassuring to children who feel confused or
embarrassed by their changing bodies and feelings.

"It's inappropriate to lie to children about sexual issues, because   9
then they learn that you're not a credible source of information," said
Debra Haffner, the executive director of the Sex Information and
Education Council of the United States (Siecus), based in New York.

"But you don't have to tell everything if you feel you may hurt the   10
child," she said. "Also, it's perfectly OK to say that you made mistakes.
Your children will listen to your advice more closely than if you
pretend you never did anything wrong."

The nature of the way adolescents think contributes to the overall   11
problem of engaging in risky behavior. As their brains mature, they are
able to see situations from new perspectives. The world is no longer
black and white to them. They can now see a drug, for example, as
having both benefits and risks.

One reason for this lack is that with the impressive growth in   12
adolescents' abilities to ponder more complex and abstract problems
comes their belief that they are invulnerable.

"Teen-agers like to take risks," Strasburger said. "It's part of find-   13
ing out what their new bodies are all about and how much they can
now do. But parents should encourage their children to take more
socially acceptable risks." He added that new athletic pursuits, like
skiing, rock climbing or scuba diving, often give them the extra thrill
they need.

"We can't control our teen-agers' behaviors," Haffner said. "All   14
we can do is provide them with decision-making skills and good
information."

Questions for Thinking and Discussion

1. In Kutner's article, Debra Haffner says, "We can't control our teenagers'
   behaviors. All we can do is provide them with decision-making skills
   and good information." Do you believe parents can control their teenagers' behaviors? How can parents guide their teenagers in decision-
   making skills? What sort of good information should parents offer their
   children?

2. Kutner assumes that the "concerns and risks are very different now
   from what they were a generation ago." Though he doesn't discuss this
   comment, what do you think he means by it? What are some areas that
   parents must consider today that they would not have had to consider
   twenty or thirty years ago? Conversely, are there some problems that
   parents in the 1960s or 1970s might have faced that no longer exist?
   What are some areas of parental concern that have always existed (and
   probably always will)?

Parents Vs. Drugs

INGRID GROLLER

BILL IS SIXTEEN. He's bright, articulate, and outgoing—and he's 1
recovering from an addiction to drugs and alcohol. Bill first started
drinking and using drugs when he was in seventh grade. At that time,
he and his mother, who's divorced, moved from Arizona to the Philadelphia area. When he started school there, he looked up to the "in"
kids, he says, "but I didn't fit in. I didn't want to be just like everybody
else. I wanted to be known and all of that.

"I found that all I had to do was dress up like a burnout—wear 2
concert T-shirts, a jeans jacket or a leather jacket, a chain around my
neck—and I was accepted," he continues. "Along with the dress came
the talk, the walk, and then the drugs."

He started with pot and alcohol. The first time his mother caught 3
him with a joint, he admitted, "Yeah, I tried it, but I don't like it. I'm
not going to do it anymore."

Both Bill and his mother feel that they had a good relationship 4
while he was growing up. "My mom gave me everything," he says. "I
think that because she and my dad were divorced, she thought she had
to make me happy. She never really enforced any kind of rules on me
when I was younger because I was a real good kid—I did real well in
school. Then when we moved here and I did stuff that was not
acceptable, she tried to make rules and put stipulations on me. I
thought, 'Forget that,' so I totally rebelled."

From pot and alcohol, which Bill says he used throughout his 5
addiction, he moved on to speed and then cocaine and acid. And, he
says, "I did crack here and there."

At one point, Bill says, "I tried to commit suicide; I was reaching 6
out for help by trying to commit suicide. I didn't want to die."

While, of course, most young people do not become addicted to 7
drugs and alcohol, Bill's story is in many ways stereotypical of how and
why teens and preteens get started using drugs. For the majority of
young people, drugs and alcohol are a way of coping with the pressures
of their world, among which being one of the gang ranks high.

PROBLEMS START EARLY AND ARE WIDESPREAD

According to Thomas Gleaton, executive director of the National 8
Parents' Resource Institute for Drug Education (PRIDE), "There's a lot

of research on drug use and certain kinds of personalities, home life, etc. But I've worked and talked with a lot of kids. They say, 'It's fun.' 'I like it.' 'My friends do it.' It has nothing to do with bad parents."

Joyce Nalepka, president of the National Federation of Parents for   9
Drug-Free Youth (NFP), agrees: "I don't believe that there are deep psychological reasons why children use drugs and alcohol. They do it because their best friends do it. It's there, it's available—like leather sneakers.

"It's an extremely serious situation," she warns, and statistics   10
support her.

With funding from the National Institute on Drug Abuse, the   11
University of Michigan Institute for Social Research has been doing a nationwide survey of high school seniors for the past twelve years. Although drug use was declining or leveling off between 1980 and 1984, the 1985 survey showed an increase in the use of some drugs, including cocaine, which had been tried by 17 percent of seniors. (This is the highest rate of cocaine use recorded in the twelve-year survey and might reflect the use of crack, which was not listed separately in the 1985 survey.)

A statewide survey during the 1985–86 school year in California   12
showed that more than 51 percent of high school juniors had tried illegal drugs. For those who were regular users, marijuana was the most popular, with one of every thirteen eleventh graders saying that he or she smoked every day of the year.

Alcohol use is even greater, according to this survey. By eleventh   13
grade, 85 percent of the students had experimented with drinking and more than 65 percent had been intoxicated.

Of the seventh graders polled, 58 percent had tried a drink and   14
11 percent had tried drugs.

Drugs and alcohol are also an issue at the grade school level.   15
Joyce Nalepka reports that 25 percent of fourth graders nationally have felt pressure to try drugs or alcohol.

It's a problem, too, that knows no geographical boundaries. Kath-   16
erine True, a member of the NFP board of directors, from Lancaster, Pennsylvania, says, "We're 25 years behind the times here and it's horrendous. The number of high school students who are drug- and alcohol-free could fit into one large conference room."

Today, then, the big question facing parents is, Can you   17
even hope to keep your children from experimenting with drugs and alcohol?

The answer is that most probably "you can't guarantee it," says   18
John Toto, president of The Bridge, a drug and alcohol rehabilitation center in Philadelphia. "The most you can do is to start early and lay

the groundwork so that their experimentation doesn't turn them into users."

"My theory," explains Anita Wooten, a licensed mental-health   19
counselor in McLean, Virginia, "is that most young people in our culture will experiment. But if everything is all right in the family—if there is support and communication—it will not amount to anything."

"Parents often wait to deal with the issue of drugs and alcohol   20
until it's too late," John Toto points out. " 'What can I do with my adolescent?' they ask. You can apply a lot of Band-Aids—it's never too late to start. But the question should have been asked almost at birth, 'How am I going to parent this child?' "

Many experts believe that children who develop a strong sense of   21
self-esteem during the early years have a better chance of avoiding drug and alcohol problems.

To help your children develop their self-esteem, Tom Farrel, a   22
high school principal in Maine and a member of the NFP board of directors, encourages parents to put their energy into the positive. "Recovering teens often can't think back to anything other than drugs and alcohol that ever made them feel good.

"You have to convince young children that they're okay," he   23
says. "Avoid saying things like, 'If you go into the road, you're a bad boy.' They have to understand that they're not a bad boy or a bad girl; they did a bad *thing.* If they did misbehave, reprimand them, then forget it. Drop what someone did last week or ten years ago. Begin each day fresh and remember that childhood is a time to make mistakes."

BUILDING SELF-ESTEEM REQUIRES PLANNING AND COMMUNICATION

Anita Wootten recommends structuring ways for young children   24
to be successful. "If they set the table, and the knife is out of place, don't correct at that time. Praise them for a job well done. The next time, teach them where the knife goes," she explains. "Don't expect them to do things like a grown-up."

To help children feel good about themselves, Anita Wootten says   25
that parents should take an active interest in their lives. "If they are watching *Scooby Doo,* sit down and watch it with them.

"Be sure the door is always open to them," she continues. "Listen   26
to them, keep the lines of communication open. Be aware that they face crises and give their crises the respect they deserve. We want to talk to our children on our own terms—when its convenient for us. A crisis is never at a convenient time. But when kids are having a crisis—it may be a D on a paper, a snub, getting left out of a trip, losing an election,

discovering that they're short, tall, or that their ears stick out—it's an opportunity to talk. Be available and let them know you're concerned."

Keeping channels of communication open is necessary, too, so   27
that parents can teach children the coping skills they need to deal with life.

"Little kids have to be taught how to be themselves and how to   28
control their lives," John Toto explains. "I don't like to overplay the influence of peer pressure because I think that you have to convey to kids that peer pressure is part of life. You can be 90 years old and still have peer pressure, so you'd better learn early on how to handle it. Kids have to learn when to say yes and when to say no."

He uses an experience he had with his son, who was six at the   29
time, to illustrate his point. "I'd come home at night, and all his toys were all over the front lawn. When I asked him what was going on, he said, 'If I don't bring my toys out, the other kids won't like me; they told me to bring out all of my toys or else they won't be my friends.' So we had this long talk—it went on for days, weeks—about how to cope with that.

"At six it's toys and bubble gum and if you don't do this, you're   30
not my friend," he concludes. "But if they can't handle the little stuff at six, at eight it becomes something bigger, and by sixteen it's drugs."

It Takes Skills to Get through Life

"Teenagers who end up in treatment do so because they lack the   31
tools for living," notes Barbara Michaels, director of community education services at The Bridge. "It seems that along the way people took care of them and they never toughened to their own life. They were never able to look at their own life as a situation that needed to be resolved." As a result they turned to drugs and alcohol for the answers.

"When a child is sixteen, there is pain, there is loneliness, there's   32
fear, there's pressure, there are setbacks, there are disappointments. If we don't teach kids to cope with those kinds of things, if we always take them away, how are they going to learn?" Michaels says.

"Or take the child who, whenever he's bored, is driven some-   33
where by his parents," she continues. "That child will never learn how to take care of his own boredom. What's he going to do when Mom and Dad aren't there. When I'm working with a group of little kids, I ask them, 'What are some of the things you like to do in your free time?' One might say, 'I like to go bike riding.' Then I ask, 'Do you like to go bike riding or does your mom like you to?' So many kids never learn what they really like to do. Those things that they really don't like are so easy to give up."

"Young kids have to be taught by their parents how to share their 34
feelings," John Toto adds. "Parents have to take time to work with
their children about what's bothering them. Where do they feel the
pressure? How are they going to cope with it? By first or second grade
a child should know, 'Not everyone is going to like me. I'm not always
going to have good days. Some days I'm going to feel really mad or
sick.'

"Kids are going to have both positive and negative emotions, and 35
parents have to teach them how to express those emotions in a proper
way," he says. "Drugs and alcohol are a problem but they are usually
the last in a sequence of problems."

Questions Parents Need to Ask Themselves

Before parents can teach communication and coping skills, par- 36
ents need to assess their own abilities in this area. "Parents can't get
their kids to do what they themselves can't do," John Toto says. "As a
parent you have to ask yourself some questions: Can I share my
feelings? Can I identify my feelings? Can I live with them? Do I know
how to make decisions? Can I handle normal life pressures? What do
I do when I suspect people don't like me? What do I do when things
aren't going well at work? Do I have a healthy way of handling my own
personal problems and putting them in perspective?"

The single most important thing that parents can do for their 37
children, Barbara Michaels believes, is to be a good role model. "If you
don't want your child to drink to excess," she advises parents, "then
don't drink in excess. If you want to give the message that whenever
you're nervous or frustrated a drink helps, then drink. But if you want
your child to see that when you're pent up and have frustrations to
alleviate, you put on jogging shoes and go out and run, then that's what
you should be teaching by role modeling."

The purpose of reaching children as early as possible is, ideally, 38
to prevent them from even trying drugs. If you wait until they're in
high school to address the issue, it's most likely too late.

"Under ten, there's a nonuse norm," explains Tom Adams, direc- 39
tor of the Just Say No Foundation. "That's the only age segment in our
society that has a nonuse norm. It's between ten and fourteen that the
norm changes. By the time kids reach high school, they're entering a
youth culture in which the norm is to use. Instead of waiting until
seventh and eighth grade to start teaching refusal skills, we need to
reinforce their nonuse norm. It's much easier to reinforce a norm than
it is to change one—to try to change one is a real struggle."

Reinforcing a Drug-free Existence

The "Just Say No" Clubs, for children in grades two through 40
seven, have been established for the very purpose of reinforcing that
nonuse norm. The message the clubs deliver, Tom Adams says, is
"You're great just the way you are and we want to keep you that way."
An important activity of the clubs, which number over 10,000 with
membership in the millions, is the annual walks and rallies held to
celebrate being drug-free. (This year's walk is May 15 and 16.)

"The clubs provide the children with the opportunity to be taken 41
seriously," Tom Adams, says. "They allow them to make a public
commitment. In a sense, we are teaching them how to overthrow the
tyranny of the older kids and of that use norm."

Adams's hope is that once the nonuse norm is reinforced in this 42
generation of second through seventh grades it will be perpetuated by
them first to junior high school and eventually to high school and
beyond.

Another means of taking an anti-drug message to middle-years 43
children is through programs such as Kids Saving Kids, a program that
works in conjunction with the NFP. Both Katherine True and her sons,
Peter, seventeen, and Chris, fourteen, are involved in such a program
in Lancaster. High school students who volunteer are trained to go into
the junior high and elementary school. They first perform improvisa-
tional skits dealing with drug and alcohol issues and then break up
into smaller groups for discussion.

"I expected them to be fairly naive," Peter says about the elemen- 44
tary students he works with. "Most don't have all the facts straight, but
they do know what it's called, where to get it, and how to use it."

Because younger children do look up to teenagers, Katherine 45
True believes that this program is highly effective in getting information out. "The younger students hang onto every word the teens say,"
she comments, "and in the process they learn that not everybody does
take drugs."

As for the current teenage generation, Peter True comments, "I 46
don't like to say that my generation is lost, but its mind is made up."
And it seems to be made up in favor of at least experimenting with
drugs and alcohol.

No one, of course, condones the use of drugs and alcohol by 47
teenagers. Joyce Nalepka states strongly that "for children drug use is
abuse. There is no responsible use of illicit drugs, ever, and no responsible use of alcohol for children under age."

Still, most experts believe that for the large majority experimen- 48
tation does not lead to addiction.

"By the age of eighteen, 90 percent will at least try drinking and   49
probably some illicit drugs," John Toto explains, "and that isn't a
problem at that point. That's probably normal adolescence. If it's there,
they're going to try it."

He is concerned though that by the age of eighteen, 60 percent   50
are drinking regularly and 40 percent are doing some drugs regularly. "Those kids are at a critical point and somebody significant
better enter their lives and help them see just what they're doing,"
he comments. "If that doesn't happen, they could be headed for
trouble, since by the time they are eighteen, one in twenty do have
serious drug and alcohol abuse problems." According to the Alcohol,
Drug Abuse and Mental Health Administration, a teenager may develop an addiction to alcohol or drugs, such as cocaine, within six
months.

REALIZING THERE IS A PROBLEM

Ideally, the significant person who steps in should be a parent.   51
The problem is that parents frequently fail to recognize that their
children are using drugs and alcohol.

Katherine True got involved with the issue when she discovered   52
that her stepson had a drug problem and she wanted to educate herself
about drugs. "I was appalled at how stupid I was," she says now. "He
had been involved with drugs for three years before we realized it."

According to a recent study done by Wade Silverman, Ph.D.,   53
head of the division of psychology at Emory University, parents under-
estimated the likelihood of their children's using alcohol or marijuana,
but they overestimated the likelihood that their teenager would confide
in them if they needed help with substance abuse. The study, which
polled Atlanta-area high school seniors and their parents, showed that
while only 35 percent of the parents thought that their children had
used alcohol in the last 30 days, in fact 65 percent of the students said
they had. Only 3 percent of the parents believed that their children had
smoked marijuana in the last 30 days, whereas 28 percent of the
children said they had.

When asked whom the teens would turn to if they had a   54
substance-abuse problem, "over 50 percent of parents elected themselves as the people to confide in," says Dr. Silverman. In reality,
however, 70 percent of the seniors said that they would go to a friend,
and only 20 percent chose their parents.

"To know if your children are using drugs, you have to know your   55
kids," John Toto states. "You have to know their normal behavior. If
you don't, that's problem number one."

There are many areas in which behavior may change, he says. 56
"Has there been a drop in grades? Has your son or daughter always
been involved in activities and now is not? Did you know all of his or
her friends and now don't known any of them? Has your child always
been outgoing and now is sullen and quiet? Did he like to be in his
room and read and now is always out of the house? Was he fairly
obedient before and now isn't? Was your child relaxed and calm and
now is fidgety?

"If you know your child's patterns and there's a significant 57
change, you have to step in and ask, 'What's going on?' When parents
or teachers start to say, 'I don't know what's wrong with him. He never
used to be this way,' there has to be some reason."

"When you get a gut feeling that something is wrong, trust it," 58
Thomas Gleaton advises. "Ask them, 'Is it a girlfriend, boyfriend,
school, drugs?' Tell them, 'Share with me, I'm concerned.' That's a
caring parent."

WHEN CONFRONTATION FAILS

What if you do confront your son or daughter, and they deny any 59
involvement with drugs or alcohol? Use your judgment, Gleaton advises, and if your instincts tell you that they're not being honest, you
are justified to go so far as searching their room for evidence. "You can't
do nothing," he says. "It's better to be wrong occasionally than to do
nothing."

Although the statistics are against them, Thomas Gleaton urges 60
parents to "encourage your kids not to try drugs at all. Ask them to
stay clear until they are adults. Then the decision to experiment is up
to them. But as adults they have a better chance of escaping problems."

PRIDE believes in a health approach to abuse prevention, and as 61
Gleaton says, "If parents understand the health effects, they can explain
to their children how drugs are harmful and hurtful and that they
cannot allow them to use drugs."

Also, parents should teach their kids how to say no and how to 62
have excuses handy, he says.

To deal with young people who are users, John Toto says, we go 63
back, again, to communication. The fact that a child comes from a
healthy home environment, doesn't guarantee that there will be no
problems, but at least in those cases there is a better chance that family
members can talk about it and work things out.

"What would you do if your ten- or twelve-year-old came home 64
and said, 'Mom, I smoked a joint'?" he asks parents. If you go into a
tirade, you've lost right there.

"Spend less time talking about drugs, and find out why," he 65
advises. "Don't yell. Ask why. What does it mean to you?"

What's Behind a Drug Problem?

"Young people use drugs for very basic reasons," he continues. 66
"Everyone has the same basic needs in life—to be loved, to feel love,
to feel a part of something, to feel responsible for something, to feel
needed, to feel that somebody thinks that he or she is important, to be
in control. These feelings are a little more exaggerated in adolescence.

"But if I don't help my kids to feel good about themselves, if I 67
don't help them see that they are wanted and that they're part of us, if
I don't let them share their love, if I don't give them control, if I don't
give them variety, they're going to go after it someplace else.

"For a lot of kids, when they hang out with druggies," he says, 68
"they're 'in.' That's their status. 'I'm a drug addict and I'm proud of it.
I'm a good drug addict. All my friends are addicts; they like me and I
like them.' "

Anita Wootten adds that children are most vulnerable to using 69
drugs when they are under stress, such as that caused by a family
move or when there are emotional restrictions in the family. "Children
are perceptive; they get messages that are not spoken," she says. "It's
not okay to be short, or look like Uncle Harry. Drugs change that
mood.

"The work of adolescence is to learn to cope," she points out. 70
"Make them understand that if they use drugs to ease the pain and
boredom adolescence can bring, they won't learn to cope naturally."

Teens have to be warned that everyone who ends up with a drug 71
or alcohol problem "started out feeling good," John Toto says, "but it
reaches a point where the drugs or alcohol become a crutch.

"What parents or friends have to get kids to see is that there are 72
ways to get what you want without hurting yourself in the end.
Initially, they don't see that eventually alcohol and drugs can kill you.
And if they don't kill you, you survive with psychological and emotional problems. The job of parents is to step in and help kids identify
what they're really after and then help them go after that. If communications have broken down, and parents are unable to get through to
their teenagers, get professional help," he advises.

What's the Attraction?

Part of the problem in convincing teenagers to stay away from 73
drugs and alcohol is that our society has made these things very

appealing to young people. "When you look at advertisements for alcohol," John Toto says, "there's a clear message—it's equated with being grown-up, success, good sex, and a good life."

"The American culture puts out a strange message for kids," Tom   74
Adams agrees. "We have this concept called a rite of passage and we've sort of said to them that one of their rites of passage is to try drugs and alcohol.

"Ours is one of the few cultures that doesn't have a ritualized rite   75
of passage. We're fumbling around trying to figure what makes the move from adolescence to manhood or womanhood. Unfortunately teenagers seem to think that is done by drinking at graduation or driving a car when you're stoned.

"There is a big difference between a rite of passage and a right to   76
use drugs," he notes. "A rite of passage—what makes you a man or what makes you a woman—should be the first time you accomplish something, or the first time you help someone. Those are the true rites of passage—not using drugs and alcohol—and that's what we should be conveying to our children."

GETTING THE MESSAGE ACROSS

Tom Farrell is asking his community to back up the antidrug   77
message his students are getting from first through twelfth grade. A big problem as far as he's concerned, is that parents often buy the keg of beer for their teenagers' parties. "The community has to decide if they want kids to drink at any age," he says. "As educators we're trying to teach what the community values."

Farrell has already sent out a newsletter asking parents not to   78
condone such parties. He also sends a letter to parents who provide alcohol, explaining that what they are doing is counterproductive.

The laws on drugs and alcohol are another way that society   79
makes a statement. But John Toto says, "If you get bogged down in the law part you're missing the whole point. It makes no difference if everything is legalized tomorrow—it's still going to have the same effect on people.

"And legal or illegal, drugs will still be available as long as there's   80
a demand," he believes. "You can bust the top drug person in Philadelphia right now, and by tonight there will be someone else in his place. I cringe when I hear that they just made the greatest raid in the history of the world. The drug kids are laughing. At the very most it might mean that they have to travel a little farther for their stuff temporarily.

"The only way it's going to stop," he believes, "is if people learn   81
to achieve their needs and goals in other ways. It has to start with the

parents. They have to help their kids gain the skills to say no, to be in charge. You have to replace drugs and alcohol, you can't just come off of them. You have to go on to something."

Questions for Thinking and Discussion

1. In this article, Joyce Nalepka says that she believes there are no deep psychological reasons kids use drugs; they do it because their friends do it. Later on, however, Tom Farrell and others refer to self-esteem problems as one reason why kids use drugs. Evaluate both positions. Which do you believe is more valid? Do they both have merit?

2. Barbara Michaels says that teenagers end up in treatment because they lack the tools for living. What does Michaels mean? How can parents ensure that their children have appropriate life skills and coping skills? What can teenagers do to help themselves learn to cope with uncomfortable situations (pressure to use drugs and alcohol, for instance)?

Are Kids Growing Up Too Fast?

SALLY WENDKOS OLDS AND DIANE E. PAPALIA

PARENTS HAVE ALWAYS WANTED SMART, CAPABLE AND CREATIVE CHILDREN 1
who grow to be confident, successful adults. Parents have always
wanted the best for their children. But are kids today being asked to
be too smart, too capable, too creative—to have skills and interests,
and an emotional maturity, that are far beyond their years? Have we
turned our yearning to give them the best into a race to turn out kids
who are better than our neighbor's kids? Are parents—and schools, the
media, big business—pushing kids too hard, too fast and forcing them
into premature adulthood? Many experts believe so.

"Children are being shortchanged," says Lee Salk, Ph.D., child 2
psychologist and professor at Cornell Medical Center in NYC. "We
hurry them toward independence before they're emotionally ready. We
rush them out of childhood."

It's dangerous, these experts believe, to put children under such 3
enormous pressures. And in this special report we'll tell you why—and
what you can do about it.

- The party is rocking as a d.j. spins the hit records. "I want your
  sex, I want your body!" one song blares. Danielle, one of the
  guests, wearing gold lamé pants, a designer blazer and dan-
  gling earrings, gyrates sinuously to the throbbing beat.
  Danielle, who is awarded first prize in the contest for the
  sexiest performance, is, like the birthday girl, in fourth grade.

- Ricky, a conscientious student, goes up to his teacher after
  class and nervously asks, "Now that I've been doing better with
  my schoolwork, do you think I'll get into a good college?"
  Ricky is in third grade.

- Michael hangs up the phone after making a play date with a
  friend and enters it into his appointment book, which also lists
  his karate, piano and tennis lessons, as well as his parents'
  work schedules. Like most of his friends, Michael is dependent
  on his calendar to keep his dates straight. Michael is in second
  grade.

Surely these can't be elementary-school–age children. But they 4
are. When these kids grow up, will they look back upon their early

years and wonder where their childhoods went? More to the point, can there be dangers in growing up too fast?

We think the answer to both questions is yes. And as the two of us—a professor of child and adult development and a writer who specializes in family issues—were researching the most recent edition of our college textbook, *A Child's World,* we discovered that our concerns are shared by many experts.

Today's parents, like parents of the past, want to do what is best for their children," says David Elkind, Ph.D., professor of child study at Tufts University, Medford, Massachusetts, and author of such influential books as *The Hurried Child* (Addison-Wesley, 1988) and *Miseducation: Preschoolers at Risk* (Knopf, 1987). "But they themselves are victims of social pressure, of media oversell and of faddish educational practices. All of these forces conspire to victimize their children, too."

What are some of the forces that are hurrying our children to age before their time?

THE SCREEN IMAGE OF CHILDREN

Kids on television and in movies are often portrayed as incisive, intelligent and uninhibited mini-adults. As *New York Times* film critic Vincent Canby writes: For "children pushing their way through the uncertain, often painful years from 5 to 15 . . . television sitcoms see them as wisecracking, lovingly impertinent pseudo-adults. This vision pleases older audiences and gives younger audiences hip role models to follow."

But hip is not necessarily *safe.* For example, when five-year-old Jason overheard his parents discussing why it would be tough for each of them to pick him up from the babysitter's house one evening, he hastened to reassure them. "It's okay," Jason said. "I can figure out a way to get home myself." He could not, of course, negotiate the one-mile walk across two busy streets. When his parents asked him why he thought he could, Jason reported that he'd heard the little boy on *Family Ties* say the same thing to his parents.

Parents often don't realize that television can put a heavy burden on youngsters who think they have to act as savvy as their TV counterparts do. The greater danger is that parents, seeing child characters act older than their years, may come to expect their own children to respond with more maturity than they are capable of. "Parents are viewing their children as little adults, as if they've been shrunk in a dryer, and the children become so good at these roles that they often fool us," says John D. Sweetland, Ph.D., a psychologist in the Port Washington, New York, public schools.

"Children see world events on the news, they're privy to the lives   11
of adults through television programming and advertising," says Ellen Wartella, Ph.D., research professor in the Institute of Communications Research at the University of Illinois at Urbana-Champaign. "Even during the Saturday morning children's hour there are announcements about drugs, alcohol, AIDS. Television *is* changing the nature of childhood."

THE HARD (KIDDIE) SELL

Television, we know from our own experience, has a direct im-   12
pact on consumer spending. And kids, the business world has found, are an impressionable and profitable market. The catchphrase of the nineties is not so much "Let the consumer beware" as "Let the child beware."

Visit any big city and you'll see toddlers strolling the streets in   13
Calvin Klein jeans, Esprit sweaters, and Weebok sneakers—expensive brand names bought by parents as symbols of status. It's no wonder kids start asking for brand-name clothing by the time they can talk. Today, fashion designers promote their styles to little girls in 4-to-6X sizes by signing them up in department stores to receive fashion newsletters. Others develop and advertise products such as $30 toilet waters for babies, $15 colognes for little boys, and elaborate cosmetic sets—including press-on fingernails and eyebrow pencils—for little girls.

The products themselves are troubling, as are the ways they're   14
advertised. One newspaper ad for a child's watch, for example, features a photo of a little girl looking at her new purchase. The caption reads: "Boys are always late." Such ads promote childhood dating and female passivity (a girl waiting, waiting, waiting for a boy), and ploys such as these show that companies look at children as fair game who need no special protection from sophisticated merchandising.

"It's nauseating to see the way people are making money on the   15
vulnerability of children," says Peggy Charren, president of Action for Children's Television (ACT), a Boston-based advocacy group that fights for diverse and nonexploitive children's programming. "But it's important to remember that most of this manipulation requires the partnership of the parent, who plunks down the money for these products. If the parent refused to play the game, the merchants would lose. And

the kids would be given back their childhood." Unfortunately, unless parents monitor what their children watch and read, the power of the media will continue to shape children's spending habits—not to mention their values—from the time they are old enough to sit upright in front of a television screen.

THE HEAD OF THE CLASS

Most children these days assume a great deal of responsibility— including responsibility for themselves—at an early age. In families where both parents work outside of the home or in single-parent families, the grandparents, aunts, uncles and other family members who in earlier times alleviated family pressures are often too far away or too busy themselves to help. 16

And because good child care is scarce and expensive, many children—latchkey children—are left on their own for at least part of the day. 17

Leisurely activities such as playing a board game together, reading a book on the front porch, or taking a walk through a park seem to have largely fallen by the wayside in parents and kids' frantic schedules. As one third-grade teacher in a suburban school put it, "Parents don't do many 'kid' things with their children. Instead of taking their children to the zoo or doing crafts projects with them, they escort them to Broadway shows and expensive restaurants—things parents enjoy more." 18

But even parents who feel that such outings are neither necessary nor desirable may be swept along by local customs, such as a school system that offers a structured preschool or a neighborhood where other children seem too busy with after-school music lessons, for example, to simply play in the yard. "If I don't send my daughter to day camp in the summer, she won't have anybody to play with," laments a Davenport, Iowa, mother who wishes her daughter could know the long, relaxed days of summer that she herself remembers from her own youth. As a result, parents have kids "enriching" themselves at breakneck speed from infancy on. 19

Many babies, for example, begin swimming lessons at three months. Toddlers can tumble in gymnastics at two years of age and go on to reading at four, soccer at five, computer camp at ten, and dating at twelve. "I hardly ever hear of boredom anymore—from parents or children," says Kay Willis, founder and president of Mothers Matter, a support and educational group based in Rutherford, New Jersey, which recognizes motherhood as a profession both for homemakers and 20 income-earning women. "Parents have so many goals for themselves and their children that they're too busy to be bored."

And, because parents are so busy, they may be relieved when   21
their children show signs of independence, and therefore encourage them to "grow up" ahead of schedule. At the same time, parents believe that their children will be well-prepared for the future, thanks to their head start in academics, athletics or the arts.

But the irony, says Fred Rogers of *Mister Rogers' Neighborhood,* the   22
popular, award-winning children's TV show, is that "it's just the opposite. If we really want children to succeed and be productive people, we'll respect them as human beings and let them grow at their own pace. Children who get a warm feeling from being read to when they're very young will develop a sense of joy in learning on their own—and in the end will do better than those children who are pushed into it."

Noted pediatrician and *Redbook* contributing editor Dr. Benjamin   23
Spock agrees: "Human beings, including children, are naturally competitive—we're a pecking-order species. But in America we've gone much too far in trying to get ahead of everyone else. So we have a kindergartner playing soccer because his father thinks, 'I would have gotten farther in life if I had been a better athlete.' Or a two-year-old looking like a scared rabbit under the pressure of learning to read, when there's no evidence in the world that a child shown flash cards in the crib will be a better reader at age eight."

What's more, says Dr. Elkind, the notion that children can be   24
programmed for success simply by being enrolled in enough classes or camps is in itself harmful. "Parents don't stop to think of the other influences on children, such as their inherited abilities and characteristics, their level of maturation, the influence they receive from society at large." In other words, parents who expect to see a certain level of accomplishment in their children might not be prepared to cope with disappointment.

THE LOSS OF INNOCENCE

In some ways our society seems to be returning to the child-   25
rearing climate of medieval times, when, according to historians, there were no sharp demarcations between childhood and adulthood. Adults did not feel a need to shelter children from information and experiences that were beyond their emotional or intellectual capacities, and children dressed like their elders and even worked at the same jobs. Some social critics point this out when making the argument that we are losing ground when it comes to our childrearing skills and values.

But, points out Dr. Wartella, "there's no documented scientific evidence that a less differentiated notion of childhood is harmful. Still, I do agree with the concerns of many contemporary child-development professionals that thoughtful, caring adults need to step in to offset some of the confusing messages that today's children are receiving."

The current generation of children is being asked to shoulder   26
even more—and more complicated—kinds of emotional burdens. Pointing to the current spate of books for preschoolers about sexual abuse, Dr. Elkind says, "Reading a book about sexual abuse to a three-year-old gives her the message that it's up to her to take care of herself. But there's no way she can protect herself against an adult, and she shouldn't have to think about this danger. Instead, it's up to *parents* to see that the people caring for their children are responsible adults." AIDS education is another problem that previous generations did not have to cope with. "Suppose eight-year-old children do learn about AIDS—what can they possibly do about it at their age?" asks Dr. Elkind. This downward shift of responsibility, he says, only makes children fearful without giving them any tools to deal with their anxieties.

Indeed, children seem to be jumping into the adult arena earlier   27
and earlier. Reports show that five- and six-year-old girls worry about getting fat, that significant numbers of 12-year-old children have sexual intercourse, and that both pregnancy rates and suicide rates among minors are alarmingly high. Although there's no proof that pressures on children are directly responsible for these disturbing trends, much informed opinion links them to the demands on children to grow up before they're ready.

"Between the increasing influence of the media and the decreas-   28
ing presence of parents in the home, it may be inevitable that children today will grow up sooner," says Neil Postman, Ph.D., professor of media ecology at New York University and author of *The Disappearance of Childhood* (Delacorte, 1982). "No social change comes without cost. But I feel this is a loss, not only to children but to society as a whole. If childhood itself becomes eroded, we're likely to lose some of the cherished values that I believe are important and worth preserving— innocence and curiosity among children and, among adults, measuring maturity by the degree of responsibility assumed for the care of the young."

WHAT PARENTS CAN DO

How can parents tell the difference between encouraging inde-   29
pendence and pushing their children beyond their emotional capabili-

ties? When does challenge turn into pressure? And what can parents do to close the door on societal influences with which they do not agree? In the 19th century, laws were enacted to protect children from laboring away their early years in harsh, restrictive environments. Today, we don't need laws so much as awareness that children have special developmental needs and that it's parents' responsibility to help set the right pace. The following guidelines, based on expert opinions, should held you help your child to reclaim his or her childhood.

- **Don't be fooled by your children's pseudosophistication.** 30 "Even while our children are mouthing off about issues and sounding very mature, we shouldn't forget that they are still children," cautions Dr. Wartella. "They are often confused, and we as adults have to help them cope with the confusing on-slaught of information that's coming their way, as well as help them to make sense of the world they're living in." This means offering explanations and reassurances. When it comes to subjects such as sex or violence, they may not know how to express their worries. Adults need to go beyond what children say to imagine what they might be thinking.

- **Trust your own instincts.** Don't let your children do, wear or 31 see things that you don't approve of. Your child may accuse you of being an old fogy, but the limits you set will be a positive influence later. Just because "all the other children" are going on dates or a ski trip does not mean that your child is ready for that particular activity.

  "If, for example, a little boy begs to go to tennis camp," 32 says Dr. Spock, "and if his parents think he is ready for it, that's not pressuring the child." But if you don't think your child is ready—even if *he* does—you need to do what you believe is right, says Dr. Spock, even if that means disappointing your child.

- **Slow down.** A recent study by three research psychologists 33 compared children from academically oriented preschools with those from more relaxed preschools. "Children who played in preschool did as well when they got to kindergarten as those who attended the academic preschool," reports one of the researchers, Kathryn Hirsh-Pasek, Ph.D., assistant professor of psychology at Temple University in Philadelphia. "Plus," she says, "the kids in the accelerated programs showed more anxiety in the testing situation and were less creative and more negative about school than the ones who went to the low-key preschools."

Additionally, enrichment programs that urge parents to   34
enroll their infants in swimming classes, toddlers in strenuous
gymnastics classes, or first-graders in competitive team sports
ignore—at the children's peril—evidence that physical exercise
undertaken too early can strain children's bone and muscle
development and cause serious injury. Joseph F. Fetto, M.D.,
associate professor of orthopedics and assistant director of
sports medicine at New York University Medical Center, cautions that, when children's bodies are too immature, such
activity can impair their growth and development and possibly
lead to permanent disability.

"Parents *should* encourage their children to have some   35
physical activity, but they need to do research," says Dr. Fetto.
"They should know the training and experience of the instructor and how well the program works for the typical child who
takes part, not just a superstar. And they should be sure that
the activity is suitable for their child's age and ability. For
example, preschoolers can be in a gymnastics class that includes simple tumbling and rolling—but not until about age
nine should children do formal floor exercises that require
training and discipline."

"Parents have to learn to ignore efforts to make children   36
grow up too fast," says Dr. Spock. "And when other people try
to rush your child into sports or reading or some other activity
that you feel isn't appropriate for your child, you need to stand
up to them and say, 'Go away! That's not what my child should
be doing.'"

• **Monitor and discuss with your child what he or she sees**   37
and reads. You don't need to watch every episode of every TV
show your children watch to determine whether it's appropriate. One episode will give you a sense of the program's flavor.
A 1988 survey commissioned by Planned Parenthood showed
a high incidence of sexual references on TV with practically no
mention of birth control or prevention of sexually transmitted
diseases. "Television gives children an opportunity to find out
about sex but not to learn about it," says ACT's Peggy Charren.

Parents, then, have to fill in the gaps. They have to initiate   38
conversations with their children—questioning the values
shown in commercials and programs and balancing the sometimes overheated and frightening news of world events.

Another option is to use home videos, which allow parents   39
more control over choosing what their children watch. "To-

day's parents have a significant alternative to television with the wide selection of children's videos available to buy, rent or borrow from the library," says Charren, who cites the book *Guide to Videocassettes for Children* (Consumer Report Books, 1989) as a helpful resource. "If home videos had been around when my children were small," says Charren, "I may not have had to start ACT."

(For more information about screening children's viewing   40
time, send a self-addressed, stamped envelope to Action for Children's Television, 20 University Road, Cambridge, MA 02138.)

- **Ease a latchkey child's worries.** A parent can minimize the   41
inherent stresses of this situation by judging whether a child is really ready to stay alone. Ask yourself: Can my child understand and remember spoken and written instructions? Is he flexible and resourceful enough to handle an emergency? Does she know what to say and do about visitors and telephone calls?

   If you feel your child is ready, Dr. Elkind suggests saying   42
something like, "I'd rather be home with you, and I know you'd rather have me at home. I know that staying alone is a big responsibility. But I'll teach you how to handle all the things you're worried about." Then give your child the names and phone numbers of people to call if he has any questions. Also help him plan the use of his time alone (to do homework, chores and so forth) and be clear about safety rules. Set up a regular time during which the two of you will check in with each other.

   (For more guidance on easing latchkey children's worries,   43
see *Redbook*'s October 1989 issue, for a feature called "Alone At Home: 10 Safety Tips For Working Parents & Their Kids.")

- **Don't make your child into a "status symbol."** It's hard   44
not to want your child to match or top other children's accomplishments—and so be a positive reflection on you as a parent. But it's important to remember that a child's time spent simply playing may, in the long run, advance his development far more than goal-oriented events. During play, children learn how to get along with others, how to plan and persevere (required for even such simple projects as building a block tower) and how to gain the self-esteem that comes from doing what they like to do in a way they like to do it.

- **Become your child's advocate at school.** If you feel your   45
child's school is putting on too much academic or athletic
pressure, speak to the teacher, the principal or both. Take
your concerns to your parent–teacher association. Chances
are that other parents share your feelings, and voices raised
in chorus can often bring results that a single individual
could not.

- **Protest and boycott businesses that exploit children.** If   46
you believe that an advertising campaign is not in the best
interests of children, write to the chief executive officer of the
company behind it. Also, let your local video and record store
know that you believe videocassettes and records that link sex
and violence are harmful to children. To make sure that the
store gets your message, say that neither you nor your children
will be shopping there if such tapes are easily available to
minors.

- **Make time for doing nothing.** Unscheduled relaxation time   47
is good for both you and your children. Try not to cave in to
pressure to make every moment you spend with your child
"meaningful."

   Says Fred Rogers, "The first years of our children's lives   48
represent the best opportunity for emotional growth. As we see
our children develop, we receive a precious second chance to
work through whatever issues were left unresolved in our own
childhood. When we rush children through their developmental stages, both generations are the poorer."

   One final bit of wisdom from school psychologist John   49
Sweetland: "Childhood is not just preparation for life. Childhood *is* life."

Questions for Thinking and Discussion

1. In the first three paragraphs of this article, the authors cite examples of
children who are much too adult for their own good. In your own
experience, either in your own life or through your observations, do
you know of children who are much too adult for their years? Why do
some children grow up too fast? What happens to them when they
become adults?

2. Part of the article discusses how parents influence their children to be
involved in too much. Children are encouraged to take all sorts of

lessons and be involved in many activities—"parents have kids 'enriching' themselves at breakneck speed from infancy on."

Are all of these activities really that detrimental for children? Can some of the lessons they take (piano, karate) or the activities they participate in be useful? Evaluate both sides of this issue and think about both the negative and the positive influences that the activities can have.

Are We Stealing Our Children's Childhood?

ANN MELVIN

IMAGES COME, UNBIDDEN, in this media age. They snag, like cobwebs on your ear, when you walk unsuspecting through, say, your own den at midnight.

A kid is talking into a handheld mike thrust at his jugular.

"I don't think it's right. Why pay a guy $16 million just to play basketball? It ain't right. I mean you just can't trust anybody these days."

I shrug with annoyance and trudge on to put clean towels in the bathrooms. Sports news reruns. Who cares?

But somehow, in the following days, the solemn face of this adolescent—and his solemn, existentialist sophistry—sift unbidden, again and again, through my consciousness.

"I mean you just can't trust anybody these days."

What does this have to do with sports? With basketball? With signing a player for $16 million? Trust?

Trust whom? Over what? And why?

This is stupid. I shake my head to shake the image.

But it persists.

And slowly it comes to me that what is persisting is the horrible image of what childhood has become for so many children. A cynical, distrusting posture of small hope and largely superficial worldliness.

Sports is not the issue here. The faceless commentator behind the mike could have been asking about school funding, Ed McMahon's million-dollar sweepstakes, news of U.N. action in Somalia or the number of calories in Coke. It doesn't matter. The message this child has for America in his 15 seconds of fame is that you just can't trust anybody these days.

And I think it is a message we should start listening to, loud and clear.

For it tells us—better than national literacy tests, better than juvenile justice statistics, better than spending patterns of the pre-teen, better than crime statistics—what is going wrong with childhood.

It reveals the common childhood of premature aging; precocious cynicism. A childhood of little joy and little hope. A childhood about which very, very little is perceived as good.

"Exactly," the ardent fix-it folks of this world exclaim. And snap-   16
ping to attention with their fingers held aloft for enumeration, they
begin:

"Therefore, we must teach the children how to protect them-   17
selves.

"We must teach them how to drop and roll in case of fire or cross   18
fire. How to do CPR and call 911 and look in the back seat before
entering the car. To never open the door to strangers and be cautious
what you tell on the telephone.

"We must teach them reproductive responsibility and about sexu-   19
ally transmitted diseases and how to use a condom.

"And we must assume their parents will not teach these things,   20
so we must shove reading and math and history aside and make more
room for teaching these life skills so they can . . ."

Can what? Not trust anything? Or anyone?   21

What are we doing here? Is this what we are supposed to be doing   22
for the children? Making cynical, drawn and frightened little survivors
out of them?

Perhaps this—this cautionary overkill—is what has parents re-   23
sisting teaching things in school like sex education and the new reproductive responsibility.

Maybe parents aren't as resistant to a little sex education as they   24
are reluctant to eschew forever life's elements of joy and victory.

Perhaps they, too, are wondering, like me, whatever happened to   25
joy, "the itsy-bitsy spider," and hope "a hard beginning maketh a good
ending."

Why are our children learning to put on condoms before we   26
have been able to read to them of John Keat's "night's starred face,
huge cloudy symbols of a high romance." Or even taken them to see
an old rerun of *The King and I*? "Shall we dance?" ever again?

I know, I know. We've got to teach them to take care of them-   27
selves. But maybe I'm not the only one worried that, in what seems a
modern overkill on what's wrong with our world, we forget to tell the
kids what's right.

I think our goal was not education for sheer survival; wasn't it   28
something about the educated mind . . . prevailing?

Questions for Thinking and Discussion

1. What does the title of this article mean? What kind of childhood
   do you believe Melvin is referring to in her title? Is that definition

of childhood compatible with the reality of childhood in modern society?

2. Melvin suggests that the fear of further stealing childhood for children is what makes many parents resist sex education in schools. What other reasons for this resistance does Melvin not address? Do you agree or disagree with this resistance? Why?

For Some Parents, Teens' Sweeties Are Welcome as Overnight Guests

LORAINE O'CONNELL

It's 6 a.m. Do you know where your teen-ager is?   1

Some liberal-minded parents can tell you exactly where their   2
teen—and their teen's significant other—are: in the bedroom. Sleeping, having sex, whatever.

While more and more school districts are preaching abstinence,   3
and popular culture is preaching promiscuity, a few parents—very few, to be sure—are coming to grips with teen-age sexuality in an unconventional way.

Eileen, a Florida bookkeeper, is one of those parents.   4

(That's not her real name. All the parents and teens interviewed   5
for this article requested anonymity.)

Her 18-year-old son, Neil, is a college freshman. For nine months   6
he dated Terry, a 16-year-old high school student. Before their breakup a few weeks ago, Neil was spending most nights at Terry's house—in her bed.

"I don't care if he's staying in her house and sleeping in her bed   7
or not," says Eileen. After all, "they can do that [have sex] anywhere they choose."

Eileen figures that forbidding the couple to sleep in the same bed   8
wouldn't have shut down their sex lives.

In fact, the overwhelming sentiment of parents such as Eileen is   9
that sexual activity among teens is an inescapable fact of life.

With the twin pressures of hormones and American culture bear-   10
ing down on them, a lot of teens are going to do what comes naturally.

"I try to be very open with her because there's so much going on,"   11
says Cindy, a customer-service representative and the mother of Terry. "I know she has learned about sex education from me and in school. I don't agree with it, but in today's time, it's inevitable [that teens will have sex.]"

Nancy Gilliland winces every time she hears those words. She's   12
the instructional support teacher for sexuality education in the Orange County (Fla.) schools.

"Parents have written off their kids," says Gilliland. "Everyone has   13
given kids the right to act [have sex] because we don't believe they can
control themselves.

"The mental attitude has got to change to tell kids we believe they   14
can control themselves, they can abstain from sex"—preferably until
marriage.

But 72 percent of all high school seniors have had intercourse,   15
according to a 1990 survey by the federal Centers for Disease Control
and Prevention.

Confronted by the reality of teen sexuality, parents who allow   16
their teens' sweeties to spend the night distinguish between casual sex
and serious sex.

"I think teen-agers having indiscriminate sex is awful," says   17
Brenda, an accountant whose son routinely spent the night at his
girlfriend's house until they broke up.

"But I think that a relationship is a relationship, whether you're   18
17 or 25. You're biologically mature and it [sexual activity] happens."

But it doesn't have to happen in your own home, school officials   19
say.

"There's just no need to aid and abet them in this kind of stunted   20
emotional development," says Beverley Freeman, director of guidance
at Lyman High School in Longwood, Fla. "I cannot see putting the
stamp of approval on it."

In addition to the obvious physical risks—pregnancy, sexually   21
transmitted diseases and AIDS—there are emotional risks, she says.

"I'm thinking more along the lines of hurt and disillusionment   22
that come with practicing sex before you know what it's really all
about," Freeman says, "and the harm that's going to come to you
psychologically and emotionally."

But parents of bed-sharing teens are convinced their kids are   23
unusually mature and can handle heart-break just as well at 17 as they
would at 27.

Both the physical and emotional hazards are less "if you have two   24
level-headed kids who respect each other,'" says Cindy, the mother of
Terry.

One high school teacher, who requested anonymity, says she has   25
talked to several kids who spend the night with their significant others.

"They'll sit right here and tell me, 'I didn't get here on time   26
because my boyfriend didn't wake me up,' " she says.

When the teacher asks where Mom is, the typical response is "in   27
her bedroom asleep."

"There's more of it going on that you'd expect."   28

Indeed.   29

Ashley, a high school senior whose parents are divorced, used to   30
stay at her boyfriend's house because her mother traveled a lot and she
didn't like being home alone.

"I get scared staying by myself, no matter how many alarms there   31
are," she says.

So her boyfriend would invite her over, they'd watch TV, get   32
sleepy and head for his bedroom.

"We slept in the same room and sometimes had sex there," she   33
says.

The two recently split up, but their playing house—at least in his   34
bedroom—for 12 months hasn't left her torn up.

"Whenever you make love, it's something special, and it does   35
make a difference," Ashley says. "Things change whenever people have
intercourse. But I don't wish I hadn't."

In fact, Ashley's reason for breaking up with the guy is refresh-   36
ingly, well, teen-age.

"I didn't want a boyfriend—I wanted to go out with my friends."   37

Not all teens are that blasé, of course.   38

Marti Wise, an Altamonte Springs, Fla., counselor who lectures   39
at schools on the value of abstinence, sees a sense of guilt and shame
developing among teens, especially girls, over their sexual behavior.

The reason: confusion bred by mixed messages.   40

Most parents still tell their kids it's best to wait until marriage—or   41
at least until you're out of high school—to have sex, Wise says. But
society imparts a very different message: Sex feels good, everyone else
is doing it, so get with it.

"When they do engage in sexual activity, especially having gotten   42
the message 'don't do it,' we see the guilt and shame," Wise says.

However, not all teens end up feeling guilty, and Wise concedes   43
that it's impossible to generalize about the emotional impact of teen
sexuality.

"There's no way to broad-brush it," she says. "Is the teen coming   44
from a home where Mom and Dad have participated in parenting?
Where they've been able to set some boundaries for the teen-ager to
grow up in? It depends upon the family's guidelines."

And the fact is, for plenty of teens the messages they get aren't   45
mixed so much as muted.

Seventeen-year-old Nancy, who has spent many nights in her   46
boyfriend's bed during the past year, says her parents didn't necessarily
want her to become sexually active, "but they knew it was my choice."

"My mother always told me that if I ever needed her to buy   47
condoms or get me on the pill, all I had to do was tell her," she says.
"But I didn't need to. His parents usually paid for things like that."

For those of us who wouldn't have dreamed of spending the night 48
in bed with our high school sweethearts, one question remains: Aren't
these kids ever nervous about, you know, being heard?

Apparently not. 49

Ashley reports that her ex-boyfriend's mother "would go to bed 50
early, and we could hear his dad snoring on the recliner."

Questions for Thinking and Discussion

1. Some of the parents in this article believe that sexual activity among
teens is an "inescapable fact of life." Given their position, how do you
feel about the parents who knowingly allow, and even encourage, their
teenage children to sleep with their partners in their own beds or their
partners' beds?

2. Identify some of the emotional and physical risks associated with teen
sex. Are these risks significant for a large population of teenagers who
have premarital sex? How do the risks stack up against the societal
message teenagers get: "Sex feels good, everyone else is doing it, so get
with it"?

Some Parents Are Wimps

Sheila Taylor

My young friend could hardly stay awake. She'd been to a slumber   1
party, and in the middle of the night, the hostess's mother had taken
the guests out wrapping houses.

I was surprised but not really shocked: unfortunately, I'd heard it   2
all before.

For those who've never been, had, known or seen kids, let me   3
explain that T.P.-ing is when you fling rolls and rolls of toilet paper into
an acquaintance's front-yard trees, so that the paper entwines and
entangles leaves and branches and is the dickens to clean up.

It's an ever so charming custom, inexpensive and relatively harm-   4
less, and its only drawback is that it negates everything the kids learn
in school, and in most homes, I like to think, about environmental
responsibility.

Well, it's against the law, too, but not a really big law, something   5
having to do with personal property, trespassing, etc.

Also, considering how many nervous homeowners keep guns at   6
the ready these days, I'd think fooling around in somebody's yard in
the middle of the night might be even more risky physically.

The one time I caught my daughter, who was then in middle   7
school, after a house-wrapping spree, I made her go over to the victim's
house the next day and clear out all the toilet paper.

A few weeks later at a parents meeting, the discussion centered   8
on setting some common rules for parties, telephone habits, curfews
and such, and one parent mentioned the perils of wrapping houses.

"What I do," one father said, "is drive them around myself to   9
wrap houses."

"You do what?" Surely, I'd mis-heard.   10

"I drive them myself. It's much better than their being out by   11
themselves at 2 a.m.," the man explained, now in full sail under the
winds of righteousness.

Well, yes. I just hadn't realized that letting 12-year-olds run   12
around by themselves at 2 a.m. was the alternative.

Here some of the mothers and fathers were punishing the chil-   13
dren for wrapping houses, and here this man was, helping them do it.

Here, too, as far as I was concerned, anyway, was a man with an   14
interesting idea of fun, as well as one in clear need of a hobby, but that's
beside the point, I guess.

Yet he explained his solution so emphatically, so proudly, that for   15
a minute or two it sounded logical, so reasonable.

"Why don't you tell 'em they can't go?" another parent finally   16
asked. "Or just lock 'em up?"

Some of us knew why. This man was scared to death of his   17
daughter, who had the tongue of a serpent.

She talked, in fact, exactly like one of those "typical" teen-agers   18
we see these days in the movies that have so consistently offered up
monster-kids and wimp-parents that both now seem the norm, rather
than the caricature they once were.

Remember *Parenthood?* The movie, not the TV show. The single   19
mother allowed her teen-age daughter a foul mouth, use of her bedroom as a motel and to be a total pain in the rear, while she, the
mother, played the role of a well-intentioned, loving and almost totally
ineffective object of pity.

The movie's redeeming factors helped make everything come out   20
all right by the final credits, but still, I wondered if other parents,
particularly single mothers, seeing the movie, mentally threw in the
towel even before they ran out of popcorn.

Take *Texasville.* What a dreary family. The kids, a teen-age son   21
with preteen siblings, are encouraged in their atrocities by the whiny
parents, whose strongest method of discipline are rueful shakes of the
head.

"Kids today. Whaddya gonna do?" they seem to be musing.   22

I certainly don't mind exaggeration for the sake of humor—   23
hyperbole is a standard tool of my own trade—but you can't help but
wonder why the make-believe parents don't simply draw the line
somewhere short of felony.

Critics said the teen-agers in *Parenthood* represented an accurate   24
portrayal of mid-America family life.

They didn't represent mid-America kids to me, just a few of the   25
more unpleasant ones, most of whom, but not all, by any means, the
product of permissive parents. Well-intentioned, certainly, and loving
. . . and almost totally ineffective.

Questions for Thinking and Discussion

1. Sheila Taylor discusses some incidents that show some parents have
   very little control over what their children do. Do you believe parents
   you have known do a good job of disciplining their children and

teaching them values? Do you see some problems, overall, with how parents handle their children? Explain with examples.

2. Both Taylor and O'Connell (in the previous article) give examples of parents whose guidance is questionable. What do you think are the likely effects of this kind of parenting on the children?

Face the Music

BARBARA MELTZ

Lead: 1
Back off, back off, bitch,
down in the gutter, dyin' in the ditch,

Text:
you better back off, back off, bitch.
face of an angel with the love of a witch,
back off, back off, bitch, back off, back off, bitch.

These are the words to a song your preteen may be listening to 2
on his headset. And if it's not this particular song—by Axl Rose of the
group Guns N' Roses—it may be something even worse, with a whole
lot of four-letter words and sexist, racist, homophobic or violent
themes. The problem is not just this group, either. Guns N' Roses'
lyrics are mild compared to those of other groups some preteens hear
such as: Nirvana, Pearl Jam, Metallica.

What's a parent to do? 3

For starters, don't jump to conclusions. Even if your child is 4
listening to this music, that doesn't mean he is listening to the words.

"There's a lot of evidence kids don't pay attention to the lyrics. 5
They go for the beat and the noise," said Donald Roberts Jr., Stanford
University communication department chairman, whose research area
is media/children.

If that's a hard line to buy, consider the experience of Lora Brody, 6
a Newton, Mass., mother of three. When her son Sam, 11, brought
home a Guns N' Roses tape, she listened—carefully—to the words.

"All I had to do was listen once to know they are not the values 7
I want for my son," Brody said. "They are very sexist, appallingly
racist."

Heated arguments ensued. She would tell Sam she didn't want 8
him to listen to the music. Sam would retort that he was the only kid
whose mother felt this way. They were getting nowhere until Brody
quoted some lyrics—unquotable here—to her son.

"Mom!" he said. "Don't say that!" 9

"You mean it's OK to listen to that on a lyric, but it's not OK to 10
say it?" she asked, somewhat incredulous.

"Yeah," he said. "I just like the music. I don't like the words." 11

296

But even if kids aren't buying the music for the lyrics and prob-   12
ably aren't buying what the lyrics say, parents should still pay attention.

"A parental laissez-faire attitude is absolutely wrong," said Mi-   13
chael T. Marsden, a dean at Northern Michigan University whose area
of research has been popular culture.

If you are hands-off, he said, "essentially, you are telling your   14
children, 'Here is our world as a family, there is that other world, and
the twain shall never meet.' You're saying you can have two sets of
values and one can be used against the other."

How you approach all this with a preteen is tricky.   15

That he likes this music at all is a sign he is trying to separate   16
from you. Think back to the music of your own preteen and teen years.
Elvis? The Stones? The Doors? Did your parents like it? Of course not.
Didn't that make you like it more?

"Societies wouldn't advance very much" if kids didn't find   17
ways to annoy their parents, said sociologist Clinton Sanders, a professor at the University of Connecticut whose area of expertise is social
deviance in popular culture. "Music is one of the first battle lines that
gets draw."

One reason is that the music is easily available. Another is that it   18
speaks to the issues the child of this age is dealing with.

"The typical preteen is coping with a number of fears and anxi-   19
eties, but especially isolation and puberty," Marsden explained. He said
horror films are another popular medium for 11- to 14-year-olds
because the monster parallels the body changes a preteen struggles
with.

"Their music serves the same function," she said. Kids "identify   20
with the music groups because they feel they don't fit in, they're
misunderstood. They find through the music an expression of their
deep-felt hopes, angst, desires, fears."

Which is why a parent needs to come at this with an "I-   21
understand-you-like-this-music" attitude. Value judgments ("This isn't
music, it's just noise!"), outrage ("We've raised you on good music!")
and lectures will make your child defensive. They will get you nowhere.

The role of the parent, after all, is to educate. Marsden, who also   22
doesn't like censorship, argues that it cuts off the possibility of education and instead prompts a child to say: "What's so bad about this? I've
gotta find out."

There's something else about censoring that bothers Roberts.   23

"It's a value statement that said to a child, 'I am teaching that it is   24
OK to control access to information.' That's a fundamental principle
parents need to be aware of and be comfortable with if they are going
to censor," he said.

Asking questions is the best thing for parents to do, according to 25
Tim Scheurer, a professor of humanities at Franklin University in
Columbus, Ohio, who studies music and popular culture. That's what
he does with his son Andy, 10.

"I want to find out what he knows about what he listens to, so I'll 26
say, 'What do you think this is about?' If I think he's confused or has
the wrong impression, I'll say, 'I think there's another way to think
about this,' " Scheurer said.

With music from groups such as Guns N' Roses, he said it is very 27
legitimate to raise such questions as, "What do you think about what
he said about blacks or gays or women? Do you agree with what he
said?"

Be prepared for almost any answer and take it in stride, Scheurer 28
advises. He's known parents who have discovered their child has sexist
feelings. He said it's also very common for a preteen to say he doesn't
like the music, but all his friends do, so he pretends he does. "That's
fine," Scheurer said. It's certainly age-appropriate. "That's just something he'll eventually work through."

The one thing parents should not be vague about is expressing 29
their opinion about the values that get espoused.

"Give your perspective on it," Sanders said. "Develop conversa- 30
tion around it."

As a father, Scheurer said, "I want to be very sure that Andy isn't 31
walking away from this thinking it's OK to think or talk about women
the way Axl Rose does. Andy tells me he likes it because it's naughty.
But he needs to know it is more than that. It's plain wrong."

Having these kinds of conversations is insurance for the future, 32
when there will be other critical topics on which you want to have
input.

Lora Brody ended up in a long conversation with her son about 33
values.

"He knows I'm not saying all this just to make his life miserable, 34
that there are values at stake here," she said.

The conversation not only enabled Brody to breathe a little easier 35
and to back off, but also, she thinks, improved their relationship. "In
some ways, it made us closer," she said.

Questions for Thinking and Discussion

1. One major conflict between children and their parents is the children's
   music—especially the music of preteens and teens. What, according to

Meltz's article, are the reasons for this conflict? What purpose, if any, does this conflict serve?

2. Many parents and others believe that listening to certain kinds of music can have negative effects on preteens and teenagers. Others believe that music is a harmless way for young people to express themselves. What do you believe? Should parents be concerned? Does some music have negative effects on preteens and teenagers, or is listening to certain kinds of music fairly harmless? Think in particular about the kind of music Meltz discusses in her article.

Build Moral Foundation at Home

USA TODAY

Parents are the primary teachers of their children, especially when it comes to values, experts say. 1

And parents need to teach—and model—their own values mindfully, says Eileen Shiff, editor of *Experts Advise Parents* (Delta, $14.95). 2

"If we don't lobby for our own beliefs, a variety of influences fill the void: music, TV, movies, magazines, peers, gangs and cults," says Shiff, of USA TODAY's Parenting Panel. 3

Says Cathy McCoy, author of *The New Teenage Body Book* (Body Press/Perigee, $14.95): "You may not hold the same values they are getting in their sex education class. The family needs to listen to the child's point of view," but also "let your child know where you stand." 4

She also says parents need to teach kids balance. "Few issues are totally black and white. Moral people can disagree." 5

Also, McCoy says parents may need to look into their own hearts. They may say they value ethnic diversity, and yet use language in their own homes that betrays hidden prejudices. 6

Shiff says, "Teaching values isn't a one-time business. It happens while you're processing children's questions, or listening to the TV news about suicide, teen pregnancy or drug-induced crime." Guidelines for parents: 7

- Discuss values early before children make "life-limiting" decisions.
- Model the values yourself. "What they see you do carries more weight than your words."
- Share what is important to you. "When we don't talk about values, we give the message they are not important."
- Help them consider the needs of others as well as their own. "Model compassion to others in need."
- Monitor the TV. "Most young people today watch a steady diet of sensationalized sex and violence."
- Help them feel good about themselves "so they won't be so vulnerable to peer pressure."
- Teach respect "by demonstrating it for yourself, your children and others."

- Role-play assertiveness skills. "Some youngsters want to stand up for their values, but don't know how."
- Be receptive to their questions. "Don't respond with anger or shock."
- Teach them to use mistakes as learning experiences.
- Help them question the values of others. "Are 'friends' who get them into trouble really friends?"

Questions for Thinking and Discussion

1. In this article, Cathy McCoy, author of *The New Teenage Body Book,* says that parents need to teach kids balance: "Few issues are totally black and white. Moral people can disagree." What issues do you know that are not "black or white"? How should parents teach balance in these issues?

2. One guideline Eileen Shiff gives parents is to "model the values your-self. What [children] see you do carries more weight than your words." Evaluate Shiff's advice here. How do children learn from parents? Is modeling the most effective way for parents to teach their children certain things? What other ways do children learn from parents? Look at some of the other guidelines. How might parents incorporate some of these suggestions into their childrearing practices?

What Makes a Bad Loser?

Lawrence M. Kutner

No child likes to lose. But there are some for whom not winning or not getting their way is a trigger for a tantrum or a pout. They'll storm off if their friends won't let them be the captain of their fantasy pirate ship. They'll knock over the checkerboard if they're losing a game.

A certain amount of this behavior is normal and reflects a child's stage of emotional development. Very young children don't yet have the words to express the intense emotions they feel. They're also experimenting with ways to handle their frustration and desire for control.

"Toddlers and preschoolers find it hard to lose, just as they find it hard to share toys," said Dr. Edward L. Deci, a professor of psychology and director of the human motivation program at the University of Rochester. He's found that older children and adults who are bad losers worry about what others think of them if they don't win or feel that winning is what makes them good people.

While the consequences of stomping off in a huff are minor when you're in kindergarten, such behavior can lead to more serious social problems among older children. Bad losers have more trouble than other children in making and maintaining friendships. For some children the problem can become self-perpetuating, since their difficulty with friendships increases their feelings of worthlessness and their need to win.

The reasons for becoming a bad loser rest in a combination of genetics and environment. Some children appear from birth to be easily frustrated and upset. Their temperaments make them more likely to become upset at situations that other children take in stride. More commonly, however, children who are bad losers are responding to the subtle messages they get from their families, teachers and the mass media.

"Children watch how their parents handle things when they're frustrated," said Dr. Sheila Ribordy, a professor of psychology and the director of clinical psychology training at DePaul University in Chicago. "They pay closer attention to what we do than to what we say."

Some children who are bad losers have parents who are bad losers, who teach through their actions that getting angry is the way to handle frustration. The example set by parents may be both subtle and blatant. Parents who never talk about their own disappointments or failures give their children an impossibly high standard to live up to. The implications of making mistakes or losing are blown out of proportion.

Even well-meaning questions like "Did you do your best?" can unintentionally give children a disturbing message. If they didn't do their best, they worry that their parents or coaches will view them as disappointments. If they did do their best and still failed, then perhaps they are hopeless.

"Parents should assume that whatever their child did, it was the best he or she could do on that particular day," advised Dr. Philip C. Kendall, a professor of psychology at Temple University in Philadelphia. "A lot of parents think that their children's negative emotions are bad. But they're healthy in the right places."

Although all children have periods when they're short-tempered and have difficulty losing, it's seldom a sign of trouble if it occurs rarely and reflects the importance of the situation. We should expect children to be more upset if they lose the finals of a local basketball tournament than if they lose a spur-of-the-moment pick-up game. Children who treat those disappointments equally are probably seeing them as tests of their self-worth.

"I'd be concerned if your child doesn't get over it quickly," said Dr. David Fassler, the director of Child and Adolescent Psychiatry at Choate Health Systems in Woburn, Mass., a suburb of Boston. "Most preschoolers can get over a moderate disappointment within a few hours. With older children, it can last a couple of days."

Questions for Thinking and Discussion

1. In this article, Kutner implies that being a bad loser will eventually be harmful to a child, but he never describes what happens to bad losers. What kinds of problems do you think bad losers experience? What are some effects of these problems? What happens when bad losers become adults?

2. Are you a good or a bad loser? What specific events in your childhood or adolescence probably contributed to your being a good or bad loser?

Teaching your Child That Losing Isn't Everything

THE NEW YORK TIMES

BECAUSE CHILDREN WHO ARE BAD LOSERS often have unrealistic expectations for themselves, one of the best things parents can do is to help them set goals that emphasize effort and improvement, as well as winning. Those goals might include passing the basketball well during the pressure of a game, or swimming two lengths of the pool nonstop. 1

Here are some other things you should keep in mind if you're concerned that your child finds it difficult to keep losses in perspective: 2

- Look at the subtle messages you're giving your children about success and failure. 3

  "When your child comes home from a game, ask whether he had fun, not whether he won," advised Dr. David Fassler, the director of Child and Adolescent Psychiatry at Choate Health Systems in Woburn, Mass., a suburb of Boston. "If you have a big celebration when your child's team wins, but you just say, 'Well, you tried,' when they don't, you're teaching that you value winning more than effort." 4

- Talk about some of your own frustrations with your children. 5

  Bad losers often worry that anything they don't succeed at will be shameful to their parents. This concern is compounded if they never see or hear about how family members handle disappointments. 6

  "Parents of healthy, achieving children share their mistakes and shortcomings, while the parents of bad losers often hide their mistakes," said Dr. Miriam Adderholdt-Elliott, an educational psychologist at the University of North Carolina at Charlotte who studies perfectionistic children. "Talk about when you didn't win the lead in the school play." 7

- Let your children practice losing as well as winning. 8

  Young children take great glee in defeating their parents at simple card and board games. It gives them a sense of power that they relish. But consistently winning such games at home may set up false expectations for when they play with their friends. 9

"Don't let them win all the time," advised Dr. Sheila 10
Ribordy, a professor of psychology at DePaul University in
Chicago. "They learn some important lessons from disappoint-
ment."

Losing a game at home can be less threatening to children 11
than losing one at a friend's house.

- Encourage your children to keep trying, even when they're 12
frustrated.

If bad losers don't feel they can be successful at an activity, 13
they may not do it at all. Letting children know that you'll be
proud of them simply for trying will often give them the
incentive they need to redouble their efforts.

"If they persevere, they may find that they can master what 14
they've been avoiding," Ribordy said.

Questions for Thinking and Discussion

1. This short piece gives parents suggestions to help their children deal
with losing. Which of Kutner's suggestions do you think would work
best? Are there any that wouldn't work at all? Explain.
2. Dr. Miriam Adderholdt-Elliott, who is quoted in this article, specializes
in "perfectionist children." What are perfectionist children? What are
such children like? If you know any, provide examples of their behavior. What childhood experiences do you think help form children? Or,
are they just born that way?

Spanking Is Opposed, Hands Down

SHARON COX

PARENTS: BEFORE DISCIPLINING YOUR KIDS with a blow to their bottom, 1
thigh or hand, stop, take a deep breath and listen to what they have to
say about physical discipline.

"I don't feel that spanking or any physical punishment is right," 2
said Margaret Brown, a 17-year-old senior at Trinity High School in
Euless [TX]. "Spanking instills a degree of fear in a child that should
not exist in a healthy parent/child relationship."

When kids get in trouble today, most prefer alternative forms of 3
punishment.

"I would ground them or send them to their room because if they 4
already got hurt for what they did [like get in a fight at school], why
hurt them again?" asked Lindsay Scott, 11, a fifth-grader at Lily B.
Clayton Elementary School in Fort Worth. "If you do spank a kid, they
will get mad and run out or they will become very scared of you."

"Spanking could also drive kids to drugs and alcohol. Children 5
may use drugs and alcohol to take away the pain," said Dawn Perkins,
seventh-grader at Watauga Middle School in Forth Worth.

"Under no circumstance should it be appropriate for anyone to 6
spank a child because it could easily be a form of child abuse," said
Tim Box, an 11-year-old student at Lily B. Clayton.

During the past 10 days, I interviewed more than 100 first- 7
through 12-grade students. Most preferred sparing the rod and spending the weekend sitting in their room for punishment *unless* being
grounded means missing a major social function like a friend's party.

When asked if they would rather be spanked or miss a party, all 8
but four said they would rather have a quick, nonviolent lick and then
head off to be with their friends.

"I'd rather be spanked than grounded. It is a quick punishment 9
and it would be over. For example, say you are going somewhere and
you go somewhere else. And when your parents find out, they would
spank you and then your punishment is over and you can go on with
your life."

Chrystal Goodwill, eighth-grader
Watauga Middle

"Spanking would be OK if you had a party and you were going   10
to be grounded. But if you were going to be put in your room, then I
don't think you should be spanked."

Emily Vance, 11
Lily B. Clayton Elementary

Emily and her classmates repeatedly emphasized the fear that   11
spanking instills in children.

"I think spanking is not appropriate because you become scared   12
of your parents. Respect is very important in a parent/child relationship. Without respect, kids have no kind of trust in their parents.
Spanking ruins that trust. Kids should be able to relate in some way
toward their parents.

Charlotte Ice, 11

Several seniors at Trinity High, however, said that younger kids,   13
like preschoolers, needed spankings as an immediate form of punishment.

"It is important to spank children during their younger years.   14
When children are in their young stages, physical discipline has a
greater effect on them as opposed to verbal discipline, and discipline
is a necessity. When children reach about fifth grade, verbal discipline
should be encouraged more than physical."

Chris Mapp, 18

Stephen Pillow, an 18-year-old student at Trinity, has a mature   15
response to the entire spanking issue:

"I believe it only is appropriate to spank a young child so long as   16
it is used only as a disciplinary measure. If it gets to the point where
the child is left with prolonged pain or bruises, then I believe the
spankings should be stopped. In this case, the child would need to be
punished by being banned from whatever he is most interested in at
the moment."

Questions for Thinking and Discussion

1. How valid are the viewpoints of the children in Cox's article? Read each
   of the children's comments and decide whether you believe the children's points are reasonable.
2. One 17-year-old high school student says, "Spanking instills a degree
   of fear in a child that should not exist in a healthy parent/child
   relationship." What are the characteristics of a healthy parent/child
   relationship? What criteria would you use to determine whether a
   parent/child relationship is healthy?

Motherhood Blues

SHEILA ANNE FEENEY

ABOUT A YEAR AGO, Nelta Brunson's little boy, B.J., looked up at her 1
and asked, "Mommy, why is your face like that? Did I do something?"

A site project manager for a construction company, Brunson 2
loved her job, hated her commute, and realized that her evenings with
B.J. were a forced march consisting of dinner, homework and bed.

"By the time I get home, it's 7 o'clock. The kid is tired by that 3
time; he's played and he's not interested in doing homework. I realized
I'm rushing him along because I wanted to get dinner ready and
showers done," just so she could hit the sack to get up again.

At that point, Brunson, a divorcee, realized she had to dig herself 4
out of the blues before her 8-year-old grew up to remember his mother
as someone who put the laundry ahead of love.

The emotional tug of war between a demanding job and demand- 5
ing kids is familiar to every parent who has ever had to leave a weeping
kid to earn a living.

There's guilt that you're not spending enough time with the kids. 6
There's guilt that you're not spending enough time at your job—
especially now with the tyranny of the recession looming over everyone. And there's a Greek chorus of critics (with grandparents,
ex-spouses and bosses singing solos) reminding you that you aren't a
good enough mother, housekeeper or employee.

In the movie *This is My Life,* mom Dottie Ingels disputes the myth 7
that a happy mom makes for happy kids.

Anything that spells joy for a single mom—a glamorous, lucrative 8
career that entails travel, a great love life—makes kids miserable,
Dottie moans.

Give kids a choice between a suicidal mother in the next room or 9
their mom ecstatic in Hawaii, and they'll choose suicidal in the next
room every time, Ingels laments.

The stress of fulfilling dual roles is "enormous," says Suzanne 10
Jones, executive director of the Single Parent Resource Center.

"Resentment is another part of it. You resent your child and you 11
resent your job and you hate yourself because you're just inadequate
to all of it. You get very depressed," says Jones.

"The teachers call these women in and tell them to spend more 12
time with their child. Well, they work all day, travel an hour and a half
each day and go to college at night."

Moms and dads may feel that their kids and their careers keep 13
them continually in a state of guilt, but "there's an expectation pro-
jected onto mothers to fix everything," says Joanne Turnbull, associate
professor at Columbia School of Social Work.

"Women have a high rate of depression," in part because of 14
the multiple roles they are expected not only to fulfill, but to excel.
"The single highest risk factor for being depressed is being female," she
adds.

Sometimes, the breaking point comes as an epiphany, as it did for 15
Brunson. She resolved to change the way she lived, and she did.

"For the first time, I'm starting to feel happy," she says. 16

B.J. is happier, too. Now he's much more likely to entice his mom 17
into his own construction project with a plea to "look at this design
and my foundation base!"

To put herself in a more energetic mood, Brunson began waking 18
up earlier—at 4:45 a.m.—to get in her exercise, prayer and medita-
tion.

She also resolved to pay the $150 more a month to take the 19
express bus home at night. The subway was cheaper, but the unpleasant ride took forever and left her in a sour mood.

"With the bus, I get 45 minutes of centering, down time," when 20
she can read a book and recharge.

Another plus is the amicable relationship she has cultivated with 21
her ex-husband. Brunson discovered a good relationship with her ex
benefits not only B.J., but her—especially when dad steps in to pinch-
hit with baby-sitting. On the weekends he's with his dad. "I take a
shower and a bath, and do my nails."

B.J. also had to face some facts. He looked forward to his week- 22
ends home as a time he got mom's attention all to himself, but Brunson
negotiated with her "male chauvinist piglet." The more he helped her
with the housework, the sooner she and he could get down to the
serious business of playing with action figures, Chinese checkers and
building blocks.

Unknowingly, Brunson implemented a lot of these techniques 23
that experts advocate:

- Frazzled moms have to take a break from the worrying and
  endless interruptions to make a list and gain some clarity,
  Jones says.

- Divide obligations into "musts" and optional chores.
    "Cleaning the house, in my mind, is trivial. Some people *24* consider ironing the curtains and reading to their child equally important."
    Forget the curtains and make sure you spend at least 20 *25* minutes each night with each child alone, Jones says. "They need that attention alone with no one competing for it." Bedtime is often the best opportunity, she adds.

- The first few minutes home is usually murder on any parent. *26* Identify the 20 minutes you are most stressed each day and make a deal with the little rascals to leave you alone then. Mom is entitled to sit and drink a cup of coffee and read the newspaper without anyone bothering her. "You're not the doormat," Jones reminds.

- While working together should never take the place of a *27* child's play time or interfere with homework or extracurricular activities, it's not a sin to have them pitch in and pull their weight.
    "Kids need to know they're important in running the fam- *28* ily. Otherwise, you have little selfish rascals," Jones says.

- Every working parent, single or not, needs a shoulder to talk *29* out the ambivalence. Eveyln Dougherty attends a working parents support group hosted by American International Group (AIG), where she works as a secretary. The group meets monthly and kicks around questions on development, discipline and family conflicts, and everyone leaves a little relieved.
    "We bring all our problems into the group and everyone *30* gives their opinions. It helps a lot," says Dougherty, mother of a 2½-year old. Too, it's nice to share the headlines of first steps, new words and cute stunts with other, similarly rapturous parents.
    In *This Is My Life,* Dottie has her daughters keep journals *31* of their daytime activities when she goes on the road.
    Because three days can seem like an eternity to a tyke, *32* Turnbull recommends letting little ones put stickers on a calendar to count off the days until mommy comes home.

- Anna Beth Benningfield, president elect of the American Asso- *33* ciation for Marriage and Family Therapy, says parents of kids who evince depression, declining grades and bad behavior should rethink their jobs.
    One of her patients told his employer that he could no *34* longer travel for his job because his sons needed him. Arrange-

ments were made for him to supervise another, more mobile employee.

"Many times, traveling and parenthood are not compat- 35 ible. I definitely think you should consider the effect it has on your kid and the effect it has on the parent. They feel they miss out on critical times, and they do," says Benningfield.

Juggling Junior and a job may seem overwhelming, conceded 36 Linda Lyon Bern, director of AIG's employee assistance program, but it also has rewards. One of her friends, a lawyer, was getting ready for work when her daughter looked up and asked, "Mommy, can men be attorneys too?"

Questions for Thinking and Discussion

1. Women in modern American society face many challenges, especially if they are single parents. Think about some of the unique challenges that single mothers face. How do these challenges affect their children?
2. Nearly all working parents feel guilty at some time with regard to both their children and their jobs. How can working parents find a compromise between family life and their jobs? How can they be good parents and good workers? Try to cite some examples of people you have known who seem to be able to be successful both as parents and as workers. What seems to be the secret of their success?

Writing Projects

1. Melvin and Olds and Papalia address the complicated issue of teaching children the skills they need to survive in a complicated and sometimes dangerous world without making them "cynical, drawn and frightened little survivors" (Melvin). Write a paper in which you develop a plan to accomplish this delicate balance. As supporting evidence for your plan, draw on examples from your own childhood or the childhoods of people you have known.

2. Reread your favorite article in this chapter, taking special note of the main parenting problem discussed in the article. Then, prepare a paper entitled "Five Parents Respond to the Experts."

   To write this paper, begin by taking notes from the article. What do the experts say about this particular parenting problem: What is the problem? Why does it exist? What solutions do the experts offer? Then, do some "research" for the paper by interviewing five parents. Summarize for them the experts' discussion in the article and ask the parents whether they agree with them.

   Finally, work up the paper itself. Do your interviews show that the parents agree with the experts? What do your findings tell you about the experts' analyses and advice?

3. Using the same approach as outlined in Writing Project #2 (above), write a paper entitled "Five Children Respond to Experts." Interview five children. Summarize for them the experts' opinions and ask the children whether they agree with them. The paper will show that the interviewees either agree or disagree with the experts. What do these findings tell you about the experts' analyses and advice?

4. Select one of the following topics covered in readings in his chapter:

   > Children Growing Up too Fast (Olds and Papalia)
   > Parents and Children's Music (Meltz)
   > Spanking Children (Cox)
   > Motherhood and Guilt (Feeney)

   Research other articles on this topic, and then prepare a report for your classmates. This report should summarize the opinions of at least two other experts. Do they agree or disagree with points made in the article in this chapter? Do they discuss areas of the problem not covered in the article?

14

Television and Children

ONE EPISODE OF THE ANIMATED SERIES *The Simpsons* opens with the baby, Maggie, watching on television the violent actions of the cartoon characters Scratchy and Itchy. Directly after watching this show, Maggie crawls to where her father, Homer, is doing some work with tools. When he isn't watching, Maggie bops Homer over the head with a hammer, the very same act she had just seen performed on *The Itchy and Scratchy Show.* This episode of *The Simpsons* illustrates what many people believe to be true: TV influences children and if shows are violent, children will be violent, too.

Experts disagree, however, about *the degree to which television affects children* and the *kinds of effects it has.* Look for ways that the first readings in this chapter deal with these two questions. For instance, look for discussions of how television can make children violent, sexually active, restless, or unimaginative; how it can put in children's heads some negative stereotypes of women; how it can force children to grow up too fast; and how it can affect children's physical well-being.

The later readings look at children and television very differently. For example, the last three readings in the chapter describe how parents and teachers use television for positive purposes.

313

Is TV Ruining Our Children?

RICHARD ZOGLIN

BEHOLD EVERY PARENT'S WORST NIGHTMARE: the six-year-old TV addict. 1
He watches in the morning before he goes off to school, plops himself
in front of the set as soon as he gets home in the afternoon and gets
another dose to calm down before he goes to bed at night. He wears
Bart Simpson T shirts, nags Mom to buy him Teenage Mutant Ninja
Turtles toys and spends hours glued to his Nintendo. His teacher says
he is restless and combative in class. What's more, he's having trouble
reading.

Does this creature really exist, or is he just a paranoid video-age 2
vision? The question is gaining urgency as the medium barges ever
more aggressively into children's lives. Except for school and the family,
no institution plays a bigger role in shaping American children. And
no institution takes more heat. TV has been blamed for just about
everything from a decrease in attention span to an increase in street
crime. Cartoons are attacked for their violence and sitcoms for their
foul language. Critics ranging from religious conservatives to consumer
groups like Action for Children's Television have kept up a steady
drumbeat of calls for reform.

Last week Congress took a small step toward obliging. Legislators 3
sent to President Bush a bill that would set limits on commercial time
in children's programming (a still generous $10^1/_2$ minutes per hour on
weekends and 12 minutes on weekdays). The bill would also require
stations to air at least some educational kids' fare as a condition for
getting their licenses renewed. Bush has argued that the bill infringes .
on broadcasters' First Amendment rights, but (unlike President Rea-
gan, who vetoed a similar measure two years ago) he is expected to
allow it to become law.

Yet these mild efforts at reform, as well as critic's persistent gripes 4
about the poor quality of children's TV, skirt the central issue. Even if
the commercialism on kidvid were reined in, even if local stations were
persuaded to air more "quality" children's fare, even if kids could be
shielded from the most objectionable material, the fact remains that
children watch a ton of TV. Almost daily, parents must grapple with a
fundamental, overriding question: What is all that TV viewing doing
to kids, and what can be done about it?

Television has, of course, been an inseparable companion for 5
most American youngsters since the early 1950s. But the baby boom-

ers, who grew up with Howdy Doody and Huckleberry Hound, experienced nothing like the barrage of video images that pepper kids
today. Cable has vastly expanded the supply of programming. The VCR
has turned favorite shows and movies into an endlessly repeatable
pastime. Video games have added to the home box's allure.

The average child will have watched 5,000 hours of TV by the
time he enters first grade and 19,000 hours by the end of high
school—more time than he will spend in class. This dismayingly
passive experience crowds out other, more active endeavors: playing
outdoors, being with friends, reading. Marie Winn, author of the 1977
book *The Plug-In Drug,* gave a memorable, if rather alarmist, description of the trancelike state TV induces: "The child's facial expression is
transformed. The jaw is relaxed and hangs open slightly; the tongue
rests on the front teeth (if there are any). The eyes have a glazed,
vacuous look . . ."

Guided by TV, today's kids are exposed to more information
about the world around them than any other generation in history. But
are they smarter for it? Many teachers and psychologists argue that TV
is largely to blame for the decline in reading skills and school performance. In his studies of children at Yale, psychologist Jerome Singer
found that kids who are heavy TV watchers tend to be less well
informed, more restless and poorer students. The frenetic pace of TV,
moreover, has seeped into the classroom. "A teacher who is going into
a lengthy explanation of an arithmetic problem will begin to lose the
audience after a while," says Singer. "Children are expecting some kind
of show." Even the much beloved *Sesame Street* has been criticized for
reinforcing the TV-inspired notion that education must be fast paced
and entertaining. Says Neil Postman, communications professor at
New York University and author of *Amusing Ourselves to Death:* "*Sesame
Street* makes kids like school only if school is like *Sesame Street.*"

Televised violence may also be having an effect on youngsters.
Singer's research has shown that prolonged viewing by children of
violent programs is associated with more aggressive behavior, such as
getting into fights and disrupting the play of others. (A link between
TV and violent crime, however, has not been clearly established.)
Other studies suggest that TV viewing can dampen kids' imagination.
Patricia Marks Greenfield, a professor of psychology at UCLA, conducted
experiments in which several groups of children were asked to tell a
story about the Smurfs. Those who were shown a Smurfs TV cartoon
beforehand were less "creative" in their storytelling than kids who first
played an unrelated connect-the-dots game.

But the evidence is flimsy for many popular complaints about TV.
In a 1988 report co-authored for the U.S. Department of Education,

Daniel Anderson, professor of psychology at the University of Massachusetts in Amherst, found no convincing evidence that TV has a "mesmirizing effect" on children, overstimulates them or reduces their attention span. In fact, the report asserted, TV may actually increase attention-focusing capabilities.

Nor, contrary to many parents' fears, have the new video technologies made matters worse. Small children who repeatedly watch their favorite cassettes are, psychologists point out, behaving no differently from toddlers who want their favorite story read to them over and over. (The VCR may actually give parents *more* control over their kids' viewing.) Video games may distress adults with their addictive potential, but researchers have found no exceptional harm in them—and even some possible benefits, like improving hand-eye coordination. 10

Yet TV may be effecting a more profound, if less widely recognized, change in the whole concept of growing up. Before the advent of television, when print was the predominant form of mass communication, parents and teachers were able to control just what and when children learned about the world outside. With TV, kids are plunged into that world almost instantly. 11

In his 1985 book, *No Sense of Place,* Joshua Meyrowitz, professor of communication at the University of New Hampshire, points out that TV reveals to children the "backstage" activity of adults. Even a seemingly innocuous program like *Father Knows Best* showed that parents aren't all-knowing authority figures: they agonize over problems in private and sometimes even conspire to fool children. "Television exposes kids to behavior that adults spent centuries trying to hide from children," says Meyrowitz. "The average child watching television sees adults hitting each other, killing each other, breaking down and crying. It teaches kids that adults don't always know what they're doing." N.Y.U.'s Postman believes TV, by revealing the "secrets" of adulthood, has virtually destroyed the notion of childhood as a discrete period of innocence. "What I see happening is a blurring of childhood and adulthood," he says. "We have more adultlike children and more childlike adults." 12

What all this implies is that TV's impact is pervasive and to a large extent inevitable. That impact cannot be wished away; all that can be done is to try to understand and control it. Reforms of the sort Congress has enacted are a salutary step. Networks and stations too— though they are in the business of entertainment, not education—must be vigilant about the content and commercialization of kids' shows. 13

The ultimate responsibility still rests with parents. The goal should not be—cannot be—to screen out every bad word or karate chop from kids' viewing, but rather to make sure TV doesn't crowd out 14 all the other activities that are part of growing up. These counterbalancing influences—family, friends, school, books—can put TV, if not out of the picture, at least in the proper focus.

Questions for Thinking and Discussion

1. Put yourself in the position of a parent dealing with a "TV addicted" child. What are some things you would do to reroute the child's interest? As a parent, how would you "detoxify" your child?

2. One section of this article focuses on the effects of television on schoolchildren. Does television negatively affect children's learning experiences? Or, are children better informed, thus better educated, because of television?

How TV Violence Affects Kids

LILIAN G. KATZ

FOR MORE THAN A QUARTER OF A CENTURY, evidence has been mount- 1
ing that children's exposure to violence on television has long-lasting
effects on their behavior. Between 1982 and 1986, the amount of
television time allocated each week to violent cartoons increased significantly. And the number of violent acts on television in the past
decade has increased from about 19 to 27 per hour. Given the amount
of time that children watch television, it has become one of their most
powerful behavioral models.

The Position Statement on Media Violence in Children's Lives, 2
recently adopted by the National Association for the Education of
Young Children, points out that preschoolers are particularly vulnerable to the negative influences of the media because they are not yet
fully able to distinguish fantasy from reality, and their grasp of the
underlying motives for behavior and the subtleties of moral conflicts is
not yet well developed. For example, the rapid recoveries of people on
TV from violent attacks give children an unrealistic picture of the
injuries that have been sustained.

EFFECTS ON PLAY

Children naturally often want the toys shown on and advertised 3
during these programs. And with these toys, their play tends to be
more imitative than imaginative. Children simply mimic the behavior
observed during the program, thus undermining both the imaginative
and the expressive functions of play. The narrow range of most
violence-related toys advertised on television jeopardizes the role of
play in helping children make better sense of their own feelings and
interpret their world. Some research even suggests that children apply
the behaviors observed on TV programs to their real-life situations.

PARENTS CAN HELP

It is a good idea for parents to monitor the amount as well as the 4
kind of television their preschooler watches. If your child appears to
be obsessed by war play and weapons, it would be a good idea to
restrict his viewing. Controlling viewing is easier to do during the

preschool years than during the school years, so you should initiate a pattern of restricted television watching now.

Help your child to interpret what she sees—to think of explanations for the events depicted and to imagine how the show is put together. Make simple critiques of a show without implying that her fascination with the drama and the weaponry makes her guilty by association.

Ask the staff of your child's preschool about their policy on war play and toy weapons. Many preschool teachers prefer not to have commercially made toy weapons brought into the classroom and welcome hearing your concerns about this matter. Look for other parents who share your views. Work together to limit the amount of violent programs watched, and the number of violent toys found, in the home. Try to arrange play dates for the children as an alternative to TV viewing. Or look for videos of wholesome, nonviolent programs for preschoolers, and encourage their use as an engaging alternative to violent television programs.

Questions for Thinking and Discussion

1. This article states that children's exposure to violence on television can have long-lasting effects on their behavior. What behaviors have you have observed in children that may be a result of watching violence on TV? What are some of the behaviors children act out as a result of watching TV violence?

2. What types of TV shows portray violence? Think about both adult shows as well as children's shows. How do cartoons, for instance, portray violence? How is that violence different from the violence in adult shows?

Fighting Mad in Iowa

ANN LANDERS

Dear Ann Landers: Our 17-year-old daughter told us she was spending the night of the Valentine Ball at her girlfriend's house, but we have since learned she and two of her girlfriends spent the night with three boys at a motel. I was disappointed but not surprised.

I have read that producers of prime-time TV have chosen to portray their teen-age role models as having sex when they turn 18. One show featured a high school girl losing her virginity on prom night. No wonder one of my daughter's friends said, "What do you think prom night is for, anyway?"

The message our kids get from TV is that teens feel there is something wrong with them if they haven't had sex by the time they're 18. What if the producers decide next year that sex at 16 is OK? Maybe the next year it will be 12.

I'm tired of television being a co-conspirator in lowering the code of ethics in this country.

When my kids were little, I didn't like the violence on cartoons so I made sure they had more worthwhile things to do on Saturday mornings. Most kids did watch that stuff, and I'm sure it is no coincidence that drive-by shootings are nothing unusual these days.

The only suggestion I've ever seen for influencing TV programming is to write the shows' sponsors. But few parents have the time to monitor all the shows on TV, even if they could stand the steady diet of garbage. Is there any way to get a list of offending shows and their sponsors, so parents who care can make their feelings known?

—Fighting Mad in Iowa

Dear Iowa: Action for Children's Television and the National Coalition Against TV Violence used to have such a list, but it no longer exists. The suggestion you mention is still the best: Parents who wish to register complaints about the TV fare that is offered should write to the producers and sponsors of the shows they find offensive.

What can be seen on daytime TV is embarrassingly provocative these days, and the stuff on at night is shocking. Your best bet is Public Broadcasting. It's clean, educational and constructive.

Questions for Thinking and Discussion

1. This mother who writes to Ann Landers blames the media for lowering the "code of ethics in this country." She holds television responsible for everything from premarital sex to drive-by shootings. To what extent is the media, especially TV, responsible for these occurrences? What other factors might also be responsible for these problems?

2. Some people feel that modern television simply depicts reality and that it can have positive influences on teens faced with complicated modern issues. How can television help teenagers work through some of the issues they face? What kinds of TV shows seem to be the most helpful?

Adults in Little Town
Don't Want MTV

Tim Nelson

To MTV, or not to MTV?   1

That's the question these days in Olivia, a town of 2,620 people   2
about two hours west of the Twin Cities.

It's "The Corn Capital," according to a sign on the east edge   3
of the city. Another across the road reminds motorists that the
town's team took the state's Class B football championship in 1990 and
1991.

But the talk up at BOLD High School (the acronym is for Bird   4
Island, Olivia and Lake Lillian District) and around town these days is
about music videos. Ten years after the town was wired for cable TV, a
group of parents say it may be time to cut MTV out of the local cable
picture.

"I guess we're just saying enough is enough," says Lynne Wiger,   5
a member of the Citizens Advisory Committee, a 25-member panel
that functions something like a PTA for the school district.

She and other parents say they aren't going to force the MTV   6
channel out of the basic cable package offered in Olivia, Bird Island
and Danube by Midwest Cablevision in Redwood Falls.

But in April, with the approval of the local school board, the   7
committee will mail to parents a warning letter about MTV. Its critics
in town call it everything from violent and sexist to incomprehensible
and anti-Christian.

Wiger, mother of a boy, 12, and a girl, 14, is credited with starting   8
the discussion about MTV—the nation's premier high-voltage, rock 'n'
roll cable offering.

The channel, which Wiger considers "the most explicit network   9
on television," occasionally features clips of scantily clad women dancing to sometimes rakish music. Madonna, Guns 'n' Roses, and Metallica come up often in discussions about the network.

"They're not all bad," Wiger says of the three- to four-minute   10
videos MTV features 24 hours a day. "But I think it's saying to kids just
the very opposite of what we want them to see and hear . . . It takes
away the innocence of children and doesn't give them a chance to be
kids."

The debate about music television started in September, at a 11
meeting of the Citizens Advisory Committee.

The committee, which includes parents, teachers and administra- 12
tors, took a look at some of MTV's programming, talked to members
of the local cable commission and invited a Midwest Cablevision
manager to speak.

Committee members debated MTV's influence and whether it 13
would contribute to premarital sex, drinking, drug use and violence—
particularly toward women.

"We talked about MTV and how we could get it off," says Linda 14
Wagermaker, who works at a furniture store in Olivia and is chair-
woman of the advisory committee. "But the cable company said there
were enough people who wanted it, and that they'd like it to stay."

A deal was finally struck a few weeks ago and approved by the 15
school board last week. Next month, the advisory committee will mail
to parents a newsletter titled "Fresh Air in April: The MTV Challenge."

It will include a $10 coupon toward the cost of a $25 device that 16
can remove MTV from subscribers' cable service. No one knows how
many will buy the device.

Mark Machart, area manager for Midwest Cablevision and an 17
MTV fan, says he isn't really sure what the flap is about. "Years ago,
people were upset about Elvis Presley, and I don't really understand
what's different about this," he says.

Students at BOLD High School are of several minds about the 18
matter, but Kelly Prochniak wants her MTV.

"I think the reason they see it as wrong is all the sex and things 19
like that on TV," she said after writing a letter to the *Olivia Times-
Journal* in defense of MTV. "But I just think that adults didn't get
exposed to this kind of stuff when they were growing up. They're just
afraid of the change."

Others, like classmate Matt Beckman, say they're not worried 20
about MTV disappearing, and understand why some parents are
concerned.

"I don't think they're being overcontrolling or anything like that," 21
Beckman says, adding that if he had small children, he doesn't know
that he'd want them watching MTV.

Questions for Thinking and Discussion

1. The question of the influence of television on children is resolved by
   the parents group in this small Minnesota town. What do you think of

the way they have decided to handle the situation? What are the pros and cons about their approach?

2. Consider your own experiences watching MTV, and then evaluate what these parents say about the negative side of it. Is it likely, for instance, that it "would contribute to premarital sex, drinking, drug use and violence—particularly toward women"?

What TV Does to Kids

NEALA S. SCHWARTZBERG

THE LATEST LURE: INTERACTIVE TOYS.   1

The newest development in the relationship between product   2
and program is the interactive toy, a toy that is actually affected by the
TV show itself. Mattel has developed several that will interact with a
new live-action program, *Captain Power and the Soldiers of the Future,*
and Axlon has introduced *Techforce and The Moto Monsters.*

While both are labeled interactive, the toys and the ways they   3
operate are as different as night and day. In the case of Captain Power,
various action-figure accessories will be able to fire at on-screen enemies for points and be hit by enemy fire for point losses. With Techforce, figures actually move across the floor in response to commands
embedded in the on-screen dialogue and can be programmed from a
special computerized command console.

Although children can play with all the toys without the TV   4
shows, and watch the show without the toys, this intimate relationship, the very interactive nature of the toy, can easily exert a subtle but
real pressure to depict situations compatible with the toys' unique
capabilities.

However fascinating and entrancing the technology behind them,   5
these toys augur a deeper level of commercialism in children's television, drawing it farther away from the writer's imagination and creativity and closer to the necessities of the marketplace.

FUTILE ATTEMPTS TO REDEEM VIOLENT CONTENTS

But regardless of the source of their shows and the financial   6
incentives involved in their presentation, broadcasters and producers
have attempted to bolster public acceptance of their programs. They
have added moralistic messages tacked on at the end of violent cartoon
shows, for example, in an attempt to convince their audience that the
programs do have some redeeming social value. However, researchers
such as Jerome L. Singer, Ph.D., at Yale University claim that the kids
watching the shows often don't get that message. What they pick up
on is the violence, and their play tends to be more aggressive after
watching such programs.

How Kids Watch TV

The way youngsters watch and understand a television show and the way they interpret what they see is crucial. In order for a child to become aware of the pro-social message underlying a program, he would need to sit down and watch most, if not all, of the program. This would be particularly important if the message was supposed to counteract the effect of aggressive content.

But children do not simply sit and watch an entire television show. They walk in and out of the room, play with a toy, or change the channel in the middle of a program. Carrie Heeter, Ph.D., and Bradley Greenberg, Ph.D., of Michigan State University found that children do a lot of channel changing, especially if they have a remote control selector or cable box. The researchers asked a sample of 1500 adults and 400 fifth and sixth graders about the way they watched television. The younger the viewer, the more likely he or she was to change channels. These "zappers," as Heeter and Greenberg call them, do less planning. They do not sit down with the intention of watching a particular show, but rather to watch television, so they catch bits and pieces of different shows as they move through the channels. They stop at the first program that looks good and then change the channel between shows, during shows, and at commercial breaks. Heeter and Greenberg found that zappers are less likely to watch a program from start to finish and often watch more than one show at a time. (Although interactive toys may focus kids' attention more on one program—an unfortunate prospect, since many of the shows the toys interact with are violent and some of the toys themselves are guns.)

But even if children sat down and watched a program from the opening scene to the closing credits, would they be able to understand and interpret what they saw? No, it seems they would not. They tend to remember the action—particularly the violent action.

What Children Remember from Television Programs

In an admittedly unscientific experiment, I asked my six-year-old son to watch one of his favorite cartoons and remember all he could about it. The show, which seemed fairly uncomplicated when I simply watched it, became quite involved when I noted every event and element. Subplots and actions irrelevant to the main plot seemed to be included to stretch out the show's length.

My son recalled very little, two or three scenes that he told me about out of order, suggesting that he had not integrated the information into any linear, coherent representation.

I tried again with another series. This time he did better, but he   12
had seen this episode before. When I sprang the question, "So, what
was the show about?" without warning, and without first asking him
to watch the whole episode, he could remember only the names of the
characters and one scene: one of the characters sent out his pet to eat
up the other character.

More formal research turns up similar results. W. Andrew Collins,   13
Ph.D., director of the Institute of Child Development at the University
of Minnesota, found that children in the early grades fail to organize
and understand the scenes in a show and the way in which two scenes
are related. They make fewer inferences about the relationships among
program elements and fail to understand the links among the motives,
acts, and consequences.

Suzanne Pingree, Ph.D., at the University of Wisconsin at Madi-   14
son edited and simplified a family situation comedy and showed it to
a group of preschoolers. She found that the characters' actions were
remembered far better than scenes offering explanations of their actions. When she divided the show into segments, she discovered that
children recalled most poorly the scenes recounting inner feelings and
emotions to explain previous events.

It seems then that due to their TV viewing habits, our young-   15
sters are less likely to pick up on the dialogue that promotes a
more positive, or even more complete, understanding of the plot
and story line. What they are catching is the physical actions and
confrontations.

And even if they do watch the whole show, kids have difficulty   16
fully understanding the entire thrust of the program, the theme or plot
that guides and integrates the action. So again they are left with the
physical actions dominating their recall.

What's Real and What's Not?

What children see on television is fiction. And how much can it   17
affect them if they know it isn't "real"? It all depends on how they think
about reality.

Children may understand that what they see is made-up, but that   18
does not stop them from believing it anyway. It now appears that even
programs that are obviously fantasy can be judged by children as at
least partly real.

Children's conception of reality is not one-dimensional, nor is it   19
simple. They are used to getting "real" information from "unreal"
sources. In children's television, for instance, words walk across the
screen to form sentences. Animated characters demonstrate science,

safety, and even nutrition. Puppets act out scenarios that the young-sters recognize as parallels to their own experiences.

Aimee Dorr, Ph.D., at UCLA interviewed youngsters in kindergar- 20
ten through sixth grade as well as thirteen-year-olds, sixteen-year-olds, and adults about what they mean when they say something is "real," and how they decide what is "real" on TV.

Up until third grade, the majority of children had great difficulty 21
in explaining what "real" meant. They said either they did not know, gave a synonym, or gave an idiosyncratic response. Around sixth grade, the children could describe what they meant by "real." Dorr found that about half used "real" to mean something that could possi-bly happen. To them, "real" meant "made-up but possible in real life."

Although by six or seven years of age youngsters generally know 22
that television programs are "made-up," the more plausible a show appears, whether fantasy or not, the more likely it is to be taken as a representation of something that could happen. Children do not even evaluate a whole show as plausible or not. They evaluate separately the genre (cartoon, drama, comedy), the characters, what they do, and what happens to them. In other words, Dorr concludes, "Television content and its reality are thought about primarily in terms of inci-dents, events, or actions carried out by characters."

WHY ATTEMPTS TO BALANCE VIOLENCE WITH PRO-SOCIAL MESSAGES FAIL

So for many youngsters, attempts to pretty-up the violence with 23
the fine words of justification and morality are not likely to do any good. The words and implications will be overlooked in their quest for and focus on the action. They are not apt to discount what they see if it seems plausible, even if television presents a distortion. And if they see characters they enjoy watching using violence to solve problems, they will view violence as an acceptable problem-solving method.

Could we make better television for children? Yes, we could. 24
Research has shown that children do pick up pro-social messages from programs when the pro-social context is not overshadowed by aggres-sion and violence. We could use TV to open up kids' worlds, to introduce them to the wonders of science and nature. The lessons of history could come alive through animation. Television could bring an appreciation for the cultures of others into out homes.

But we have allowed the content of one of the most powerful 25
tools ever created to be controlled by the quest for profit rather than for excellence. The quality of children's television is poorer than ever,

and our children still sit in front of the television set and learn lessons that society may have cause to regret.

Questions for Thinking and Discussion.

1. Schwartzberg says that television can and does change the way children see themselves and their roles, as well as the roles of others. What are some of the roles that children are likely to interpret as realistic? What problems are associated, in particular, with stereotypical roles children view on television?

2. Children's programs often seem to be a "front" for advertisers. Schwartzberg says, "the quality of the program is secondary to its ability to display and entice children into wanting the products. . . ." What does he mean by this? What advertisements for children seem to fit this description?

How Super Are Heroes?

SUE WOODMAN

ONE MORNING IN THE PLAYGROUND of River Park Nursery and Kinder-   1
garten in New York City, principal Desiré Ford overheard 4-year-old
Walter tell his friend Billy: "Go ahead and bend my finger back. You
can't hurt me because I'm Superman and Superman feels no pain."
Billy needed no further invitation. In an instant, Superman was on his
knees howling, his finger almost broken. "That was the incident that
made me decide to ban Superhero play and paraphernalia from my
school," Ford says.

Kids have always been captivated by larger-than-life figures. But   2
the pervasiveness of today's mass-marketed heroes—including Ghostbusters, Teenage Mutant Ninja Turtles, Batman and Superman—makes
them far more influential than they used to be. The images flex their
collective muscle and commercial might over every corner of children's
lives—from the TV screen to the toothpaste tube.

Sure, thousands of '50s kids donned coonskin caps and their   3
chests swelled under the giant "S" logo. But Davy Crockett and the
original Superman were featured on TV for just a half hour a week at
most, whereas many of the current characters are on TV daily and
show up in movies, and their myriad spin-off products scream from
toy and grocery stores.

Superheroes' biggest fans are youngsters age 3 to 6. Experts say   4
the heroes—whether bold turtles or mighty men—seem to appeal to a
particular sense of powerlessness that little kids feel in dealing with the
adult world. The idols of older kids (10 and up)—from rock stars to
Bart Simpson—are more often like anti-heroes who appeal to kids'
sense of rebellion and "apartness."

As the popularity of these fictitious figures mounts, so do con-   5
cerns of parents, teachers and child psychologists about the strangle-
hold the characters seem to have on young kids' minds. Some experts
think the heroes are primarily catalysts for fun. But others fear that
preoccupation with superheroes engenders sexual stereotyping, promotes violence, blurs a child's ability to separate fantasy from reality
and cramps the creativity of children's play.

"From waking up in the morning to going to bed at night my son   6
does nothing but play Ninja Turtles," says the mother of a 4-year-old.
"He has Turtles on his underpants, Turtles on his lunchbox and he

330

wears a Turtle mask for most of the day. Sometimes I worry that he'll grow up warped in some way: I mean, just how much time can you spend communing with turtles?"

HARMLESS OR HURTFUL?

Psychologists who say parents should stop fretting think we   7
should just let kids be kids. Superhero play continues the tradition of falling-down-dead, cops-and-robbers-type play, says John Condry, Ph.D., a professor of human development and family studies at Cornell University. "It's a real old part of childhood. Even before there was TV, people told stories about superheroes," he says.

"All people need myth and fantasy in their lives, especially kids,"   8
agrees Brian Sutton-Smith, Ph.D., professor emeritus of education at the University of Pennsylvania, and author of *Toys As Culture* (Gardner Press Inc., 1986). "Kids are having a great time pretending to be heroes, defeating villains. These superheroes make our kids happy. There can't be much wrong with that."

But critics are concerned that these characters are sending out   9
signals that may have a profound effect on the development of kids under age six. For example, dozens of studies from around the world gathered by the National Coalition on Television Violence have demonstrated that violence in children's shows causes heightened levels of aggression in the kids who watch them.

One of the biggest gripes about the current slew of heroes is that   10
they are ubiquitous. The easy availability of these characters—and the fact that their shows are constantly repeating the same themes— discourages children's imaginations, believes Peggy Charren, president of Action for Children's Television. "Kids don't have to make up their own stories anymore. They don't pile leaves or play 'King of the Hill.' It has become, 'You are what you watch,' rather than 'You are what you think about and design.' "

"Any time my son walked into a room with other kids his age, a   11
Ghostbusters game would instantly get going," agrees one father, re- calling the days when every waking moment of his 3-year-old's life was consumed with the search for protoplasm and slime. "Every kid knew the story. They knew every word of the script. It was like mass hypnosis."

But Mark Runco, Ph.D., an associate of child development at   12
California State University at Fullerton and editor of the *Creativity Research Journal,* thinks such role playing can actually foster imagina- tiveness in certain slightly older kids. Research suggests that around

fourth grade children become much more realistic in their thinking, and can fall into a creative slump. So allowing kids to remain ensconced in the fantasy land of their superheroes can help feed their imaginations, Runco says.

Although most superheroes are foes of evil, Bart Simpson advocates values that parents and teachers find particularly troubling. "He tells kids every week, 'I'm an underachiever and proud of it,' " says Frank Farley, Ph.D., a psychologist at the University of Wisconsin at Madison. "American education is in a real state of crisis; the last thing we need is a major TV show that extols the virtues of being a below-average student," he says. 13

The creators of *The Simpsons* are aware of Bart's influence on a generation of youngsters with severe literacy problems, and point to the fact that Bart expresses shame in his shortcomings: "O.K., I'm dumb as a post. Think I'm happy about it?" 14

SUPER STEREOTYPES

While devoted young followers know by rote how their favorite hero would act in any given situation, they also absorb skewed notions about how each gender predictably behaves. The most publicized superheroes are male, and research suggests that 3- and 4-year-old girls often identify with the more dominant characters of the opposite sex. But girls also have their own set of role models who come to live in their homes and heads—from Barbie to My Little Pony to the newest heroine, The Little Mermaid. 15

One disgruntled mother bemoans her 5-year-old daughter's fixation with Ariel, Disney's redheaded mermaid: "This latest dose of sexual stereotyping for the very young still suggests that you have to give up your identity in order to achieve perfect happiness with your own square-jawed prince. It seems to me a very retro message." Other female characters—like April, the dim reporter in *Ninja Turtles,* and the office girl, Janine, in *Ghostbusters*—are passive, tending to watch action from the sidelines. 16

Similarly, male heroes still strongly reflect cliché masculine behavior. Whether man or beast, all (with the possible exception of Ghostbusters) are tough and confrontational, and resort to force to solve their dilemmas. And aggressive acts aren't done just by the bad guys. According to the National Coalition on Television Violence, 107 of the 194 violent acts in the *Teenage Mutant Ninja Turtles* movie are committed by the heroes. "The message is always 'Might is Right,' " 17 says Ford. "But kids need to learn to value human life, and that there are ways to solve problems without killing people off."

THE UNREAL WORLD

For most critics, however, the most serious concern is that so 18 many of the characters *don't* die: They walk through a hail of bullets and carry on, unharmed. As a result, experts say, children get a warped perspective of what's really dangerous and what isn't. If heroes can have their fingers bent back and feel no pain, then why can't Walter? If Superman can fly. . . .

Although there have been isolated incidents of children throwing 19 themselves out of windows thinking they could fly, psychologists agree that this particular fantasy is not a problem for most kids. Still, professionals such as Runco feel that until around age six, children's inability to discriminate between fantasy and reality complicates their involvement with superheroes.

"It's hard to tell how frequently kids seriously confuse reality and 20 fantasy because we don't know the thinking that underlies children's actions," Runco says. "But there are studies by the Swiss psychologist Jean Piaget and others that suggest that children do confuse the two." Particularly since kids are bombarded from every direction by images of the latest heroes, it's hard for youngsters to grasp that the characters might not really exist.

Experts are generally confident that most children's identification 21 with heroes begins to fade around age seven to nine. "As with Santa Claus, kids generally come to realize these are part of a fantasy world,'" says Condry. "When they start asking serious questions about society—such as what people in different cultures are like—and don't find answers in *The Little Mermaid* or *Ninja Turtles* they usually move on," he says. As they become increasingly aware of the adult world, most young people become more interested in real heroes, such as entertainment, sports, or political figures like Martin Luther King Jr., says Farley.

Parents' acceptance of make-believe heroes generally parallels 22 kids' preoccupation with them. At first, parents encourage fantasizing: They buy the toys, sanction watching the shows, even let their children record episodes on the VCR. "Kids get signals that their parents think their interest in superheroes is OK," Condy says. "We indulge our 3- and 4-year-olds to think that there really are ghosts and goblins and Santa. When they're 5 and 6, we're a little more leery. But by the time they're 7 and 8, we don't want our kids to believe in them anymore. It really bothers us if, by 9 or 10, they still believe in Santa or Batman."

HEROES RUN AMOK

So how much Turtles is too much Turtles? Most experts say that's hard to quantify. But they suggest that if superhero play seems to blot out interest in anything else, or if a child is imitating negative or violent behavior in the name of a character, then it may be time for parents to intervene. Try to limit TV watching, and help your child develop a liking for other stories too. "Get as much other content in front of your kids as possible, and eventually they'll be attracted to that as well," says Charren.

While most children do eventually manage to find a happy medium between green slime and more material forms of life, professionals admit that some do not. At her school, Ford occasionally comes across children who cannot be weaned from superhero play. Their obsessions may indicate other problems, she believes. "Some kids find the idea of power and control—which they play out with these characters—so attractive, it's almost like a drug," she says. "The reason may be that they don't have enough control in their lives."

Ford encourages the parents of these kids to look at issues such as toilet training, meals and bedtime, and ask themselves whether they are giving their children enough say. "Sometimes it's difficult for parents to know how much to let kids decide for themselves and how much they need to be guided," she says. "But kids need real power, not just superhuman symbols of it."

For the majority of kids, the symbolism encapsulated in superheroes belongs to a particular, passing phase of childhood. Most kids—enough for experts not to be unduly concerned—will outgrow their superheroes and move on to other things. The minority who do have trouble letting go may benefit from having parents step in to help create the right balance: a little Batman and a bit of baseball, a touch of Turtles and a smattering of Mark Twain. By encouraging kids to have a wide variety of interests, chances are that eventually they'll come to think of Leonardo and Michelangelo as Renaissance painters.

Questions for Thinking and Discussion

1. Superheroes serve a purpose for many children. With what superheroes are you familiar, and what purpose do they serve for children?

As a child, who were some of your "larger than life" heroes? What did they do for you?

2. Some experts believe there is little, if any, harm in children imitating superheroes. Others argue, however, that children worshiping superheroes is detrimental and has negative effects. What do you believe? Based on your own observations and what you have read, are superheroes generally a good influence on children, or are they generally a bad influence?

Couch-Potato Habits Catching Up with Kids

ASSOCIATED PRESS

DANNY WILLIAMS, 10, is exhausted after a long school day and the 1
one-mile walk from Flour Bluff [TX] Intermediate School to his home.

Often, he recuperates by plopping down in front of the television 2
and snacking on microwaved bacon or cookies. He usually plays video
games and sometimes he plays with his GI Joe, Transformers or dinosaurs. Later, it's time for more television.

Rick Fette, 11, another Flour Bluff fifth-grader, enjoys video 3
games, too, averaging 45 minutes a day, he said. He likes to play with
his trains and race cars but rarely participates in sand lot sport. His
family seldom gets together for recreation sports, and candy bars and
pizza are among his favorite foods, he said.

The lifestyles Danny and Rick have adopted are common among 4
today's children, fitness experts say.

The active, energetic kids who once played tag and touch football 5
have grown up to have children who have grown fatter and more
sedentary as they "play" Nintendo and eat junk food.

Studies show only half the nation's children get enough exercise. 6

Obesity in children has jumped by 50 percent in 10 years, ac- 7
cording to the President's Council on Physical Fitness and Sports.
Ten-year-old children weigh an average of 72 pounds, about three
pounds heavier than their parents weighed at the same age.

Dr. John K. Russell, present of the American Fitness Association, 8
believes that unless something is done to alter children's lifestyles they
eventually will suffer from increases in weight, heart disease and skele-
tal disorders.

"Kids are much more out of shape now they they ever were," he 9
said. "Kids are becoming couch potatoes at a much earlier age."

Dr. Robert Pankey, assistant professor of kinesiology at Corpus 10
Christi State University, recently surveyed 338 Corpus Christi middle
school children and found them to be prime candidates for heart disease with too much body fat and too little cardiovascular conditioning.

Pankey, who chairs CCSU's kinesiology department, said the 11
study conducted in March 1990 with George Taylor of the University
of Texas-San Antonio and Lola Grundy of the Corpus Christi Inde-

pendent School District, tested fitness levels of South Texas boys and
girls age 11 to 13.

Students were selected randomly from three Corpus Christi mid-   12
dle schools and tested in these areas: one-mile runwalk as a measure
of cardiovascular fitness; two-minute timed bent-knee sit-ups for mus-
cular endurance; shuttle run for agility; sit and reach to assess ham-
string and lower back flexibility; percentage of body fat.

The study found a majority of the children had normal blood   13
pressure and higher than normal muscle endurance, but they scored
below normal on cardiovascular endurance, flexibility and speed. They
study also found the percentage of body fat was above normal except
among black males, Pankey said.

Pankey chose to study middle school students because children   14
start to form their own eating habits at that age, he said.

"That's where we see the beginning stages of cardiovascular dis-   15
ease," he said.

Kids today are at greater risk for cardiovascular disease and   16
although the study did not examine the reasons for poor fitness,
Pankey believes inactivity, automated recreation—such as video
games—and fast food are among the culprits.

"Kids probably need more activity, not only in school, but at   17
home," he said.

Research indicates the average American child under age 12   18
watches 24 hours of television a week. Parents should pry their children from the TV and Nintendo and take them for walks or go bike
riding, Pankey said.

Francis Perry, who teaches the fifth-grade physical education   19
class in which Danny and Rick are enrolled, said she has tried to get
parents involved by sending letters home with each student outlining
their weaknesses and what can be done to correct them.

The changing American diet is as much to blame for kids' lack of   20
fitness as the lack of exercise, experts agree.

Questions for Thinking and Discussion

1. Based on your own observations and reading, do you think that TV can
   play a *positive* role in the goal of getting and staying healthy?
2. According to this article, American young people are very out of shape
   and unfit. Although television is one culprit, what other reasons explain why American children and teenagers are unfit? What sort of
   long-term plan could families, schools, or communities implement to
   get control of this problem?

TV Can Lower Kids' Metabolic Rate

Marilyn Elias

TV CAN DRAMATICALLY LOWER A CHILD'S METABOLISM—a possible clue 1
to why frequent viewers are more likely to be overweight, a new study
finds.

Watching just 30 minutes of *The Wonder Years* reduced children's 2
metabolic rates 14 percent below their resting rates, says Robert C.
Klesges, Memphis State University. "In other words, they're burning
more calories doing nothing."

TV may induce deep relaxation, which lowers metabolism, he 3
speculates. This metabolic drop alone could lead kids who watch
several hours of TV a day to gain a few extra pounds a year, Klesges
adds. He'll report findings to the Society of Behavioral Medicine today
in New York City.

Past research has shown the more TV kids watch, the more likely 4
they are to be obese. Snacking in front of the tube and substituting TV
for play were believed to be reasons.

But scientists have never looked at how viewing affects metabo- 5
lism—the rate at which your body uses calories. It's easier to gain
weight with a slower metabolism because the calories don't burn off as
quickly and may turn to fat.

Klesges measured resting metabolic levels for 32 girls—half 6
normal weight, half obese—7 to 11 years old. He then rechecked
rates after they watched one half-hour episode of *The Wonder Years*.
Results:

- TV viewing lowered metabolism by an average 14 percent.
- The drop was worse for already obese girls: 16 percent vs. 12
  percent for normal-weight kids.

The findings are important, says Dr. William Dietz, Tufts Univer- 7
sity School of Medicine, Boston. "It's one potential explanation, but
activity and diet also play a role."

Questions for Thinking and Discussion

1. Studies have shown that TV watching can substantially reduce children's metabolic rate. If this study is accurate, what are some health implications for these children? Think about both short-term and long-term problems they might experience.
2. This study reflects modern America's sedentary lifestyle. How do children learn this lifestyle? What kind of activity program could you offer young people to help them become more fit?

TV & Family Life:
Do They Mix?

INGRID GROLLER

IT'S A LOVE-HATE RELATIONSHIP—that which we have with our tele-   1
vision sets. In a national telephone survey conducted by *Parents* Magazine, television was strongly criticized. Parents, especially, were
concerned about their children's viewing. Still, everyone's watching.

Of those polled: 2

60 percent said that most TV programs are not worth watching;

72 percent said there is too much violence on TV.

While what's worth watching is a matter of personal taste, the fact   3
that there's too much violence is "indisputable," according to George
Gerbner, Ph.D., dean of The Annenberg School of Communications at
the University of Pennsylvania. "There are between six and eight acts
of violence an hour during prime time with two entertaining murders
a night."

According to this survey, viewing habits are passed down from   4
parent to child. Children of heavy viewers are also heavy viewers.
"Viewing is a ritual," Dr. Gerbner says, "We call it a new religion; it's
something that you're born into. Children develop viewing habits in
the first four, five, or six years of life. Of course, that means essentially
that parents set an example not by what they say, but by what they do."

In general, however, adults are more concerned about children's   5
viewing habits than they are about their own. Of the respondents (who
averaged 2.3 hours of television in a given evening):

28 percent said they watch too much;

61 percent said they watch the right amount;

9 percent said they don't watch enough;

2 percent weren't sure.

Of the parents polled: 6

40 percent said that their children (who averaged 2.02 hours of
    television viewing on a given evening) watch too much;
57 percent said they watch the right amount;
 2 percent weren't sure;
 1 percent said they didn't watch enough.

"I think the fact that 40 percent say their children watch too   7
much reflects a discomfort that parents feel about their children and
television," says John Condry, Ph.D., director of the Human Development and Television Research Lab and Archive at Cornell University.
"Television is kind of an uncontrolled part of the culture. Parents are
worried about the effect it's having, but they don't know what to do
about it."

When asked about the effects of television on children: 8

40 percent said the effects are negative;
34 percent said neutral;
19 percent said positive;
 8 percent were unsure.

Peggy Charren, president of Action for Children's Television   9
(ACT), says that there are two negative aspects to television: "One,
what children are not learning or doing while they're watching television. And, two, what they are learning and doing while they're watching television. When you watch TV, you're not talking to anybody, and
if you're watching MTV you're learning that it's nice to hang women by
their wrists and beat them up while you sing."

On the other hand, Charren also agrees with the 19 percent who   10
say television is positive. "If you're careful how you use the set, it can
turn from a Pandora's box into an Aladdin's lamp."

As to how they monitor TV in their homes, of the parents sur-   11
veyed:

29 percent said the child watches whatever he or she wants;
36 percent said the child picks whatever programs he or she
    wants to watch, though the parent has veto power;
30 percent tell the child what programs to watch;
 5 percent said it varies, or were unsure.

Parents of young children were most likely to make the selections   12
for the child, while parents of teenagers allowed them to watch what
they wanted.

Selective viewing should be everyone's goal, Charren believes.   13
"ACT has never said that there is some number of hours that is right
for every family," she comments. "You shouldn't think in terms of
hours; you should think in terms of program choices. You don't go to
the movies for three hours; you go to see *Hannah and Her Sisters*." "The
ability to evaluate and judge is a powerful immunizing factor," Dr.
Gerbner agrees. When you have that, you're no longer controlled by
the television, he says, "you're taking the first step to controlling it."

Questions for Thinking and Discussion

1. According to the *Parents* survey discussed in Groller's article, TV viewing habits are passed down from parents to children. Children of heavy
   viewers also tend to be heavy viewers. As role models, what activities
   could parents engage in to ensure that their children will not be heavy
   TV viewers?

2. John Condry, Ph.D., director of the Human Development and Television Research Lab and Archive at Cornell University says, "Television
   is kind of an uncontrolled part of the culture. Parents are worried about
   the effect its having, but they don't know what to do about it." Do you
   believe television is an uncontrolled part of American culture? Explain.

Don't Touch That Dial, Parents

ROBERT A. FRAHM

LOTS OF PARENTS BLAME TELEVISION for turning their children into 1 glassy-eyed couch potatoes, but a recently released study says TV can be a good thing, too, especially for bright kids.

Parents who turn off the TV may actually be depriving high-IQ 2 children of an important source of learning, says a study published by a center for gifted children, based at the University of Connecticut.

"Gifted children . . . enjoy learning tasks that are often unstruc- 3 tured and flexible," the report says. "Television seems to fit the bill and should be considered a viable learning tool rather than as the detractor of attention, literacy and learning skills."

The study, "Some Children Under Some Conditions: TV and the 4 High Potential Kid," criticizes much programming as inappropriate for children but says some television viewing can benefit young viewers.

"The catastrophic impact of television on youth, as depicted in 5 the popular press, is . . . fictitious," says the study released by the National Research Center on the Gifted and Talented.

"For some children, under some conditions, some television is 6 harmful. For other children under the same conditions, or for the same children under other conditions, it may be beneficial," the study concludes.

"That's the bottom line—it depends on the child," said the study's 7 author, Robert Abelman, a professor at Cleveland (Ohio) State University who has worked as a consultant for Children's Television Workshop and commercial television networks.

"I think the study is right," said Peggy Charren, a nationally 8 known children's television activist who has pushed for more choice of programs and less commercialism on TV.

"People who blame TV for children not doing well in school are 9 using TV as a scapegoat," she said. "When TV is nifty, it's really very good for kids if they don't watch too much of it." With good programs, she said, "I think TV can be as productive for children as good movies, good games."

The study, which includes a review of decades of research find- 10 ings on television viewing by children, is based in part on findings used in Abelman's 1992 book *Television and the Exceptional Child: A Forgotten Audience.*

The 72-page study cites research showing that gifted preschool   11
children typically watch two to three more hours of television per week
than to other children of the same age. However, gifted children reduce
their TV viewing sharply once they reach school age, generally watching less TV than do other school-age children, the study reported.

It also said that gifted children: 12

- Are more likely to be involved in plot and story line and least
  likely to be confused by TV programs.
- Quickly outgrow educational and instructional programs such
  as *Mr. Rogers' Neighborhood.*
- Are less likely to be influenced by television violence, which
  studies have shown to have more effect on low achievers or
  naturally aggressive children.

Another prominent television researcher, however, cautioned   13
against generalizing from the study, saying its conclusions seem
skewed because it focuses only on high-IQ children.

"It's the average kid and the below-average kid we have to worry   14
about," said professor Jerome Singer of the Yale University Family
Television Research and Consultation Center.

"There is no question one can learn useful things from television,"   15
said Singer, who had not seen the Abelman study. "It depends on what
the program is and if parents play a mediating role."

Singer said television's potential harm to children is a serious   16
matter.

"I do think heavy television viewing of commercial TV, particu-   17
larly, by the average preschooler, can displace the likelihood of reading
and learning how to read." And he said heavy viewing "has consistently
been shown to be linked with aggressive behavior."

Abelman's study—based on more than a decade of interviews,   18
experiments and surveys with intellectually gifted children from Hartford, Austin, Washington and Cleveland—produced several guidelines
for parents.

It found, for example, that the extra amount of time spent in front   19
of the television set by bright preschoolers does not necessarily warrant
concern by parents or reductions in viewing time.

The report says the attraction to television at an early age "is   20
reflective of gifted children's natural attraction to accessible and interesting sources of information."

The study advises parents not to use TV viewing as a reward or   21
punishment. It says their best course of action is to select programs.

They should seek programming that is sufficiently challenging and includes a solid story line and plot.

"Viewing gives gifted children an opportunity to observe and familiarize themselves with advanced or abstract concepts" that are normally learned at a later age through other means, including books, the study says. 22

It also warns parents to avoid programs specifically designed to sell products or toys, such as the hard-sell programming and advertising prominent in many Saturday morning shows. 23

Cable TV and video rentals are likely to provide more reliable children's programming than prime-time television, which includes inadequate and inappropriate role models for gifted children, the study found. It also says that children rarely appear in starring roles, and gifted children are "typically depicted as social misfits." 24

Questions for Thinking and Discussion

1. Frahm quotes Peggy Charren, a nationally known children's television advocate, who says that, for some children, TV watching can be beneficial. Charren says, "People who blame TV for children not doing well in school are using TV as a scapegoat." Do you agree or disagree with Charren? How big a role does television play in how children perform in school?

2. Jerome Singer, a professor of the Yale University Family Television Research and Consultation Center, says in Frahm's article that television's potential to harm children is a serious matter. Singer suggests that heavy TV watching can lead to aggression, as well as displacement of other activities such as reading. Evaluate Singer's position. What effects can heavy TV viewing have on children? What can parents do to help control the effects of heavy TV watching by their children?

VCRs Unite Kids and Parents, Research Shows

Felix Gutierrez

VCRs ARE TURNING TELEVISION VIEWING into video campfire gather-   1
ings—with kids and parents not only watching more prime-time TV
together but also talking to each other more, recent studies show.

"When a VCR comes into a household and the household has   2
children, people tend to talk to each other more," said Southern Illinois
University professor Carolyn Lin, who has studied home video cultures
since 1984.

"They have to negotiate about what videos to rent and when to   3
play these videos," Lin said. "If someone wants to 'time-shift' (record)
a show for later viewing, the person will have to get consent from the
other people as well."

More communication is only one side effect of families' adding   4
videocassette recorders to their television sets. Although many homes
have more than one set, VCRs are bringing people to watch a single
screen, much like the campfires of yesteryear.

In a survey of 233 VCR homes in three Midwestern communities,   5
Lin found that, after adding a video recorder, 58 percent of the people
spent more time watching TV with the family and 35 percent spent
more time having video parties at home.

"Prerecorded cassettes appear to have brought back 'family view-   6
ing' during prime time," said Debra Krayson of AGB Television Research, which tracked VCR use in April. Prime-time tape viewing "not
only brings the family together but also appears to be a social event.
AGB data show a significant number of guests in the audience."

Children are the VCRs' most avid users, spending 50 percent   7
more time watching tapes than adults. According to the AGB study
released last month, children under 18 spend an average of 3.4 hours
a week watching videotapes, while adults average 2.3 hours weekly.

Teen-agers developed their own versions of video campfires,   8
often watching tapes in groups at parties. Often they have little adult
supervision, Lin said.

Despite parent-group fears that racy adult videos are the biggest   9
video moneymakers, 1987 Video Software Dealers Association figures
show comedy and action/adventure tapes are tops, with nearly 20

percent of the dollar volume apiece. Adult videos rank fourth behind drama, at 11.4 percent.

Tape rental prices averaged $2.45 per tape in 1987, video stores   10
stock averaged 2,832 titles, and the number of videos rented per visit averaged 2.3, the survey revealed.

Of the seven hours of an average week when the VCR is in use,   11
2.4 hours are spent recording programs and 4.7 hours are spent viewing tapes, AGB reported last March. Twenty-three percent of the time is used taping shows for later viewing, known as "time-shifting."

Homes with pay cable channels spent more time recording and   12
less time playing tapes than those without cable, the study found. Most taping is during evening prime-time hours or during weekdays, and most viewing is during weekend days, late nights and early mornings.

Questions for Thinking and Discussion

1. Gutierrez refers to work by Southern Illinois University professor Carolyn Lin, who says, "When a VCR comes into a household and the household has children, people tend to talk to each other more." How do you account for Lin's observation? Is this the case when you have been around a household where a VCR is being used? Why or why not?

2. Gutierrez' article shows how VCRs offer parents control over what their children see on television. What kinds of guidelines do you believe are feasible for parents who allow their children VCR time? Why are these guidelines important for both parents and children?

Mayberry a Moral Beacon for Real Life

J. Peder Zane

MICHAEL A. CHAMBERS used to spank his 7-year-old son. But a year   1
ago he changed his way of thinking as he watched reruns of his favorite
program, *The Andy Griffith Show.*

"I saw that the character played by Andy Griffith never laid a   2
hand on his boy but talked through their problems," he said. "It made
me realize that there was a better way."

Chambers, 32, a graphics designer from Houston, is not the only   3
fan who says he has gotten more than laughs from the show about the
cozy Southern hamlet of Mayberry. Among the roughly 5 million
people who visit Sheriff Andy Taylor, his son Opie and Aunt Bee each
day (shown here weekdays at noon on KTXA/Channel 21) are parents
who use the show to teach values, ministers who quote it in Sunday
sermons and other viewers who use it as a moral compass in a sometimes frightening modern world.

"It's like religion to a lot of people," said James Clark, founder of   4
the Andy Griffith Show Rerun Watchers Club, which he says has
20,000 members. "Andy's very wise, he's the Solomon, the Abe Lincoln
of Mayberry. And so many of us in real life will ask: 'What would Andy
do? How would he handle this situation?' "

The devotion of those fans has also attracted a coterie of scholars   5
who say the program is not just an escape from the real world, but a
demonstration of how television teaches what families or towns once
taught.

"The program does not merely reflect society, but suggests val-   6
ues," said Richard Kelly, a University of Tennessee English professor
who wrote a book on the program in 1981. "At a time when a lot of
the standards have broken down, it represents a kind of lost paradise
founded on the best hopes of people."

In Mayberry the men swap tall tales, but the women are tight-   7
lipped about their pickle recipes. The only substance abuser is a
hiccuping town drunk named Otis. Law and order is kept by a sheriff
who never wears a gun and is the best fisherman in town.

Of course there are problems. There was the bully who used to   8
take Opie's milk money, and those burly vegetable farmers who

348

wouldn't listen when Andy's goofily officious deputy, Barney Fife, told them to close down their roadside stand.

"Mayberry was about the best things of small-town life when there were still small towns left," Andy Griffith, who also helped write the show, said in a recent interview. 9

"Every problem could be solved in a half hour and usually by someone taking an interest in someone else." 10

The show began in 1960 and left the air in 1968 as the top-rated series. 11

Now in reruns in 127 television markets, its appeal is stronger than ever. *Andy Griffith Show* trading cards were introduced last year, and fans have scooped up 25 million of them. *Aunt Bee's Mayberry Cookbook*—which includes recipes for Poke Sallet, Sweet Tater Pone and Hoot Owl Pie—has sold 200,000 copies since April. It was put together for Rutledge Hill Press in part by Clark, the "presiding goober" of the rerun watchers club's 600 chapters, who otherwise writes corporate newsletters for a living. 12

The show's enduring influence still astonishes Jack Elinson, a Bronx, N.Y., native who co-wrote about half the first season's episodes with Charles Stewart, a native of Seattle. He said the moral elements were standard television fare in the 1960s, though he sees why it is so popular by contrast to what he calls the "raunchy in the sex gutter" mentality of today's shows. 13

"All we were trying to do was write a wholesome show that would get some sponsors and an audience," he said in a telephone interview from his Los Angeles home. "In this business, you never know what you're going to do and most of the time you never know what you did." 14

Grant T. Byrd, a Texas Baptist minister in McKinney, uses the show in lectures to youth groups because "television is so much a part of their world." He said the patience Andy has for his bumbling deputy, allowing him to find solutions without butting in, is a model for a parent-child relationship founded on empathy and love. 15

Robert J. Curtis of Colorado Springs, Colo.—who has nearly all 249 episodes on videotape—said the show conjures warm memories of watching it with his parents. 16

Now he encourages his 5-year-old daughter to watch as one way of sharing his own childhood with her. That kind of memory—television watching creating nostalgia for earlier episodes of television watching—shows one peculiar opportunity given to the first generation that grew up on television: it can relive chunks of its childhood through reruns. 17

Curtis says he also lets his daughter watch because he knows children copy what they see on television. 18

"It teaches kids to be respectful instead of smart-alecky," he said.   19
"I want my child to be like Opie, not Bart Simpson."

Questions for Thinking and Discussion

1. In part, Zane's article discusses the values that Americans used to learn from their towns. Do you or your children still learn values in this way? Which values did you learn from your community, and which did you learn from your family? Besides positive values, what negative things have you learned from your community and family?

2. Think about the Taylor family in the *Andy Griffith Show* of the 1960s. How are modern television families different from the Taylor family? In what ways are they similar?

Writing Projects

1. Write a self-study describing the influence of television on your life as a child. What kinds of shows did you watch? Did they influence you? Were the influences negative or positive?

2. Write a paper based on the criticisms of children's television programs provided by Katz and Schwartzberg. Begin your work by identifying the five or so major objections that these two writers have toward these programs. Then, schedule time to watch at least three hours of children's programs. Take notes during your viewing and write a paper that answers this question:

   Do these programs illustrate the problems that Katz and Schwartzberg describe?

3. Based on your reading of research pertaining to children and television, assume that you have been asked to present a paper to a group of concerned parents. You have been asked to discuss two things: (a) whether you believe television is a serious threat to the well-being of children and (b) how you believe that parents can deal with television viewing by their children. Write your paper drawing on the studies by experts from your reading in this chapter. You may want to read your paper to classmates and have them critique what you have to say.

4. In her article, Woodman looks at both sides of the superheroes question. Some experts believe there is little, if any, harm in children imitating superheroes. Others think that children worshiping superheroes is detrimental. What do you think? Based on your own observations and reading, write a paper in which you argue for or against the presence of superheroes in the lives of children today.

Index

"4,200 Teens Fatally Shot in '90, Study Shows" by Christopher Connell. *Fort Worth Star-Telegram*, March 24, 1993. Copyright © 1993 The Associated Press. Reprinted with permission.

"Guns are Death For Our Children" by Carolyn Poirot. *Fort Worth Star-Telegram*, September 10, 1992. Copyright © 1992 by the *Fort Worth Star-Telegram*. Reprinted courtesy of the *Fort Worth Star-Telegram*.

" 'Bang, Bang, You're Dead' Isn't A Game" by Clarence Page, as it appeared in the *Fort Worth Star-Telegram*, June 17, 1993. Copyright © 1993, Chicago Tribune Company. All rights reserved. Used with permission.

"Federal Programs Just Intensify the 'Who Me?' Factor" by Mike Royko. *Dallas Morning News*, March 20, 1993. Copyright 1993. Reprinted with permission.

"Violence, A Problem in our Society Today" by Roderick Richardson. Copyright 1993. Reprinted with permission.

"The Dating Game" by Merrill Markoe. *Time*, Fall 1992. Copyright © 1992 Time Inc. Reprinted with permission.

"Breaking the Ice" by Dave Barry, appeared as "Fear of Failure" in the *Fort Worth Star-Telegram*, February 16, 1992. From DAVE BARRY IS NOT MAKING THIS UP by Dave Barry. Copyright © 1994 Dave Barry. Reprinted by permission of Crown Publishers, Inc.

"Creative Dating" by Don Oldenburg. *The Washington Post*, February 13, 1992. Copyright © 1992 The Washington Post. Reprinted with permission.

"With This Headhunter, $10K Defines a Spouse" by Deidre Fanning. *The New York Times*, November 18, 1990. Copyright © 1990 by The New York Times Company. Reprinted by permission.

"Interracial Relationships" by Ingrid Watson. *Fort Worth Star-Telegram*, February 2, 1993. Copyright © 1993 by the *Fort Worth Star-Telegram*. Reprinted courtesy of the *Fort Worth Star-Telegram*.

"Being Alone Doesn't Have to Mean Being Lonely" by Karen Peterson. *USA TODAY*, March 10, 1992. Copyright 1992, *USA TODAY*. Reprinted with permission.

"Wide Gender Gap Found in Schools" by Mary Jordan. *The Washington Post*, February 12, 1992. Copyright © 1992 *The Washington Post*. Reprinted with permission.

"U. Can't Ignore It" by Sheila Taylor. *Fort Worth Star-Telegram*, March 15, 1992. Copyright © 1992 by the *Fort Worth Star-Telegram*. Reprinted courtesy of the *Fort Worth Star-Telegram*.

"How Do You Teach a Girl To Value Herself?" by Debbie Price. *Fort Worth Star-Telegram*, January 29, 1992. Copyright © 1992 by the *Fort Worth Star-Telegram*. Reprinted courtesy of the *Fort Worth Star-Telegram*.

"Bias Against Girls" by the Forth Worth Star-Telegram. *Fort Worth Star-Telegram*, February 18, 1992. Copyright © 1992 by the *Fort Worth Star-Telegram*. Reprinted courtesy of the *Fort Worth Star-Telegram*.

" 'Western Wall' Syndrome Hampers Girls of Today" by Kathleen Parker, as it appeared in the *Fort Worth Star-Telegram*, March 9, 1993. Copyright © 1993 by the Orlando Sentinel. Reprinted with permission.

"Ohio College Says Women Learn Differently, So It Teaches That Way" by Susan Chira. *The New York Times*, May 13, 1992. Copyright © 1992 by The New York Times Company. Reprinted by permission.

"Tomorrow's Lesson: Learn or Perish" by Michael Lemonick. *Time*, Fall 1992. Copyright © 1992 Time, Inc. Reprinted with permission.

"Guiding Kids with a Curriculum of Compassion" by Karen Peterson. *USA TODAY*, December 14, 1992. Copyright 1992, USA TODAY. Reprinted with permission.

"New Grading System Earns an 'F' from Houston Parents" by The Associated Press, as it appeared in *The Chicago Tribune*, November 17, 1993. Copyright © 1993. Reprinted with permission.

"State Board of Education Studies Proposal for Year-Round Schools" by Tony Tucci. Reprinted with permission.

"Schools at the Workplace Bringing Families Together" by Mary Jordan, as it appeared in the *Fort Worth Star-Telegram*, March 14, 1993. Copyright 1993 © *The Washington Post*. Reprinted with permission.

"Commuter Students Up to Speed on Learning" by Elizabeth Mehren. *Los Angeles Times*, November 2, 1993. Copyright © 1993. *Los Angeles Times*. Reprinted by permission.

"Mother, Son at Odds on Education" by Abigail Van Buren. Taken from A DEAR ABBY column by Abigail Van Buren, as it appeared in the *Stephensville* [TX] *Empire Tribune*, August 30, 1990. Dist. by UNIVERSAL PRESS SYNDICATE. Reprinted with permission. All rights reserved.

"Letter by Linda Kaufman," by Ann Landers. *Ann Landers* column as it appeared in the *Fort Worth Star-Telegram*, March 13, 1993. Copyright © 1993. Permission granted by Ann Landers and Creators Syndicate.

"What's a Diploma Worth? A Thousand Bucks a Month" by The Associated Press, as it appeared in the *Stephensville* [TX] *Empire Tribune*, January 29, 1993. Copyright © 1993. Reprinted with permission.

"Useless U" by Jacob Weisberg, as it appeared in *Mademoiselle*, August 1993. Copyright © 1993 by Jacob Weisberg. Reprinted with permission.

"New Elitism: The College Class" by BettiJane Levine. *Los Angeles Times*, August 17, 1993. Copyright © 1993, *Los Angeles Times*, Reprinted by permission.

"Graduation Address: Spring, 1993" by Christopher Guthrie. Reprinted with permission.

"Hey, Give Us A Break!" by William Booth. *The Washington Post*, April 4, 1993. Copyright © 1993 *The Washington Post*. Reprinted with permission.

"Cities Eager to Follow Lead of Lauderdale" by Tao Woolfe, as it appeared in the *Fort Worth Star-Telegram*, April 4, 1993. Copyright © 1993. Reprinted with permission from the *Sun-Sentinel,* Fort Lauderdale, Florida.

"Party Schools Find the Image is Difficult to Shed as Efforts to Curb Alcohol Abuse Have Limited Success" by Christopher Shea. *The Chronicle of Higher Education*, April 7, 1993. Copyright © 1993 *The Chronicle of Higher Education*. Reprinted with permission.

"Letters from College Students" by Ann Landers. *Ann Landers* column as it appeared in the *Fort Worth Star-Telegram*, February 17, 1992. Copyright © 1992. Permission granted by Ann Landers and Creators Syndicate.

"College Students and Alcohol" by Ann Landers. *Ann Landers* column as it appeared in the *Fort Worth Star-Telegram*, January 6, 1993. Copyright © 1993. Permission granted by Ann Landers and Creators Syndicate.

"The Athletic Department Vs. The University" excerpted from *College Sports, Inc.* by Murray Sperber. Copyright 1990 by Murray Sperber. Reprinted by permission of Henry Holt and Company, Inc.

"UNLV Basketball Star Suspended After Review of His English Paper" by Douglas Lederman. *The Chronicle of Higher Education*, March 24, 1993. Copyright © 1993 *The Chronicle of Higher Education*. Reprinted with permission.

"Teaching Your Child That Losing Isn't Everything" by Lawrence M. Kutner. *The New York Times,* January 26, 1992. Copyright © 1992 by The New York Times Company. Reprinted with permission.

"Spanking Is Opposed, Hands Down" by Sharon Cox. *Fort Worth Star-Telegram,* February 16, 1993. Copyright © 1993 by the *Fort Worth Star-Telegram.* Reprinted courtesy of the *Fort Worth Star-Telegram.*

"Motherhood Blues: Stop the Guilt Trip, I Wanna Get Off" by Sheila Anne Feeney, as it appeared in the *Fort Worth Star-Telegram,* April 16, 1992. Copyright © 1992 The New York Daily News, used with permission, and cannot be reproduced without alteration.

"Is TV Ruining Our Children?" by Richard Zoglin. *Time,* October 15, 1990. Copyright © 1990 Time Inc. Reprinted with permission.

"How TV Violence Affects Kids" by Lilian Katz. *Parents,* January 1991. Copyright © 1991 Gruner & Jahr USA Publishing. Reprinted from PARENTS Magazine by permission.

"Fighting Mad in Iowa" by Ann Landers. *Ann Landers* column as it appeared in the *Fort Worth Star-Telegram,* April 14, 1992. Copyright © 1992. Permission granted by Ann Landers and Creators Syndicate.

"Adults in Little Town Don't Want MTV" by Tim Nelson. *Fort Worth Star-Telegram,* March 27, 1993. Copyright 1993 by the *Fort Worth Star-Telegram.* Reprinted courtesy of the *Fort Worth Star-Telegram.*

"What TV Does to Kids" by Neala S. Schwartzberg. *Parents,* June 1987. Copyright © 1987 Gruner & Jahr USA Publishing. Reprinted from PARENTS Magazine by permission.

"How Super Are Heroes?" by Sue Woodman, *Health,* May 1991, 23(4) pp. 40+. Copyright © 1990 by Sue Woodman. Reprinted with permission.

"Couch Potato Habits Catching Up with Kids" by The Associated Press. Copyright © 1993. Reprinted with permission.

"TV Can Lower Kids' Metabolic Rate" by Marilyn Elias. *USA TODAY,* March 26, 1993. Copyright 1993, USA TODAY. Reprinted with permission.

"TV and Family Life: Do They Mix?" by Ingrid Groller. *Parents,* May 1987. Copyright © 1987 Gruner & Jahr USA Publishing. Reprinted from PARENTS Magazine by permission.

"Don't Touch That Dial, Parents" by Robert Frahm, as it appeared in the *Fort Worth Star-Telegram,* May 25, 1993. Copyright © 1993 *The Hartford Courant.* Reprinted by permission.

"VCRs Unite Kids and Parents, Research Shows" by Felix Gutierrez. *Dallas Morning News,* August 21, 1988. Copyright © 1988 The Associated Press. Reprinted with permission.

"Ideas & Trends; Lessons for Living, From the Lapsed Town of Mayberry" by J. Peder Zane. *The New York Times,* December 7, 1991. Copyright © 1991 by the New York Times Company. Reprinted with permission.